Using surveys in language programs

CAMBRIDGE LANGUAGE TEACHING LIBRARY

A series covering central issues in language teaching and learning, by authors who have expert knowledge in their field.

In this series:

Using Surveys in Language Programs

James Dean Brown

University of Hawaii at Manoa
Honolulu, Hawaii

CAMBRIDGE
UNIVERSITY PRESS

PUBLISHED BY THE PRESS SYNDICATE OF THE UNIVERSITY OF CAMBRIDGE
The Pitt Building, Trumpington Street, Cambridge, United Kingdom

CAMBRIDGE UNIVERSITY PRESS
The Edinburgh Building, Cambridge CB2 2RU, UK
40 West 20th Street, New York, NY 10011-4211, USA
10 Stamford Road, Oakleigh, Melbourne 3166, Australia
Ruiz de Alarcón 13, 28014 Madrid, Spain
Dock House, The Waterfront, Cape Town 8001, South Africa

http://www.cambridge.org

First published 2001

Printed in the United States of America

Typeface Sabon 10½/12 pt.

A catalog record for this book is available from the British Library.

Library of Congress Cataloging-in-Publication Data

Brown, James Dean.
Using surveys in language programs / James Dean Brown.
p. cm. – (Cambridge language teaching library)
Includes bibliographical references and index.
ISBN 0-521-79216-9 – ISBN 0-521-79656-3 (pbk.)
1. language surveys. I. Title. II. Series.

P128.L35 B76 2000
418′.0071 – dc21   00-040344

ISBN 0 521 792169 hardback
ISBN 0 521 796563 paperback

The extract on pages 297 to 298 is reprinted from *Learning styles in adult migrant education* (1988) by Ken Willing with permission from the National Centre for English Language Teaching and Research (NCELTR), Australia. © Macquarie University.

This book is dedicated with love to Kimi.

Contents

Contents

Preface

Using Surveys in Language Programs arose out of a need that has existed for years. In teaching curriculum and research design courses, in serving as an administrator of English as a Second Language/English as a Foreign Language (ESL/EFL) programs, and in consulting on curriculum development and research projects in various EFL/ESL programs, I have found myself repeatedly explaining the basics of survey research for both curriculum development and research purposes: how to plan a survey project, how to create sound interview or questionnaire instruments, how to gather and compile the survey data, how to analyze the data quantitatively and qualitatively, and how to report the results. Over time, my reading, thinking, explaining, and hands-on experience with these topics converged into the material of this book.

Using Surveys in Language Programs consists of six chapters, which correspond to the topics that I have found the most useful for language teachers:

1. Planning a survey project
2. Designing a survey instrument
3. Gathering and compiling survey data
4. Analyzing survey data statistically
5. Analyzing survey data qualitatively
6. Reporting on a survey project

I chose this organizational structure because planning, designing, gathering, compiling, analyzing, and reporting are the steps that I have most often found necessary in carrying out survey projects. Each of the six chapters contains extensive examples drawn from my experience in survey development and use as an ESL teacher, professor, administrator, and researcher.

Using Surveys in Language Programs presents a comprehensive, but practical, overview of the different phases and activities involved in developing and implementing sound, rational, and effective survey projects. I tailored the explanations to be useful for graduate students, language teachers, administrators, and researchers. As such, I present both the theoretical and the practical issues involved in survey design in digestible chunks. And, I explain all concepts in a step-by-step recipe manner, with many examples and checklists throughout the discussions. Each chapter also includes a summary, suggestions for further reading, a list of important terms, review questions, and application exercises, all of which should make the survey design concepts more meaningful.

In short, I wrote this book to help you do whatever survey research is important in your particular language teaching situation. I will have succeeded only if you actually apply what you learn here to solving some of the many problems you face as a language teaching professional.

JD Brown

Using surveys in language programs

1 Planning a survey project

Research in the language teaching professions is done by many different types of people and comes in many forms. Figure 1.1 is my attempt to show where survey research fits into all of these forms of research. Notice that the figure shows two basic categories of research: **secondary research** (that is, studies based on secondary sources such as other researchers' books and articles), including library research and literature reviews; and **primary research** (that is, studies based on primary, or original, data sources, such as classroom observations of real students, or their test scores, or their responses to a questionnaire), including qualitative, survey, and statistical research. Further subdividing primary research, *qualitative research* can be thought of in terms of the many research traditions encompassed by the term "qualitative" (holistic ethnography, ethnography of communication, discourse analysis, phenomenology, etc. – for more on this topic, see Lazaraton, 1995) or in terms of many different qualitative data-gathering techniques (diaries, field notes, case studies, etc.). Continuing the subdivisions, *survey research* (the topic of this book) includes interviews and questionnaires, and *statistical research* includes descriptive studies, exploratory research, quasi-experimental studies, and experimental research.

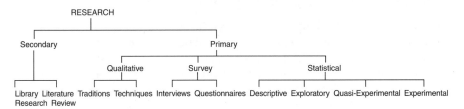

Figure 1.1 Broad categories of research.

Much has been written about these various types of research and the ways they are interrelated, so I will not elaborate on all of them here. However, even without elaboration, Figure 1.1 illustrates four important characteristics of **survey research:** (1) It is primary research and therefore data-based; (2) it is based on interviews and questionnaires; (3) it is distinct from qualitative research and statistical research (for instance, see any of the numerous books cited in the References on *survey research*

1

methods); and (4) it is somehow sandwiched between qualitative and statistical research in that survey research can draw on both qualitative and statistical techniques, and conversely in that qualitative and statistical research studies sometimes include survey techniques. In practice, this last point means that survey research can take four forms in terms of how the results are analyzed: purely statistical, statistical with some qualitative, qualitative with some statistics, and purely qualitative. Given all the distinctions shown in Figure 1.1 and discussed here, any general definition of **research** will obviously need to be very broad, perhaps something like the following: Research is any systematic and principled inquiry (for many other definitions of research, see Brown, 1992c).

The purpose of this book is to focus on and explore the issues involved in one type of survey research methodology: language surveys. **Language surveys** are any survey research studies that gather data on the characteristics and views of informants about the nature of language or language learning through the use of oral interviews or written questionnaires. In this book, *data* will be defined as all of the information, quantitative or qualitative, that results from a survey. (Note that in American English, the plural term *data* is often used in the singular, as in *the data is ready for processing*. In this book, I will use **data** only for the plural noun, as in *the data are ready for processing;* the singular **data point** will also be used in lieu of *datum*. In deciding whether to use the plural or singular usage, no correct answer exists; you will simply have to follow your personal preference. However, you should probably decide on using *data* one way or the other, as I have here, and use it consistently.)

Available tools for gathering information

Before deciding on a language survey as the appropriate research methodology for gathering information in a particular situation, you should consider all of the available tools so you are sure that you have chosen the most appropriate and efficient instruments available. Many tools are available for gathering information about language or language learning, as shown in Table 1.1. Notice that I have organized the available research tools into four categories useful for gathering non-survey information (existing information, tests, observations, and meetings) and two categories useful for gathering survey information (interviews and questionnaires).

Non-survey information

EXISTING INFORMATION

You should always consider existing information before wasting energy developing brand-new information-gathering tools. Existing information

TABLE 1.1. TOOLS FOR GATHERING INFORMATION

Type of information	*Type of tool*	*Research tools*
Non-survey	Existing information	Records analysis
		Systems analysis
		Literature review
		Letter writing
	Tests	Proficiency
		Aptitude
		Placement
		Diagnostic
		Progress
		Achievement
	Observations	Case studies
		Diary studies
		Behavior observation
		Interactional analysis
		Inventory
	Meetings	Advisory
		Interest group
		Review
		Delphi technique
Survey	Interviews	Individual
		Group
		Telephone
	Questionnaires	Self-administered
		Group-administered

may include *existing records* of any kind. For instance, in a language program, databases of student records may exist (in computer format or in paper files) that would be worth analyzing. Such records might include biodata information about the students that would eliminate the need to do a survey, or at least the need to do a survey of biodata information. *Systems analysis* of existing records is similar but is conducted more broadly – for instance, across years or among different language programs. A *literature review* may also prove useful for finding out whether other language professionals have been concerned about gathering information similar to what you are interested in. Perhaps, answers to your questions already exist, and even if they do not, such a literature review may provide useful ideas for developing your own survey instruments. In addition, a literature review may lead you to identifying individuals or institutions that have interests similar to yours. Then, *letter writing* (or variations such as phoning, faxing, or e-mailing) may prove useful for gathering information that already exists in other programs. As mentioned above, you should definitely consider existing information first, in order to avoid the problem of reinventing a wheel that already exists.

TESTS

Tests may also prove useful for gathering information in a language teaching setting. Language *proficiency tests* are particularly useful for gathering information about the general skill or knowledge levels of language students. *Aptitude tests* provide information about each student's general ability or aptitude to learn languages. *Placement tests* are useful for gathering information about the level of study that would be most appropriate for students. *Diagnostic tests* are useful for gathering information about the specific strengths and weaknesses of individual students with regard to a clearly identified body of language knowledge or set of language skills. *Progress tests* are similar to diagnostic tests, except that progress tests are administered while the course is still in progress to determine how much (of the material or skills being taught) the students have learned. Finally, *achievement tests* can provide information about the amount that has been learned in a particular language course or program with regard to a clearly identified body of language knowledge or set of language skills. All in all, tests can provide fairly efficient ways of gathering large-scale information on students' abilities, knowledge, or skills. The different types of tests I listed above are distinct from each other in that they are designed to gather information for a variety of purposes (for more information on the different types of tests, see Brown, 1995, 1996).

OBSERVATIONS

Observations involve direct on-the-spot examination of language use, learning, or training. *Case studies* usually involve carefully observing a single individual or a few individuals over a relatively long period of time. *Diary studies* include any procedures wherein an individual or group of people keep a journal or diary on a regular basis about a particular issue or set of issues. The diaries are then analyzed systematically. *Behavior observation* includes any investigation in which language production or language learning behaviors are examined, systematically recorded, and analyzed. *Interactional analysis* would be used as the label if such behavior observations focused on interpersonal language interactions. *Inventories* are simple counts, as in a count of lexical tokens, or number of each part of speech in a given corpus of language. In a language teaching setting, an inventory could include a count of the number of students per teacher, chairs per classroom, parking spots per student, number of books in the library, and so forth. Observations, regardless of the type used, are often appropriate for providing direct information about language, language learning, or language learning situations.

MEETINGS

In language teaching settings, meetings are generally structured so that the participants can accomplish certain tasks. However, the process of trying to accomplish a task may provide unforeseen information about the people or issues involved. *Advisory meetings* should be set up to inform the participants about new conditions, or policies that may have occurred in a particular institution. *Interest group meetings* are most effective at airing differences that may have arisen. There may be differences in views between individuals or between interest groups within a program. The point is that groups should convene and argue the relative merits of their different ideas. *Review meetings* should draw participants into the process of sifting through and analyzing the information gathered with other procedures. All types of meetings provide opportunities to gather data with relative efficiency, particularly about the interactions of the participants. One other meeting-related technique deserves mention here because it can be used to avoid meetings. The *delphi technique* is "a communications process which permits a group to achieve consensus in the solution of a complex problem without face-to-face interaction or confrontation" (Uhl, 1990, p. 81; for more on this topic, see this source).

Survey data

INTERVIEWS

Interviews are procedures used for gathering oral data in particular categories (if the interview is well planned and structured in advance), but also for gathering data that was not anticipated at the outset. Interviews can be conducted with individuals, in groups, or by telephone.

Individual interviews are interviews with respondents on a one-to-one basis. Such personal interviews allow for gathering data privately. As a result, you can establish a certain level of confidentiality and trust, which, if handled correctly, is more likely to lead to the "true" views of the respondents than, say, group interviews. However, such interviews also have a drawback, which is that they are very time-consuming. As a result, individual interviews are best used for exploring which questions, views, or issues are worthy of later follow-up study through structured questionnaires, which are much easier to administer.

Group interviews might at first seem to be procedures that could circumvent the time-consuming nature of individual interviews. Unfortunately, any information obtained in a group interview is not confidential. For personal, political, psychological, or even emotional reasons, the opinions expressed when participants are together may be quite different from the views they would express if they were interviewed individually.

This difference between individual and group interviews can sometimes prove useful. By comparing the opinions of people when they have been interviewed in a group interview with what they say individually, you can actually study the disparities.

Telephone interviews offer a kind of compromise in the sense that they are confidential, but somewhat less time-consuming because the interviewer need not spend time traveling to the respondents. However, telephone interviews also have several drawbacks. For instance, in a telephone interview, some data are lost because the interviewer cannot observe the facial expressions, gestures, and surroundings of the respondents. A telephone survey also eliminates the possibility of showing respondents any kind of realia. In addition, at least in the United States, people have become very wary of telephone sales promotions and surveys, and therefore, may instantly shut down communication or be hesitant to cooperate.

QUESTIONNAIRES

Interviews can clearly be used to gain insights into the questions, topics, views, and opinions that may be of interest in a particular language setting. However, if those issues are worth pursuing on a broader scale (in terms of the number of people you survey), questionnaires may prove easier to develop and more efficient to use.

Questionnaires are any written instruments that present respondents with a series of questions or statements to which they are to react either by writing out their answers or selecting from among existing answers. Questionnaires are particularly efficient for gathering data on a large-scale basis. For example, whereas interviews might be used effectively with a few of the participants in a language program, a survey would be more effective for obtaining the views of all the participants.

When you think of a questionnaire, you probably think of the self-administered type. A **self-administered questionnaire** is most often mailed out and filled in by the respondents whenever and wherever they like (that is, it is self-administered), and then returned by mail. Questionnaires of this type have three inherent problems: (1) they often get a low return rate; (2) they must be completely self-contained and self-explanatory, because on-the-spot clarification is not possible; and (3) you do not know the conditions under which the questionnaire was filled out.

A **group-administered questionnaire,** which is administered to groups of individuals all at one time and place, may solve all three of the problems listed in the previous paragraph. For instance, if you want to survey the students in a particular language school, you could go to each of the classrooms and ask the teachers to spend the 15 or 20 minutes necessary for all the students to fill out the questionnaire together. In such a situation, you will have solved problem (1) because the students will be a captive audience, who will generally feel obliged to fill out the questionnaire. Thus the return rate will be high. In fact, you can make it even higher by tracking down any students who were absent on the day of the questionnaire administration and having them fill out the questionnaire on the spot. You will also have solved problem (2) because you can be present to explain any ambiguities or confusions that arise. And you will have solved problem (3) because you will know exactly what the conditions were when the students filled out the questionnaires.

When the respondents are other than students – for example, the parents of students – you may need to call a meeting that will attract them for some other reason (for instance, parent–teacher conferences, an all-school talent night that involves every student, or some other meeting that is likely to attract all or most of the parents). Once they have been attracted to the meeting, you will once again have a captive audience to respond to your questionnaire. Note, however, that you will definitely want them to fill out the questionnaire (with your profuse thanks) on the spot. If they are allowed to take the questionnaires home, all of the problems discussed above will once again be present.

Clearly, the group administration strategy offers a relatively efficient way of administering questionnaires. However, if the geographic distribution of the respondents is wide, or the number is very large, the self-administered approach may make more sense.

The steps in a survey project

You should never view a survey in isolation. Instead, you should consider any survey, whether an interview, a questionnaire, or both, as a part of a larger survey project. Such a survey project requires careful and complete planning before you administer the survey interviews or questionnaires. You must decide a number of issues: (1) how the survey fits into the bigger picture of the field as a whole or into a particular language program, (2) what the purpose of the project is, (3) what formats and types of questions you will use in the survey, (4) whom you will sample in the survey, (5) how you will administer the survey so as to obtain the maximum amount of quality data, (6) how you will analyze the data you get, and (7) how you will report the resulting data, and to whom. And, as I pointed out at the beginning of this paragraph, you must make all these decisions before you actually conduct the research so you do not waste all your efforts because of oversights and blunders caused by unforeseen circumstances. In short, in setting up a survey research project, you must become clairvoyant – at least with regard to the potential pitfalls of your specific project.

Stacey and Moyer (1982) suggest the following ten steps for the construction of surveys:

1. Specifying survey objectives and research questions
2. Reviewing the literature
3. Defining abstract concepts
4. Selecting question formats
5. Selecting the statistical analysis
6. Writing the survey questions
7. Ordering the questions in the survey
8. Adjusting the physical appearance of the survey
9. Preparing the cover letter and instructions
10. Validating the survey

These ten steps are fine if all you are concerned about is producing a survey instrument. However, this book will take the point of view that a language survey instrument is part of a larger survey project, which involves the following steps:

1. Planning a survey project
2. Designing a survey instrument
3. Gathering and compiling survey data
4. Analyzing survey data statistically
5. Analyzing survey data qualitatively
6. Reporting survey results

As you will see in the chapters that follow, these steps, though fewer in number than those suggested by Stacey and Moyer (1982), are broader. In other words, these six steps form categories that include all of the ten steps listed by those authors, but also much more. These steps correspond to the titles of this chapter and the other five chapters in this book, so the steps clearly form the basis for the book's organization. By way of previewing the rest of the book, I will briefly describe each of these steps in turn.

1. Planning a survey project

During the planning stage of a survey research project, you should recognize that survey interviews and questionnaires are only two of the tools available. As discussed in the previous section, tools other than surveys may prove more appropriate for gathering certain types of data. Thus, before investing a great deal of energy in a survey project, you should consider potential alternatives to survey interviews and questionnaires, such as existing information, tests, observations, and meetings. Your goal should be to find the most appropriate tools for gathering data – the tools that will best serve the purposes of your particular project.

If it turns out that survey interviews or questionnaires are the most appropriate tools for your project (or for part of a larger project), the next part of the planning process is to delineate the goals of the language survey. Such surveys are often used to perform needs analysis and program evaluation (for a classic needs analysis from Europe, see Richterich & Chancerel, 1980, or more recently, the Japanese language learning needs analysis reported by Iwai, Kondo, Lim, Ray, Shimizu, & Brown, 1999), but surveys can also be used to conduct other types of research (for an example from Australia, see Willing, 1988, or the questionnaire in Appendix I). To delineate the survey project goals, you may need to think over and define all key concepts that are important to the project.

The last part of the planning stage is to formulate tentative survey research questions. Of course, the research questions may change, but at least if they are put into writing they can serve as a tentative starting point for the project. Even if the survey is for curriculum development rather than for research, research questions should probably be used so they can serve as a starting point and working basis for whatever investigations will follow.

I will cover all of these issues that make up the planning stage in a survey project in much more detail later in this chapter.

2. Designing a survey instrument

Designing a survey instrument, whether an interview or a questionnaire, involves thinking about a number of different issues. To begin with, consider the questions themselves. Language teaching professionals may find themselves wanting to address a wide variety of different types of questions. Generally speaking, these questions fall into one or the other of the following categories: behaviors, opinions, feelings, knowledge, and sensory; or problems, priorities, abilities, attitudes, and solutions. You must also consider the different functions that can be served by the questions in a survey. Will the survey include biodata, opinion questions, self-ratings, judgmental ratings, or Q-sort?[1] Equally fundamental decisions must be made with regard to question formats. Will the questions be closed-response (questions that can be answered by selecting from among options), or open-response (questions that require the respondent to produce a spoken or written answer), or some combination of the two?

The actual creation of the questions in a survey instrument involves thinking about the form of the questions, the meaning of the questions, and the reactions of the respondents. However, even with good questions in hand, a number of steps must still be followed before the survey

1 For those who are not familiar with the Q-sort, it is a procedure for rank-ordering items in a survey, often done in a face-to-face interview with separate cards for each of a number of items that the interviewee is asked to sort in order, from the items they most agree with to those they most disagree with, or the items they most like to those they most dislike. For much more on this topic, see McKeown & Thomas (1988).

instrument is ready to use: (1) The order of presentation of the questions must be considered, (2) the formatting of the instrument must be made maximally effective, (3) the clarity of the directions should be checked, and (4) the whole product should be carefully edited.

Chapter 2 covers all of these survey design issues in much more depth.

3. Gathering and compiling survey data

Gathering any kind of survey data involves deciding which people to administer the instrument to. This procedure, called *sampling,* is generally designed so that a relatively small number of people can be taken to represent a larger population. For instance, 1,000 people might be sampled from the population of the United States in order to study the current political views of the entire population.

Once decisions have been made about the sampling, you might want to consider the different survey tools that are available. Would an interview survey be more appropriate than a questionnaire survey? If so, what kind? Individual interviews? Group interviews? Or a telephone survey? And if a questionnaire would be better, which type? – Self-administered, or group-administered? Or should some combination of these tools be used sequentially?

If an interview is being administered, the interviewers should all follow certain basic guidelines. Thus you will have to develop very clear directions for the interviewers. In addition, training sessions for interviewers may be necessary, to make sure that the interviewers all understand the procedures and that they all conduct the interviews in a similar way.

If a questionnaire is being administered, the biggest problem with self-administered questionnaires is return rate. People fail to return a mailed questionnaire for many reasons. Fortunately, a number of strategies can help increase such return rates. Even if the questionnaire is to be administered to a large group in a single sitting, steps should be taken to maximize the efficiency of the administration.

Having successfully gathered the survey data, you next need to compile the data into some form that will be relatively easy to store, access, sort, and analyze. This process of compiling survey data may involve a range of activities, from data coding for the numerical answers to closed-response questions to transcribing the answers to open-response questions.

Chapter 3 covers all of the issues involved in gathering and compiling survey data in much more depth.

4. Analyzing a survey statistically

Once you have coded the closed-response answers numerically, you may want to analyze the resulting data statistically to look for patterns in the answers that are interesting or illuminating.

Descriptive statistics may prove useful in the initial analysis. These include statistics for central tendency (mean, mode, and median), dispersion (range and standard deviation), as well as various ways of examining frequencies (raw data, percentages, and graphical displays).

More complex statistics may also prove useful for making inferences from the basic descriptive statistics. These include statistics for comparing means, comparing frequencies, and examining correlation coefficients.

Finally, you should consider the reliability and validity of any survey instruments that you develop. *Reliability analyses* (in the form of internal consistency estimates and/or interrater correlations) are important because they indicate the degree to which an instrument is consistent in its measurement. *Validity analyses* are important because they indicate the degree to which an instrument is measuring what it was intended to measure. Moreover, the results of your survey project can only be as reliable and valid as the instruments and procedures on which the project is based.

Chapter 4 covers all of these statistical analyses in more depth.

5. Analyzing a survey qualitatively

Some parts of a survey may not be particularly amenable to statistical analysis – especially open-response questions. In such cases, data transcription may replace data coding. For instance, you may need to tape-record interviews, and eventually use a word processor to make written transcripts. Then, you may need to organize the data by grouping the responses to particular questions together. The same may be true even for a written questionnaire if open-response questions are used.

Once you have recorded and organized the data, you may need to analyze all of the resulting data. To do so, you may need to rely fairly heavily on the human ability to find patterns in the data. However, certain types of computer software may also prove useful in analyzing open-response data. Some grammar checkers, for instance, provide lexical frequencies that can be used advantageously. In addition, almost all word processors provide a search function that may prove helpful in sorting through the mountains of data involved in analyzing open-response questions.

Once patterns are found in the data, you will need to reduce those patterns to manageable proportions. Naturally, such reduction will involve some analysis, some synthesis, and a great deal of summarization.

Issues similar to reliability and validity are also important for any open-response results that are reported in a survey project. Four qualitative research techniques, called dependability, credibility, confirmability, and transferability, will be covered in this book. These concepts are as important for open-response data as reliability and validity are for closed-response data, because the results of a survey project can be no better than the instruments and procedures on which they are based.

Chapter 5 covers the qualitative analysis of data in considerably more detail.

6. Reporting the results of a survey

In reporting the results of a survey, you will need to sort through masses of data and decide what should be included in the report. Such reports may take several forms.

In reporting predominantly statistical research, you might want to follow the format for organizing reports suggested by the American Psychological Association (APA, 1994). The APA organizational structure includes the following sections: Introduction (including literature review and statement of purpose), Method (including descriptions of Participants, Materials, and Procedures), Results, and Discussion and/or Conclusions sections.

Another important consideration in explaining the results of a predominantly statistical study is the use, especially in the Results section, of clear, concise tables. The columns and rows of such tables should be clearly labeled. Different ways for presenting numerical results in tables and graphs should be considered. In addition, combining various types of information together in tables or graphs may prove efficient and enlightening.

In reporting predominantly qualitative research, more flexibility appears to be the norm. Most qualitative research studies generally have Introduction, Methods, and Conclusion sections of some sort. However, what the author puts within and between these three sections seems to vary considerably depending on the type of qualitative research involved and on the nature of the individual research project. One important characteristic of qualitative research appears to be that it needs to tell the story of the research and of the people involved. Since such stories may differ from project to project, so will their structures.

Naturally, hybrid forms of organization may evolve if a study combines major aspects of statistical and qualitative research. Above all else, you should explain your study, its results, and your interpretations very clearly, so that readers will be able to understand what happened in the project and what the study means to them and to the language teaching profession as a whole.

Chapter 6 covers the central issues involved in reporting statistical and qualitative survey results in considerably more depth.

The goals of language surveys

The most common uses of surveys in language education are for curriculum development and for research. For both of these uses, a wide variety of tools can be used to gather data (as listed earlier, in Table 1.1). However, very often the types of data that language researchers need are those they can best gather using survey interviews or questionnaires.

Language programs, whether government-funded or commercial, are essentially providing a service to students who want to learn the language in question. If the administrators and teachers in a program are interested in what their students think about the service, then some form of curriculum analysis and research must be conducted. The best way to find out what people think about any aspect of a language program is to ask them directly in an interview or on a questionnaire.

Surveys for curriculum development

The curriculum model shown in Figure 1.2 (adapted from Brown, 1989, 1995) is one that I have used profitably in the development of curriculum in a number of different language programs. The curriculum model is derived from the widely accepted systems approach used in educational curriculum design (particularly from the work of Mager, 1975, and Dick & Carey, 1985). The curriculum model can be viewed as a set of chronological stages, which can be followed in developing a new program from scratch and as a set of components for the processes of improvement and maintenance of an existing language program. In providing a description of the continuing process of curriculum development and maintenance, the model also accounts for possible interactions among the various components of the design, as indicated by the arrows, which connect all elements in all directions. (For much more discussion of this model and its application in language classrooms, see Brown, 1995.)

The two components of curriculum design that benefit most from survey research are needs analysis and program evaluation. Although surveys can be designed to study many aspects of curriculum (including objectives, tests, materials, and teaching), interviews and questionnaires are most commonly used in needs analysis and program evaluation.

NEEDS ANALYSIS

Needs analysis in language programs is often viewed as the study of the vocabulary, grammar, and functions that students will probably need to use in the target language when they actually try to use it in a real-life situation. The focus is on the learners, and their needs are stated as **language needs,** that is, the linguistic material they should learn. In fact, such a focus seems reasonable. After all, they are the clients, and their needs should be served. However, this view may be somewhat shortsighted in the sense that other participants in the program, such as teachers, administrators, employers, or politicians, have needs that may also be important for a particular language program.

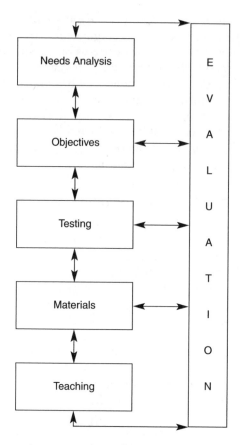

Figure 1.2 Systematic approach to designing and maintaining language curriculum. (Adapted from Brown, 1989, 1995.)

Even if a needs analysis were 100 percent focused on the students, it seems evident that they would have needs other than linguistic ones. These other needs might best be termed **situation needs** (that is, the financial, physical, political, or other nonlinguistic needs of the participants in the program). Any situation needs that affect the teaching and learning of language should be included in a needs analysis. Thus the participants' needs as human beings should be considered in addition to their language needs. This addition means that the definition given in the first sentence of the previous paragraph should be broadened to include this wider view of needs. **Needs analysis** will be defined here as the systematic collection and analysis of all relevant information necessary to satisfy the language learning needs of the students within the context of the particular institutions involved in the learning/teaching situation (after Brown, 1995).

If needs analysis is viewed as relying on input from a variety of different groups and consisting of data on both language and situation needs, survey projects may prove particularly useful. In gathering data from the various interested groups in a program, using interviews and questionnaires may become inevitable because they work well for efficiently gathering many different types of data from a wide variety of sources.

PROGRAM EVALUATION

According to Brown (1995, p. 218), *program evaluation* is "the systematic collection and analysis of all relevant information necessary to promote the improvement of the curriculum and assess its effectiveness within the context of the particular institutions involved." Because this definition is very similar to the one given above for needs analysis, the evaluation process should probably be seen as an ongoing needs assessment – one based on considerably more and clearer information. Whereas a needs analysis is typically conducted in the initial stages of curriculum development and must often depend on interview procedures, questionnaires, linguistic analyses, conjecture, and a good deal of professional judgment, program evaluation can take advantage of all of the above information and tools to assess the effectiveness of a program but can also utilize all information previously gathered in the processes of developing objectives, writing and using the tests, developing materials, and teaching. **Program evaluation** will be defined here as the ongoing process of data gathering, analysis, and synthesis, the entire purpose of which is constantly to improve each element of a curriculum on the basis of what is known about all of the other elements, separately as well as collectively.

Survey research is as crucial for program evaluation as it was for needs analysis – for exactly the same reasons. Although survey projects used in curriculum development generally remain in-house, some find their way into print (for examples, see Richterich & Chancerel, 1980, and Johns, 1981).

Surveys for language research

Surveys are also used in other types of language research that are not related directly to language curriculum. For instance, Ochsner (1980) used surveys to study the characteristics of M.A.-level teacher training programs, and Brown, Knowles, Murray, Neu, & Violand-Hainer (1992b) used surveys to investigate the opinions and attitudes of members of a national professional organization. Of all the research methods, survey research may be the most practical and usable in one sense: It relies more on common sense and less on complex statistics. Often, results reported as percentages and averages are sufficient to explain the results of a survey research project.

Survey research is particularly useful in language research because of the many types of data that can be gathered using surveys. Survey research can describe, explore, or explain physical characteristics, phenomena, behaviors, attitudes, and so forth. Certainly, you can address many useful questions by doing survey research. The possibilities for doing language survey research seem even greater when you consider that any research that is done today might usefully be repeated in five or ten years to investigate how people's ideas, attitudes, opinions, and so forth, have changed over time.

Operationalizing key concepts

In performing statistical research of any kind, you must recognize the difference between any theoretical concept being studied and the numbers derived from some measure of that concept (that is, between the concept and the numbers that are used to define the concept). For instance, if an attitude questionnaire is developed to measure Japanese students' attitudes toward American culture before and after they study English, the theoretical concept that is being measured is attitude, or more precisely, attitude toward American culture. The scores, or other numbers, that are derived from the questionnaire provide a numerical representation of the students' attitudes. However, such representations are, at best, indirect reflections of the concepts involved and are not the concepts themselves. Such indirect measures often serve as the variables in survey research studies. Thus, understanding exactly how variables are related to the measures and underlying concepts is very important.

Links between constructs and variables

In discussing these issues, researchers will often use special terminology to make these relationships clear. The theoretical concepts under investigation in language studies are called **psychological constructs.** Such constructs are the underlying psychological traits or characteristics that are operating in the participants' brains. Nobody can observe psychological constructs directly, because they are going on inside peoples' heads. Instead, the constructs are **operationalized,** which means that measures or other means of quantifying the constructs are used to define the constructs in numerical terms. Such measures may be tests, questionnaires, physical measurements, and so forth. In turn, these operationalizations of constructs become the variables in language studies. **Variables** are things that can vary over time or among people; variables are what language researchers manipulate or focus on in doing their research.

For example, consider a construct such as language aptitude. Language aptitude is a psychological construct. Theoretically, people vary in their aptitude to learn languages. The Modern Language Aptitude Test (Carroll & Sapon, 1958) is considered by some to be an indirect measure of this psychological construct (for more discussion of the pros and cons of language aptitude testing, see Parry & Stansfield, 1990). Thus the scores on this test are sometimes used to operationalize the language aptitude construct so that language aptitude can be used as a variable in a study. Similarly, questionnaires are used to operationalize constructs such as cultural attitudes, aggressiveness, motivation, anxiety, personality characteristics, preferred learning styles and strategies, and so forth. The point is that psychological constructs must be operationalized as numerical quantities before they can be used as variables in quantitative research studies.

Scales of measurement

In the process of operationalizing constructs as variables in a study, they are quantified. However, they can be quantified in a number of different ways because the facts of the world around us can be tallied, classified, counted, or measured in a variety of ways. Essentially, four ways exist to quantify the world, each of which involves numerically representing reality in terms of a specific **scale of measurement.** The four types of scales are nominal, ordinal, interval, and ratio scales. Each is useful for organizing data in a unique way. In addition, these scales are hierarchical in the sense that they provide data that have varying degrees of precision.

Nominal scales are appropriate when you want to quantify a construct, or variable, as a set of categories or groups. For instance, a questionnaire might focus on the various categories into which language learners fall. Such categories can be naturally occurring or artificially created. Naturally occurring categories might include gender (female/male), native language (Farsi, Spanish, Mandarin Chinese, and so forth), nationality (Iranian, Mexican, Taiwanese, and so forth), academic status (undergraduate, graduate, unclassified), and so forth. Artificially created categories might include groupings such as levels of study in a language program (elementary, intermediate, or advanced), or assignment by researchers to an experimental group or a control group. Variables that use nominal scales are also sometimes called **categorical scales;** or, if there are only two categories, such as female/male, they may be called **dichotomous scales.** Regardless of the label, such scales are nominal because they identify and name the categories involved.

Ordinal scales are similar to nominal scales in that they classify a named group of observations on a scale. However, ordinal scales also order or rank points along the scale. For instance, a questionnaire might be designed to ask students to rank the ten types of classroom activities that are used in their language course, from least to most interesting, using the numbers 1 through 10. The most interesting activity would be ranked first, the second most interesting would be ranked second, and so forth. Thus ordinal scales can be thought of as creating ordinal numbers to represent the variable. Sometimes, variables that use ordinal scales are also called **ranked scales.** Regardless of the label, such scales order or rank people, concepts, objects, and so forth, with each point on the scale being *more than* and *less than* the other points on the scale.

Interval scales also describe the rankings (like an ordinal scale) within a particular group (like a nominal scale). However, an interval scale is a scale that has equal distances along it. Whereas ordinal scales simply show the order of things, without regard to how far apart they are, an interval scale shows the order of things with equal distances or intervals between the points on the scale. Test scores are the most common interval scales used in language studies. However, some questionnaire results, such as attitude scales, are also treated as interval scales.

Ratio scales are different from interval scales in that ratio scales have a zero value and points along the scale make sense as ratios. For example, a scale such as number of years of language study can take on a zero value, and it does make sense to think of two years of study as twice as much as one year. Other variables that could be considered ratio scales on questionnaires are the number of languages studied, years of education, number of pages in each book, and so forth.

Formulating language survey research questions

In order to provide at least a basic idea of some of the types of research questions that can be addressed by conducting surveys and to give some idea of how they might be formulated, I want to clarify the characteristics and purposes of good research questions as well as provide some example questions to illustrate those characteristics and purposes.

Characteristics of good research questions

First, good survey research questions should provide a survey project with focus and direction. Thus they should be appropriately specific, answerable, relevant, and clear.

Research questions should be *specific* in the sense that they should be neither too broad nor too narrow. A research question such as "What is the meaning of life?" is obviously too broad. However, if the questions in a project are too narrow and specific, they may number in the dozens; worse, they may not help much in providing focus and direction for the project.

In order to find the correct level of specificity for research questions, consider the fact that such questions should be *answerable.* Research questions should be specific enough so that real answers, based on real survey questions, can be found for them. For instance, if you are interested in the attitudes of a group of language teachers toward the language proficiency of students in a particular program, an appropriate research question might be "What are the views of the teachers toward the proficiency of the students in terms of both fluency and accuracy?" To answer this research question, several survey questions might be posed about the students' fluency in oral and written language and several others about the accuracy of their oral and written language. In short, the research question is neither too broad nor too specific, and is answerable by using several questions on a survey.

Next, the research questions should be *relevant.* A research question can be appropriately specific and answerable without being particularly relevant to a project. A good deal of energy goes into formulating survey questions, gathering data, analyzing those data, and so forth. What a shame it would be to waste all of that energy on a research question of doubtful relevance.

Finally, each research question must also be *clear,* which means that it should be stated so explicitly that its intent will be evident to anyone working on the survey project, including the respondents. A research question must also be clear enough to communicate the same intent over time, that is, from start to finish of the project, and perhaps long after, if the report of the results of a project continues to have any influence. Indeed, research questions must be clear enough so that, in reporting the results of the survey, the research questions will provide a useful starting point for explaining to the readers where the project is headed.

The purposes of research questions

Research questions can serve three primary purposes in survey projects: descriptive, exploratory, and explanatory.

DESCRIPTIVE

Surveys provide relatively efficient tools for gathering simple demographic or other descriptive information. Consider the following descriptive questions, which might usefully be answered through the use of survey tools:

1. What are the numbers, genders, ages, nationalities, educational statuses, and majors of foreign students at University X?
2. What characteristics do the different types of students in language program X have?
3. What types of equipment, materials, and facilities are available in various language programs across the United States?

EXPLORATORY

Surveys also provide tools for in-depth investigations of people's experiences with language. For instance, you might appropriately use survey tools to study people's ideas, attitudes, opinions, and evaluations of the following types of issues:

1. What are students' and teachers views' of practices used in the language learning and teaching processes?
2. What are students', teachers', and administrators' views of specific elements of the curriculum of a language program?
3. What are teachers' views on aspects of their professional lives?

Surveys are also useful for in-depth investigations of people's ideas, attitudes, opinions, and evaluations with regard to a particular language, nationality, or culture:

1. What are students' and teachers views' of native speakers of the target language? Of native speakers in the various countries where the language is spoken? Of the native speakers of various dialects of the language?
2. What are students' and teachers' views of the target culture(s) involved?
3. What are students' and teachers' views of the different registers of the target language? Of the use of slang and swearing?

EXPLANATORY

Survey research can also lead to inferences that help to explain what is observed in the process. In the case of open-response (like short-answer) questions, ethnographic data analysis techniques may be brought to bear on the data to help find patterns and trends that have explanatory power. In many cases, such analyses may result in the formation of new hypotheses, which is why ethnographic methods are often referred to as "hypothesis forming." In the case of closed-response (like yes–no) questions, which can easily be analyzed numerically, descriptive and inferential statistics may help in investigating any existing patterns, similarities, differences, and so forth. The particular benefit that can be derived from using inferential statistics is that results can be analyzed in terms of the probabilities that they have occurred by chance alone. As will be explained in Chapter 4, if carefully employed, such probabilities can increase the explanatory power of the resulting inferences.

Example research questions for different groups

Research questions may also vary according to the different groups that might be studied. Consider some questions formulated to study the native speakers of a particular target language. Native speakers are often important because they can provide baseline data on what the language is like when it is actually used. When surveying native speakers, questions such as the following can be addressed:

1. How many speakers are there of different dialects of the language, and how are they distributed geographically?
2. What vocabulary, structures, registers, and so forth, are acceptable to native speakers in various situations?
3. What are native speakers' attitudes toward non-native speakers of their language?
4. What degree of accentedness is acceptable to native speakers?

Language students provide another interesting and useful source of data. Students can help you to answer questions such as the following:

1. What are the characteristics of the students in language program X, or across various language programs?
2. What are their attitudes toward native speakers of the target language?
3. What aspects of the language should they be learning with regard to pronunciation, vocabulary, structures, functions, sociolinguistics, pragmatics, and so forth?
4. What are their attitudes toward the target culture?
5. What do they think of the existing language curriculum, especially the objectives, tests, materials, and teaching methods?
6. What changes would they recommend in the existing language program?

Teachers can also be a rich source of answers to questions such as the following:

1. What are the characteristics of the teachers in language program X, or across various language programs?
2. What are teachers' views of the students' language learning needs? How well do the teachers think they met the students' needs in each of their classes?
3. What do they think of the existing language curriculum, especially the objectives, tests, materials, and teaching methods?
4. What changes would they recommend in the existing language program?
5. How good was the performance of the administrators in a particular language program?

Administrators have views too, and their opinions may be crucial from a political point of view in answering questions such as the following:

1. What are the characteristics of the administrators in language program X, or across various language programs?

2. What do they think of the performance of students, teachers, staff, and so forth, in their language program(s)?
3. What problems and solutions do they see for the curriculum of the language program that they administer?

Students' parents may also prove useful as a source of data about their own attitudes as well as the attitudes of the students. Once again, this is a group that may be particularly important from a political standpoint in answering questions such as the following:

1. What are the characteristics of the parents of the students in language program X, or in various language programs?
2. Why do they want their children to learn the target language?
3. What uses do they think that their children will eventually have for the target language?
4. What aspects of the language do they want their children to learn?
5. What are their attitudes toward native speakers of the target language? Toward the target culture?

Especially in using surveys to do needs analysis, you may want to survey those people who will be involved in the students' future. Such people might include (1) professors, lecturers, and/or teachers with whom students will study after they have finished language training, (2) the employers who will hire them some day, or (3) any other persons who can provide insight into the language that students will need to use in the future. In a survey of professors, lecturers, and teachers, questions such as the following might be answered:

1. What are the language needs of students who must eventually perform academically in the language?
2. What are the strengths and weaknesses of non-native speakers who are currently performing academically in the target language?

In the case of employers, similar questions might be phrased as follows:

1. What are the on-the-job language needs of students who must eventually perform professionally in the language?
2. What are the strengths and weakness of non-native speakers who are currently performing on the job in the target language?

In short, you should consider surveying anyone of interest in the particular research or curriculum development project, and should consider all the myriad questions that can be asked and studied. In fact, the lists of people and questions given above are not meant to be exhaustive, but rather to be illustrative of the people and types of research questions that might be answered using surveys in language research or curriculum development.

Examples of survey planning

At the end of each chapter of this book, example survey research projects will be described. Each chapter will include a running example that is common to all chapters, and rotating examples that are different in each chapter. In this chapter, the running example will begin with a description of a research survey of English as a Second Language (ESL) professionals around the world. The rotating example will be drawn from a curriculum survey project conducted at the English Language Institute at the main (Manoa) campus of the University of Hawaii.

Running example: Planning a survey research project

The first example in this chapter is a research project. This project was conducted within the professional organization TESOL (Teachers of English to Speakers of Other Languages) International[2] to explore the views of the organization's membership on the place of research in TESOL International. Because I was personally involved in all stages of this project, I will be able to describe it in detail as an example of a real survey research project. Hence this project will serve as a running example in all the chapters of this book. Naturally, I will describe only those aspects of the project that are related to the topic of the chapter in question. For instance, in this chapter I will provide some background information and describe the planning aspects of the project. In Chapter 2, examples will be drawn from this project to illustrate the design of a survey instrument. In Chapter 3, the project will be discussed in terms of gathering and compiling survey data, and so forth.

To provide some background, this project was the work of the TESOL Research Task Force, which was created by the TESOL Executive Board to look into the place of research within the organization. The task force was created at the TESOL Executive Board mid-year meeting in October 1990 with the purpose of making recommendations on the role and status of research interests in TESOL in terms compatible with TESOL International's overall mission, objectives, and long-range planning. The

---

2 For those who are unfamiliar with TESOL, it is an international organization whose mission is to "develop the expertise of its members and others involved in teaching English to speakers of other languages to help them foster effective communication in diverse settings while respecting individuals' language rights. To this end: TESOL articulates and advances standards for professional preparation and employment, continuing education, and student programs; TESOL links groups worldwide to enhance communication among language specialists; TESOL produces high-quality programs, services, and products; TESOL promotes advocacy to further the profession." (TESOL, http://www.tesol.edu). For more information, contact TESOL, International, 700 South Washington Street, Suite 200, Alexandria, Virginia 22314 USA, visit their Web site at www.tesol.edu, or e-mail them at info@tesol.edu.

task force consisted of J. D. Brown (chair), Marjorie Knowles (second vice-president), Denise Murray (chair of Research Special Interest Group), Joyce Neu (chair of Applied Linguistics Special Interest Group), and Emma Violand-Hainer (Arlington Public Schools, to represent interests of teachers and public school educators). Thus the individuals appointed by the president of TESOL to the task force were from a variety of backgrounds and locations around the United States.

The task force was charged with examining at least seven general concerns:

1. The views of the general membership and of researchers on the role of research in TESOL
2. The place of research interests in the TESOL Convention
3. The role of research in promoting scholarship within the association
4. The function of research in generating grants
5. The place of research in other services in TESOL
6. Means for increasing communication between researchers and classroom teachers
7. Possibilities for coordinating meetings, publications, and/or missions with the American Association of Applied Linguistics (AAAL), Second Language Research Forum (SLRF), and Language Testing Research Colloquium (LTRC)

The task force met twice during 1991: once in San Jose, California, and again at the TESOL convention in New York. The discussion in both meetings was very productive, resulting in many observations about the problems of research and ideas for solving those problems. One important observation was that there were many rumors about research and researchers within TESOL, but very little factual information. To address that issue, the task force created this survey research project with the goal of obtaining concrete data about the attitudes of the general membership about research issues, while tapping the views of researchers as well. To those ends, the following general research questions were formulated as a framework for our inquiries:

1. Which TESOL members do research?
2. What are members' views on the state of the profession?
3. What are members' views on TESOL publications?
4. What are members' views on the TESOL convention?
5. What are members' views on the place of research in TESOL?

A questionnaire was developed (as described at the end of Chapter 2), and sent out in April 1991 (as described in Chapter 3). The resulting data were coded and transcribed (also described in Chapter 3), as well as analyzed from a statistical perspective (as described in Chapter 4) and qualitatively (as described in Chapter 5). Finally, the results were written up in a report to the Executive Board of TESOL (Brown et al., 1992b) in a typical research format (as described in Chapter 6), and disseminated through the newsletter of the TESOL organization to inform the membership of the findings (Brown, 1992a, 1992b, 1992d, 1992e; Brown, Knowles, Murray, Neu, & Violand-Hainer, 1992a).

On the basis of this survey, various recommendations were made to the Executive Board of TESOL, the primary one being that a permanent Research Advisory Committee should be created to foster research and communication of research issues between formal researchers and teachers, and vice versa. We also recommended that this new committee base its work on the findings of this survey project (which will be further described at the end of each chapter of this book).

Rotating example: Planning a curriculum survey project

The rotating example in this chapter is a curriculum survey project. More precisely, this project was a needs analysis conducted for the English Language Institute (ELI) at the University of Hawaii at Manoa (UHM). The ELI was a long-established academic ESL teaching unit, when this project began, but the curriculum needed considerable work. Fortunately, the ELI was associated directly with an M.A. program in ESL, from which talent and energy could be drawn in the form of graduate student projects.

Because I was director of the ELI and co-teaching a course in language curriculum development at the same time, I was able to encourage teams of M.A. students to do needs analyses and objectives setting for ELI courses. The report of Kimzin and Proctor (1986) was a result of just such a project. Their manuscript served not only as the basis for developing the tests, materials, and teaching in the ELI listening courses, but also as a model for other needs analyses that were subsequently performed, for instance, Weaver, Pickett, Kiu, & Cook (1987) for foreign teaching assistant speaking skills, and Loschky, Stanley, Cunha, & Singh (1987) for academic reading.

A brief summary of Kimzin and Proctor's report (1986) will give a feeling for what a curriculum survey project might be like, at least in an academic ESL setting. Notice in particular the number and types of different data-gathering procedures (selected from those listed in Table 1.1) that were used in this project.

LITERATURE REVIEW

Kimzin and Proctor first turned to a search of the literature on teaching academic listening in order to find any existing information on the state of the art in teaching academic listening courses. Thus, in their needs analysis they began by citing a number of relevant articles from the

25

language teaching literature. Then they reviewed several in-house reports, which proved to be out of date but had some bearing on the issues involved.

INITIAL SURVEY

Before they actually began full-scale research, Kimzin and Proctor conducted a quick preliminary survey during Spring semester 1986 in one intermediate listening class and one advanced listening class ($N = 52$), to identify the general types of content-area courses the students were taking in addition to their ELI requirements.

CASE-STUDY OBSERVATIONS

Based on the initial survey, Art 474, Physics 274, Public Health 777, and Economics 150 were chosen for further investigation because they were representative courses in areas of liberal arts, science, and business – common majors for our ESL students. These particular courses were also selected because they ranged in type from small seminars to large (150-student) lecture settings. Case study observations were conducted in each course in order to investigate the listening, note taking, and discussion skills needed for these particular types of classes in these particular fields of study.

Each class was observed twice. Kimzin and Proctor carefully observed and took notes. In the process, they chose to focus on: (1) difficulties that both instructors and international students had during classroom communication, (2) learning styles that international students preferred, and (3) coping strategies that these students used. To those ends, each class session was analyzed for various aspects of lecture style, organization, and discourse.

INTERVIEWS

Next, interviews were conducted with the course instructors, as well as with ELI students who were concurrently enrolled in the courses. The interviews, though time-consuming, proved valuable for gaining detailed data about the professors' views of what aspects of the language the ESL students needed to learn and their perceptions of the lecture listening processes involved in a variety of settings.

MEETINGS

Based on the literature review, case study observations, and interviews, Kimzin and Proctor developed tentative goals, microskills, and objectives for the courses. At several points in the process, review meetings were held with the ELI listening course instructors to get their comments and suggestions about these goals, microskills, and objectives as they were being developed.

QUESTIONNAIRES

An ELI student questionnaire was then developed to investigate whether these tentative goals, microskills, and objectives were consistent with the self-perceived listening needs of the general ELI population. One section of the ELI intermediate listening course was surveyed, along with three sections of the Advanced Listening course ($N = 67$). Along with biodata information, the questionnaire provided a checklist of twenty-seven tentative microskills under the following categories: lecture listening, note taking, and discussion skills. Students were asked to check *yes, no,* or *not sure* to questions about (1) the need for each skill and (2) the degree to which it was taught in the ELI listening courses that they were taking.

CONCLUSIONS

On the basis of the data gathered in this survey project, a first set of course objectives was formulated. These were later used as the basis for test development, materials development, and teaching. The resulting list of goals, microskills, and objectives was the best available at the time, because it was based on a wide variety of data sources and professional judgment within the ELI. In the ensuing years, the ELI perceptions of students' needs have shifted considerably and so have the objectives. Nevertheless, Kimzin and Proctor (1986) provided a sound foundation with their literature review, their case studies, their meetings, and their interview and questionnaire surveys.

Notice that they planned their curriculum development efforts so that a variety of different types of instruments were used to gather data – some were survey techniques and some were not. Real projects may often work this way; that is, they may require a variety of different data-gathering procedures. Thus survey(s) may serve only as part of the larger curriculum development and revision processes.

Summary

In this chapter I showed where survey research fits into the many types of research done by language professionals. Then I introduced some of the basic concepts necessary in setting up a survey project. I first discussed the tools available for gathering data related to language and language learning. These tools included many for gathering non-survey information, and two for gathering survey data: interviews and questionnaires. Second, I covered the six overall steps involved in a survey project: planning the survey project, designing the survey instrument, administering the survey, analyzing the survey statistically, analyzing the survey qualitatively, and reporting the results of the survey. Third, I explored the two most common uses of surveys in language education: curriculum development and language research. Fourth, I discussed the issues related to operationalizing key concepts, including the links between psychological constructs and variables, as well as the four scales of measurement that can be used to operationalize variables (nominal, ordinal, interval, and ratio). Fifth, I explained the problems of formulating language survey research questions by discussing the characteristics of good research questions (specific, answerable, relevant, and clear) and the primary purposes of research questions (descriptive, exploratory, and explanatory). I also supplied example research questions as they might be formulated for different groups of people in a language teaching/learning situation. Finally, to illustrate several contexts in which survey projects would make sense, I ended the chapter with two examples: a running example project based on a research survey conducted by the TESOL Research Task Force, and a rotating example curriculum survey project drawn from a needs analysis performed by Kimzin and Proctor for the ESL listening courses in the ELI at UHM.

Suggestions for further reading

The literature on survey research methods offers a number of general books covering widely ranging and differing aspects of survey research, including classics such as Babbie (1973, 1975), Bailey (1982), and Oppenheim (1966), any of which may be available at a used book store. More recent and more readily available efforts include Babbie (1990), Berdie, Anderson, and Niebuhr (1986), Fink (1995a), and Fowler (1993). Since each covers a wide variety of topics in its own distinctive way, several of these books might prove useful in combination.

Important terms

categorical scales
data
data point
dichotomous scales
group interviews
group-administered questionnaire
individual interviews
interval scales
interviews
language needs

language surveys
needs analysis
nominal scales
operationalized
ordinal scales
primary research
program evaluation
psychological constructs
questionnaires
ranked scales

ratio scales
research
scale of measurement
secondary research
self-administered questionnaire

situation needs
survey research
telephone interviews
variables

Review questions

1. How does this chapter define a *language survey?*
2. What are the four main types of information that can be gathered using nonsurvey tools?
3. What are three procedures discussed in this chapter for conducting interview surveys?
4. What two procedures are described for questionnaire surveys?
5. What are the six broad steps that this chapter outlines for conducting a survey project?
6. What are psychological constructs? How does the concept of operationalization link psychological constructs to the variables examined in a project?
7. What are the four scales of measurement? How do they differ?
8. What are the four characteristics of good research questions?
9. What are the three purposes of research questions?

Applications

A. Think of a survey project that you would like to conduct. Quickly list the six steps given in this chapter for such projects leaving plenty of space for expanding on them. Then begin to make notes on what each of the six steps means in terms of the particular project that you have in mind.
B. In a second list, sketch out the general goals of your survey, list any psychological constructs or variables that may be involved, and decide what scales of measurement should be used to operationalize each variable. You may want to discuss your ideas with another language professional so that you can further elaborate on your ideas.
C. In a third list, write out preliminary research questions for the project that you have in mind. Next, consider your questions in light of the four characteristics of good research questions, and discard them or revise as necessary. Then, consider the three purposes of research questions. Have you accomplished all of the appropriate purposes?

2 Designing a survey instrument

In this chapter I will cover the problems involved in designing any survey instrument, whether it is a questionnaire or an interview. To that end, I will address a number of issues: (1) the types of questions that surveys can answer, (2) the functions of surveys, (3) the different response and question formats, (4) guidelines for writing good survey questions, and (5) guidelines for producing a polished questionnaire. The chapter will end as usual with running and rotating examples, and a summary.

Types of questions surveys can answer

The example research questions presented and discussed in the previous chapter, as well as the individual questions on any survey, can generally be classified into a relatively small number of categories. Question categories have been suggested by both Patton (1987) and Rossett (1982).

Patton's question types

Patton (1987) lists six types of questions that can be used in designing a survey: (1) behavior/experience, (2) opinion/value, (3) feelings, (4) knowledge, (5) sensory, and (6) demographic/background.

BEHAVIOR/EXPERIENCE QUESTIONS

Behavior/experience questions try to get at what happens under certain circumstances – more specifically, what respondents do, how they behave/act, what they experience/encounter, how they respond, or just what happens/occurs. Such questions can be asked of any respondents. The following are examples of questions that might be asked of four groups:

1. *Language students:* What do you experience when you are reading?
2. *Language teachers:* What do you do when students challenge your authority?
3. *Content-area teachers:* What do students have to do in your course?
4. *Language program administrators:* What happens to the students step by step during the placement examination?

OPINION/VALUE QUESTIONS

Opinion/value questions explore the respondents' thoughts, reactions, impressions, attitudes, and outlook on various aspects of language or language learning processes. For example, you might ask questions such as the following of language students:

1. What is the most important aspect of the language class for you?
2. How do you like the textbook used in your language class?
3. Which do you think is most important, learning oral or written French?
4. When do you think we should have the class party?

FEELINGS QUESTIONS

Feelings questions seek to investigate the respondents' emotions or emotional reactions about a particular topic. For instance, you might ask questions such as the following of language teachers:

1. Is there anything in this language program that you do not like?
2. How do you feel about the classroom observations that the program director does every semester?
3. What is your emotional reaction when students criticize your teaching?
4. How do you feel about all the testing we do in this program?

KNOWLEDGE QUESTIONS

Knowledge questions tend to tap into facts, knowledge, and information about language teaching and learning processes. For example, you might ask questions similar to the following of language program administrators:

1. How many teachers work in this program?
2. What is the schedule of classes for this program?
3. How long is each class?
4. What textbooks do you use?

SENSORY QUESTIONS

Sensory questions explore the visual, tactile, auditory, and even olfactory aspects of the language teaching and learning processes. For example, you might ask questions such as the following of language program administrators:

1. What are the noise levels like outside the classrooms?
2. Is the air conditioning set at the right level in the classrooms?
3. Is there enough light in the teachers' room to work properly?
4. What are your classrooms like physically?

DEMOGRAPHIC/BACKGROUND QUESTIONS

Demographic/background questions tend to elicit biographical or historical information. For instance, you might ask questions such as the following of language students:

1. How many years have you studied Spanish?
2. How old are you?
3. What other languages do you speak?
4. What courses are you taking this semester?

Rossett's question types

Pattons' six question types may help you to think of some possibilities in designing a survey, but I have found Rossett's (1982) list of five basic question types more effective for making sure that important issues are covered in a survey: (1) problems, (2) priorities, (3) abilities, (4) attitudes, and (5) solutions.

PROBLEMS QUESTIONS

The broadest of the five categories of questions has to do with problems. The purpose of **problems questions** is to identify problems that the respondents perceive in a some given context. For example, you might ask language students what kinds of problems they are having learning English, or inquire of language teachers what they think are the most pressing issues in a particular language program. You could also ask content-area teachers what they think is the biggest problem that chemistry students from other countries have with their English, or ask language program administrators what they think are the biggest organizational and institutional impediments to student learning in their language program.

Notice that the examples given above are very broad and exploratory. Such problem questions could equally well be very structured and narrowly focused and still be questions about problems.

PRIORITIES QUESTIONS

The second category of questions is about priorities. **Priorities questions** are posed in order to find out which topics, functions, skills, activities, grammar points, and so forth, are believed by the respondents to be most important, second most important, and so forth. For example, in learning the writing skill, the following elements might turn out to be those considered most important by a particular group of respondents: using correct spelling and punctuation, organizing information well, doing library research before writing, proofreading, and so forth. Such priorities questions may require the respondents to select those elements to which they would give priority, or may require the respondents to put the elements in order by priority. Naturally, the priorities of different groups may differ considerably, even within a single language program. In fact, students, teachers, and administrators may see the world in very different ways (for more on the differences in the views of students and teachers, see Nunan, 1986, 1991, or Willing, 1988).

ABILITIES QUESTIONS

The third category of question has to do with abilities. Many different abilities may be the focus of **abilities questions.** Often, in language curriculum development or research, language aptitude or proficiency are the abilities of interest. For instance, an ability question might be designed to determine students' abilities at the time of admissions into a particular institution. Such questions could be answered by testing students using overall language proficiency exams in order to diagnose initial strengths and weaknesses, or could be addressed in a survey by having the students assess their own strengths and weaknesses. In either case, this type of information can be very important for establishing a starting point for a given language program, and for delineating the top and bottom abilities in the total range of students. In short, questions about abilities are often important for getting a sense of the boundaries or scope of a language program.

ATTITUDES QUESTIONS

Attitudes questions are typically used to obtain data about participants' feelings, wishes, and attitudes toward the language being studied, toward native speakers of the language and their culture, toward the elements of a language curriculum, and so forth. Thus, attitude questions might include questions about how well students like studying *grammar points* as compared to *functions* of the language (such as *asking directions,* or *seeking information on the telephone*). You might elicit teachers' attitudes on the same issue by asking an attitude question such as: "Do you feel that your students learn English better and more efficiently by studying grammar points, language functions, or some combination of the two?" These are both examples of a broad class of questions that researchers use to describe and investigate the differences in attitudes of various groups of people.

SOLUTIONS QUESTIONS

Solutions questions do just what their name implies: They seek solutions to whatever perceived problems were uncovered in the previous question types. The ideas for solving problems that arise from such questions are often the best possible solutions from a political standpoint, because solutions that are perceived as having come from within a group or institution tend to have greater backing and continued support. Researchers usually position solutions questions late in a survey, after the respondents have expressed and thought about their views on the problems.

Functions of surveys

While you are formulating different types of questions as outlined in the previous section, you should remember that different parts of a survey can function in different ways. Some parts may function as brief biodata surveys, whereas others may act as brief opinion surveys, self-ratings, judgmental ratings, or Q-sorts. Naturally, you can also combine any or all of these functions so they can be contained in one questionnaire or interview.

Biodata surveys typically elicit biographical background data from the respondents. Such data might include each respondent's age, place of birth, sex, marital status, occupation, number of years of language study, years of education, salary, and so forth.

Opinion surveys usually seek to uncover the opinions and attitudes of the respondents about specific issues. For instance, questions might be developed to find out what a group of teachers think about the existing language program, its objectives, the materials, the teaching, and the tests, as well as how all of the above elements relate to the students' needs.

Self-ratings typically require the respondents to rate their own abilities, interest levels, motivations, and so forth. Such ratings can provide practical insights into the self-image of the individuals, even if the ratings themselves are not 100 percent accurate.

Judgments about various aspects of language learning usually require respondents to briefly write their views down or select those descriptions that best match their views. For example, researchers might ask teachers to judge the effectiveness of a language program's objectives and materials in terms of how useful they are to the students, how necessary they are to the students' future language use, or how easy they are to teach. In all cases, the teachers are simply providing their judgments, judgments that may form a very important part of the information revealed by a survey.

Q-sort procedures combine aspects of the opinion survey discussed earlier and the judgments discussed immediately above. You can accomplish this combination by asking the respondents to provide their views, attitudes, and/or opinions, and then rank them in terms of how important they think each of the issues is (also see the first footnote in the previous chapter for more on Q-sorts).

Remember, researchers do occasionally design entire survey instruments to accomplish one of the five functions listed above, but surveys are seldom so unidimensional. They are more likely to develop a survey to accomplish a combination of the functions listed above and answer a variety of the question types listed at the beginning of the chapter.

Different response and question formats

A quick glance at the example surveys provided in the appendixes of this book will quickly reveal that interview and questionnaire instruments contain a variety of question formats. The choices that you make among these different formats will naturally depend on the general goals of your questionnaire or interview, the types of analyses that you want to perform, the specific purpose of each question, and so forth. I will present the discussion of these question types in two basic response formats: open responses and closed responses. In the process, I will focus on questionnaire design, but you should recognize that exactly the same issues arise in designing interviews.

Response format definitions

So far in this book, I have written a great deal about survey questions. Indeed, in the previous two sections, I noted that survey questions can address eleven different types of questions and can serve five different functions. However, you may not yet understand clearly what a *question* is, because I have not defined the concept. Confusion may arise because survey questions can come in so many different forms. They may indeed be written as direct questions, but on other occasions, respondents may be asked to react to statements, a checklist, or any other type of stimulus. The point is that any part of a questionnaire that produces an individual, discrete response will be referred to as a **question** in this book, because the intent of a survey is always to question, or elicit data, even if a statement or checklist is used to do so.

Fortunately, the variety of question formats need not be as confusing as you might at first glance think, because all survey questions can be classified into one of two general **response formats** based on the ways that respondents are required to answer the questions. Quite simply, some questions require closed responses, whereas others require open responses.

Closed responses are responses for which optional answers are presented as part of the question, and the respondents are required to select the answer of their choice. For instance, a questionnaire might include a series of closed-response statements such as the following (which only require the respondents to circle agree or disagree):

35

Specific grammar points can be effectively practiced by using (circle one):

substitution drills	agree	disagree
transformation drills	agree	disagree
sentence combination drills	agree	disagree
communicative exercises	agree	disagree
. . . and so forth		

Open responses require the respondents to create the answer in their own words. For instance, if a questionnaire designer wanted to know what type of grammar drills respondents prefer, an open-response approach to this issue could simply ask a question such as: "What type of grammar drills do you think are best for effective learning?" The respondents would then be given sufficient space on a questionnaire (or time in an interview) to answer the question in their own words.

Pros and cons of closed and open responses

As shown in Table 2.1, open-response and closed-response questions each have advantages and disadvantages.

For the open-response questions (ones for which the respondents create the answers orally or in writing), the first of the advantages is that open-response questions give the respondents a great deal of flexibility in answering. This flexibility can result in a wide range of possible answers. Thus open-response questions are particularly good for finding unexpected answers. In turn, the possibility of unexpected answers makes open-response questions particularly useful for exploring the dimensions of an issue. Often, researchers can use the data gained from open-response questions to formulate narrower, more easily interpretable questions for future surveys. Open-response questions may also turn out to be easier to write when first creating a survey.

However, along with the advantages of open-response questions come some distinct disadvantages. For instance, open-response questions typically turn out to be relatively difficult and time-consuming for the respondents to answer. Thus respondents may be more likely to skip such questions. In addition, open-response questions tend to be relatively difficult to code, analyze, and interpret. As a by-product of the flexibility afforded to respondents in open-response questions, some of the answers may turn out to be irrelevant to the purposes of the survey. Also, the responses may tend to be, or at least appear to be, rather subjective. Finally, demonstration of the reliability and validity of open-response questions may prove more difficult because open-response questions do not lend themselves to statistical analysis of these important characteristics in the same way that closed-response questions do.

TABLE 2.1. OPEN-RESPONSE VS. CLOSED-RESPONSE QUESTIONS

Type of questions	Advantages	Disadvantages
Open-response	Wide range of possible answers Exploratory in nature Relatively easy to write	Relatively difficult to answer Respondents more likely to skip Relatively difficult to code Relatively difficult to analyze Relatively difficult to interpret Some answers may be irrelevant Answers relatively subjective Relatively difficult to show reliability Relatively difficult to show validity
Closed-response	More uniformity across questions Relatively easy to answer Relatively easy to code Relatively easy to analyze Relatively easy to interpret Answers relatively objective Relatively easy to show reliability Relatively easy to show validity	Narrower range of possible answers Not so exploratory in nature Relatively difficult to write

Similarly, closed-response questions (or questions for which respondents must select from among optional answers presented as part of the question) also have both advantages and disadvantages. One advantage of closed-response questions is that they provide more uniformity across questions in terms of the types and specificity of data that are obtained. Closed-response questions are also easier to answer and less likely to be skipped by respondents. Closed-response questions are also relatively easy to code, analyze, and interpret because the data can readily be expressed numerically. This characteristic also makes the answers at least appear to be relatively objective. The potential for numerical analysis of closed-response questions also lends itself to easier demonstration of the reliability and validity of the instrument as a whole.

However, there are disadvantages to closed-response questions as well.

First, closed-response questions generally provide a fairly narrow range of possible answers. One danger inherent in this narrow range of answers is that the survey designer may overlook some potential responses that are in fact important. In addition, closed-response questions are less exploratory in nature. Thus survey designers may be more likely to find what they are looking for in closed-response questions, rather than finding unexpected responses as they might in open-response questions. Finally, clear, concise, closed-response questions are relatively difficult to write, at least in my experience.

The choices that must be made between open-response and closed-response questions are not easy ones. Each format has its strengths and weaknesses. A cursory examination of Table 2.1 might lead the reader to conclude that there are many more disadvantages to open-response questions and advantages to closed-response questions because of the relatively large number of items in each of these categories in the table. However, if a survey is exploratory and a wide range of possible answers is crucial to its purpose, open-response questions are essential, and any advantages that closed-response questions might have simply do not matter.

In general, I have found that both question formats can serve useful, though different, purposes in any given survey instrument. Some questions might usefully be exploratory, while others are more structured. As a consequence, all of the instruments that I have created have involved some of each format.

Open-response questions

Within the open-response format, two forms of questions are typically used to elicit data: fill-in questions and short-answer questions.

FILL-IN QUESTIONS

Fill-in questions are exactly what they sound like; that is, they are questions that require the respondents to fill in information in their own words. However, in comparison to the short-answer questions discussed next, fill-in questions are relatively restricted in what they require the respondents to produce. For example, the following biodata questions (taken from the example questionnaire in Appendix C) are all relatively restricted in what they require of the respondents:

Major _____
Native language _____
Other languages _____
Time in the U.S.A. (in years) _____
Time at University of Hawaii _____
                              (in semesters)

SHORT-ANSWER QUESTIONS

The difference, then, between fill-in and short-answer questions is one of length. Whereas fill-in questions might call for a word or phrase, **short-answer questions** usually require a few phrases or sentences. (Please note that no long-answer question formats are discussed here because of the general inadvisability of having questions in an interview or questionnaire that call for extensive answers.) Examples of short-answer questions are provided by the following, taken from the same example questionnaire in Appendix C:

13. What are the most effective classroom activities your teacher uses? Please describe.

---

14. If you could add or change anything about this reading class, what would your changes be? Please explain your ideas.

Examples of short-answer questions in an interview are the following (taken from the example interview in Appendix D):

1. What are your personal goals for the students in your class?
2. What would you say their needs are?
3. What are your biggest problems in teaching reading?
4. How do you feel about the objectives?
5. Has having the objectives altered your teaching approach?
6. How would you describe your teaching approach?
7. What kind of learner does best in this class?

Closed-response questions

Within the closed-response category, at least four forms of questions can be used to elicit data: alternative-answer questions, Likert-scale questions, checklist questions, and ranking questions.

ALTERNATIVE-ANSWER QUESTIONS

Any questions that provide alternative answers from which respondents must select can be considered **alternative-answer questions.** The following examples (taken from the example questionnaire in Appendix B) illustrate the general form of such questions:

11. Do you feel that you stay current with the research in EFL/ESL? YES NO

12. Do you regularly read the *TESOL Quarterly?* YES NO
13. Do you feel that the research reported in *TESOL Quarterly* is of high quality? YES NO
14. Do you believe that *TESOL Quarterly* provides you with usable research information? YES NO

Note that alternative-answer questions need not necessarily be in the form of YES/NO questions, as indicated by Question 5 from the same questionnaire:

5. On what basis are you employed? (circle one) FULL-TIME PART-TIME

It is also worth noting that such questions can include more than two categories, as indicated by Question 8 from the same source:

8. Type(s) of institution(s) where you do most of your TESOL-related work (circle as many as applicable):
ADULT ED.   ELEMENTARY   HIGH SCHOOL
INTERMEDIATE   REFUGEE
UNIVERSITY (UNDERGRADUATE)
UNIVERSITY (GRADUATE)
OTHER _____

Clearly, alternative-answer questions come in many different forms, and the only limitations in creating useful questions of this sort are those imposed by the imagination of the questionnaire designer.

LIKERT-SCALE QUESTIONS

Likert-scale questions are very common on questionnaires, though they might prove harder to use in an interview because you would probably have to show the questions to the interviewee. **Likert-scale questions** are typically used to investigate how respondents feel about a series of statements. (Note that *Likert* is pronounced with what is traditionally called a short *i* sound, or /I/ in the International Phonetic Alphabet.) The respondents' attitudes are registered by having them circle or check numbered categories (for instance, 1 2 3 4 5), which have descriptors above them as in the following examples (taken from the example questionnaire in Appendix B):

19. Professionally, how much importance do you attach to each of the following items? (Circle the number that best describes the degree of importance that you attach to the item on the left.)

	IMPORTANCE			
	NONE	LITTLE	MOD.	MUCH
TESOL Quarterly	0	1 2	3	4 5
book reviews	0	1 2	3	4 5
brief reports	0	1 2	3	4 5
classroom research articles	0	1 2	3	4 5
classroom teaching articles	0	1 2	3	4 5
statistical research articles	0	1 2	3	4 5
TESOL Matters	0	1 2	3	4 5
TESOL Convention	0	1 2	3	4 5

Likert-scale questions are effective for gathering respondents' views, opinions, and attitudes about various language-related issues ranging on dimensions such as the following: very serious to slight, important to unimportant, like to dislike, and agree to disagree. Of course, other dimensions may prove necessary, depending on the purposes of a particular language survey.

One problem with Likert-scale questions has arisen often at UHM. Some types of students tend to "sit on the fence" on Likert questions. In other words, given a neutral non-opinion option (such as 3 for *moderate* in the above example), they will tend to take that option. If you need to force respondents to express a definite opinion, that is, to jump one way or the other, on each question, you may find it useful to have an even number of options from which they must choose, as in the following modification of the above example:

19. Professionally, how much importance do you attach to each of the following items? (Circle the number that best describes the degree of importance that you attach to the item on the left.)

	IMPORTANCE			
	NOT IMPORTANT		VERY IMPORTANT	
TESOL Quarterly	1	2	3	4
book reviews	1	2	3	4
brief reports	1	2	3	4
. . .				

In this example, even respondents who want to remain neutral are forced to select in one direction or the other (that is, a 2 or 3), which will give at least a hint of a direction to their opinions. Naturally, there are times when a fence-sitting option may be desirable. If that is the case, you may wish to include a clear *No opinion* option in the middle of the scale.

Of course, there are many variations of this Likert scale (variations that are often referred to as Likert-like. For instance, the following example (from the example questionnaire in Appendix C) is clearly related to the Likert scale:

4. What is your biggest problem with reading? (please check the appropriate blanks)

	very serious	moderate	slight
a. understanding main idea	_____	_____	_____
b. understanding details	_____	_____	_____
c. making inferences	_____	_____	_____
d. interpreting figures of speech and idioms	_____	_____	_____
e. summarizing or synthesizing materials	_____	_____	_____
f. recognizing the author's point of view	_____	_____	_____

CHECKLIST QUESTIONS

Checklist questions are any questions that present a list in which the respondents can check or circle all of the items that apply to them. For example, in Question 18 (in Appendix B), the respondents were required to check as many of the descriptors as applied to their attitudes toward language research as follows:

18. In general, do you find research in the language teaching field to be (check all which apply):

_____ boring	_____ pointless
_____ challenging	_____ too theoretical
_____ difficult to understand	_____ too practical
_____ easy to understand	_____ about the right mix
_____ interesting	of theory and
_____ useful	practice
_____ others	

Note that this example was not 100 percent effective, as indicated by the fact that many respondents in the TESOL survey filled in the *others* category, and many respondents also wrote qualifying adjectives in the margins for those answers that they did check. Nonetheless, interesting patterns did emerge that showed trends in the descriptors that went together for different types of language teaching professionals.

Other variations of the checklist type of question may come in a form that is more like an inventory, as in the following example (from Appendix E), which asked content-area teachers to inventory the types of tests that they give in their courses:

8. What types of tests do you give?
   a. multiple-choice _____
   b. fill-in-the-blank _____
   c. short-answer _____
   d. essay _____
   e. other _____

Naturally, such inventories can be applied to anything that can be checked off on a list.

RANKING QUESTIONS

Ranking questions are questions that require the respondents to rank order concepts, objects, people, and so forth. The ranking is usually done in terms of some overall scale, such as least to most interesting, least to most important, least to most time involved, and so forth. The following is an example of this type of question (from Appendix E):

10. Please indicate by rank order the amount of time your students must spend for each of the following areas. (1 = most time; 4 = least time)
    listening to lectures _____
    speaking in class _____
    reading for class _____
    writing for class _____

Combining different question types

There are two principal reasons for combining different questions within a questionnaire: (1) to provide a more compact questionnaire, and (2) to get general information *and* related follow-up details at the same time. For instance, two ranking questions could be combined to provide a more compact format as shown on the next page (from student evaluations questionnaires that I use when I teach ESL courses).

Directions: In the column to the left, please rank (1 = high through
9 = low) the following classroom activities in terms of the USEFUL-
NESS that you think they had for your learning of English. In the
column to the right, also rank them in terms of INTEREST level that
you had for each activity.

USEFULNESS	ACTIVITY	INTEREST
_____	Lectures	_____
_____	Grammar drills	_____
_____	Pronunciations drills	_____
_____	Pair work	_____
_____	Group work	_____
_____	Timed readings	_____
_____	Reduced forms dictations	_____
_____	Taped news items	_____
_____	Singing songs	_____

Notice in the above example that two distinctly different types of data
are being gathered. And both are necessary because many students at the
University of Hawaii at Manoa typically rank lectures and grammar
drills very high in terms of useful, but relatively low in terms of interest.
In contrast, they rank taped news items and singing songs relatively low
in terms of usefulness, but high in terms of interest. These two rankings
could have been separated into two different ranking lists, but the combined form given here is more compact and reduces repetitiveness.

Here is how two questions can be combined in order to obtain general
information *and* related follow-up details (from Appendix B):

10. Have you taken any statistics or research design courses?
    (circle one)   YES   NO
    What were the course titles (roughly)?
    . . .
15. Do you conduct research of any kind?   YES   NO
    If so, what kind?

In both Questions 10 and 15, an alternative-answer question is combined
with a short-answer question so that general and follow-up information
can be gathered.

Questions can be combined in many other ways, and you should explore such combinations as the need arises to make the questionnaire more
compact and to obtain follow-up information on previous questions.

Guidelines for writing good survey questions

Once you have made decisions about which response formats and question forms to use in a survey (or more likely, which combinations), you
still need to write those questions. Unfortunately, writing good questions

TABLE 2.2. GUIDELINES FOR WRITING GOOD SURVEY QUESTIONS

Think about the form
    Don't write overly long questions.
    Don't write unclear or ambiguous questions.
    Don't write negative questions.
    Don't write incomplete questions.
    Don't write overlapping choices in questions.
    Don't write questions across two pages.

Think about the meaning
    Don't write double-barreled questions.
    Don't write loaded questions.
    Don't write leading questions.
    Don't write prestige questions.
    Don't write embarrassing questions.
    Don't write biased questions.

Think about the respondents
    Don't use the wrong level of language.
    Don't use questions that respondents may be unable to answer.
    Don't assume that everyone has an answer.
    Don't make respondents answer questions that don't apply.
    Don't use irrelevant questions.
    Don't write superfluous information into questions.

can prove surprisingly difficult. Even more unfortunate, you may clearly recognize problem questions when it comes time to analyze the results (respondents may even point out the problems) – but by then it will be too late. Your goal at this stage should be to avoid such problems. The guidelines in Table 2.2 should help. The guidelines are organized into three categories that suggest you think about three aspects of the questions: the form, the meaning, and the respondents. The overall goal in writing questions should be to make them so precise and clear that the respondents know exactly what is being asked of them.

Think about the form

QUESTION LENGTH

To begin with, avoid writing overly long questions. As a rule of thumb, short questions are good questions. Keeping questions short is desirable for two reasons: First, you want the respondents to finish the questionnaire, and short questions will help ensure that they do not get discouraged; and second, respondents are often busy people who feel that their time is valuable, so they may want to read and answer the questions quickly. It is therefore wise for questionnaire designers to provide questions that will be effective and valid under those conditions.

Consider the following example question: "Do you think that language teaching is a rewarding career option at this point in the twenty-first century for educators in American public elementary schools, intermediate schools, and high schools?" (30 words). Now consider how much easier the following question is to process even though it contains virtually all of the same information: "Do you think that language teaching is currently a rewarding occupation in American public schools?" (15 words).

In a nutshell, questions should be as parsimonious as possible. One way of achieving parsimony is to include all and only the information necessary to answer the question. Another way of looking at the issue is to remember that questions should be short enough that the respondents can read them quickly, understand their meaning and intent, and answer them easily. One final bit of advice comes from Stacey and Moyer (1982): They suggest keeping question length to 20 words or less.

QUESTION CLARITY

You should also make sure that questions are clear and unambiguous. My experience indicates that a researcher can become so immersed in the issues and questions involved that all of the questions seem clear. In other words, because of familiarity with the questions and their purposes, you may not be able to spot ambiguities and double meanings.

Consider the following example (from Appendix B): "29. Why do you think that some research articles are inaccessible to some of the readers in our field?" This question seemed clear to me when I wrote the questionnaire. My intent was to ask a short-answer question that would find out why readers find statistical research articles difficult to understand. However, a number of the respondents found the word *inaccessible* to be ambiguous, because *inaccessible* can mean difficult to read or physically difficult to get. As a result, some respondents gave answers such as "because the library is so far away," or "because our libraries do not have journals," or "because the journals do not arrive by mail."

The only solution that I have found for this problem is to have many colleagues look over the questionnaire critically – perhaps with a checklist in hand like the one shown in Table 2.2. However, this strategy is far from foolproof, as indicated by the fact that the question in the previous paragraph was indeed examined by many colleagues. In fact, one of them had pointed out that the term *inaccessible* was ambiguous. Unfortunately, I had dismissed the criticism, assuming that the problem existed in only one variety of English (the colleague was British). So it is obviously important not only to get people to evaluate the questions, but also to listen to them in the sense of interpreting and doing something about their criticisms. Remember, the goal in writing questions (and in critiquing them) should be to make them so precise that the respondent knows exactly what you are asking.

NEGATIVE QUESTIONS

Next, you should avoid writing negative or double-negative questions, because the presence of a negative or double negative in a question can lead to misinterpretation and confusion.

Consider the following example: "Pronunciation in French is not difficult. (Circle one): Agree Disagree Don't know." In this case, respondents are likely to circle the "Don't know" option simply because the negative phrasing is confusing. It would have been much more straightforward to phrase the statement positively: "Pronunciation in French is easy. (Circle one): Agree Disagree Don't know." As you can see, the positive version of this question is far easier to answer.

Generally speaking, the best solution to this problem is to examine questions that use negatives or double negatives very carefully, to see whether you can find a positive way to restate the question. If it is absolutely necessary to use a negative, make sure that the wording is as clear as possible. You may want to emphasize the negative by making it bold, putting it in italics, underlining it, or combining all three types of emphasis to make sure that respondents notice it when reading the question.

INCOMPLETE QUESTIONS

You should also avoid writing incomplete questions. An incomplete question most often occurs when the question is not exhaustive in the sense that it does not include all possible answers.

Consider the following example (from Appendix B):

4. Please indicate approximately the percentage of your work time that you spend doing the following:
   ADMINISTRATION _____
   CLASSROOM TEACHING _____
   COMMUNITY SERVICE _____
   COUNSELING STUDENTS _____
   MATERIALS WRITING _____
   MEETINGS _____
   RESEARCH _____
   SERVICE (INSTITUTIONAL) _____
   TEACHER TRAINING _____
   OTHER _____ _____
   TOTAL _____
   [Please check that your TOTAL is 100%, even if you put in 200% days.]

The problem that arose in this example was that it did not include enough categories of activities. Although an OTHER category like that shown above is generally a good solution to this problem, in this particular case the respondents added so many other categories that the results became difficult to interpret. (Note also that there is a problem of ambiguity in this question. Although the distinction between CLASSROOM TEACH-ING and TEACHER TRAINING made sense for public school and adult education teachers, the university-level teachers often found that they were the same thing.)

The best solutions to the problem of incomplete answers are to try out such questions with a small group of respondents to make sure the possible categories in a question are exhaustive, and to use an *other* category as shown in the example.

OVERLAPPING CHOICES

The next suggestion is to avoid writing overlapping choices in survey questions. Expressed positively, this restriction means that the options, or answer categories, should be mutually exclusive. In other words, the respondents should generally not be put in a situation where they feel that they should select more than one option, or cannot decide between two.

Consider the following example: "Students should begin learning languages before what age? (Circle one): 5   7   9   11   13   15   17 adults   age not important." In this example, the categories overlap in that starting language learning before age 5 is also starting before ages 7, 9, 11, and so forth.

Consider another example in which the categories are once more over-lapping (that is, are not exclusive):

> The best location for the new foreign languages building would be:
> ____ In Shenandoah County   ____ In Lehigh County
> ____ In the city of Shenandoah   ____ Lehigh High School
> ____ Shenandoah High School   ____ Courtney High School
> ____ Other: _____

These options are overlapping in the sense that Shenandoah High School is probably in the city and county of the same name. There is a similar problem with Lehigh High School. The respondent is faced with a dilemma, because more than one of these overlapping options may make sense.

The best solution to this potential problem is to consider each combination of categories as you are writing or revising the questions to make sure that they are mutually exclusive and do not overlap. If you find overlap, you may want to consider breaking the question into two nonoverlapping questions, or eliminating whatever aspect of the question is causing the overlap.

One other hint here: If you find yourself using "Select the best answer" in your instructions, it may be worth checking to see if that instruction is necessary because you have categories that are not clearly different, or categories that overlap.

QUESTIONS ACROSS PAGES

In today's age of computers and word processors, you should pay special attention to avoid writing questions that cross page boundaries. The point is that respondents may miss part of the question if it stretches across two pages, or they may have to look back and forth awkwardly between pages to answer it. In either case, the problem can be avoided by simply checking to see that all parts of each question are on the same page. You should especially check this whenever you are editing or otherwise making changes in the questionnaire on a word processor because of the way word processors move the whole text up or down when even small additions or deletions are made.

Think about the meaning

DOUBLE-BARRELED QUESTIONS

The first issue related to thinking about meaning is that you should avoid double-barreled questions. Double-barreled questions are ones that really ask two or more questions at the same time. Such multiple purposes may make a question difficult to answer and certainly will make accurate interpretation of the answers nearly impossible.

Consider the following example: "The United States should spend less on the military and more on education (especially language education). (Circle one): Agree Disagree." This example is really a *triple* barreled question. Three factors are included (military, education, and language education spending). Respondents may have no problem answering the whole question, but interpretation of their responses will be problematic. Consider respondents who respond negatively. They may do so because they favor high military spending even though they would support more spending on education, or they may do so because they favor low military spending and high spending on education, but with no preferential treatment for language education. The problem with such questions is that respondents cannot agree or disagree without producing potentially misleading results. Some of the respondents will realize that a problem exists and may become confused. You will probably recognize the problem when you turn to analyzing the results – but by then it will be too late to do anything about it.

The best solution is to examine questions carefully for multiple purposes. Specifically, whenever the word *and* or *or* is used in a question, check to make sure that the question is not actually asking two or more questions at the same time.

LOADED WORDS

Next, avoid using what are referred to as "loaded words." Loaded words in this context are words that suggest an automatic positive or negative response because they are emotionally charged.

Consider the following example: "Spanish is obviously the language to study if you live in the Southwestern United States. (Circle one): Agree   Disagree   Don't know." The loaded word *obviously* has a positive coloring that might lead respondents to answer in a positive manner regardless of what they feel personally.

The best solutions to this problem are to avoid terms such as *obviously, clearly, usually,* and so forth, and look over each question in the survey with this specific problem in mind.

LEADING QUESTIONS

You can avoid another set of problems by making sure that there are no leading questions. Leading questions are questions that encourage respondents to answer in a certain way.

Consider the following example: "Although a French program has already been approved by the school administration, do you think that it should be started?" The information about the administration's prior approval may be leading in a positive or negative manner, depending on how the respondents feel about the administration. The question could be made far less leading by removing the comment about the administration as follows: "Do you think that a French program should be started at our school?"

Another variation of this problem is represented in the following example: "You don't use flash cards to study vocabulary even though it is considered passé, do you?" This is an extreme example, but it illustrates the problem. The question would obviously be much more neutral if it were phrased as follows: "Do you use flash cards to study vocabulary?"

The following provides one last and perhaps more subtle example of this phenomenon (from Appendix B):

16. Would you support the creation of a Research Advisory Committee within the TESOL organization designed to increase communication between researchers and teachers, encourage sound research on theory and practice, involve TESOL in seeking research grants, increase cooperation with other organizations, etc?
    YES   NO

The first problem is that this question is probably too long. In analyzing the results, however, I realized that this might also be a leading question when I read a note penciled in the margin by one of the respondents, who wrote: "and I would also support motherhood and apple pie." In retrospect, the question was clearly leading the respondents to answer in the positive way that I wanted them to answer. Indeed, they did so overwhelmingly. (It is also interesting to note that this question could be regarded as at least a quadruple-barreled question as described earlier.) Unfortunately, none of my colleagues noticed these problems in advance of distributing 1,800 questionnaires, and, of course, neither did I.

In my experience, the best solutions to this problem are to avoid qualifying phrases like those found in the first two examples, and to examine each question in the survey with this specific problem in mind.

PRESTIGE QUESTIONS

You should also be aware that some questions might inadvertently include issues of prestige. For example, when asked, some people will claim that they read more than they do, or that they study more than is true, or that they speak a language better than they actually do, because that is the prestigious way to answer.

This problem can be solved in a couple of ways. First, you could use questions that make the low prestige answer equally plausible. For instance, instead of "Have you read any books in English this week?" you might try "Have you had time to read any books in English this week?" Second, the directions should stress that accuracy is of primary importance and that a negative answer is just as valuable as a positive one.

EMBARRASSING QUESTIONS

Another issue that may arise is that of embarrassing questions. This can be a particularly knotty problem in language questionnaires, because the values of more than one culture may be involved.

Consider a question designed to find out what a group of language teachers think about teaching swear words in class. If swear words were actually included in the question, some teachers would be shocked and embarrassed because of the very presence of those words in the item, even though the words were intended as linguistic examples. The question could have gotten at the same issue without including the swear words and without being embarrassing as follows: "Swear words should be taught in the language classroom. (Circle one): Agree Disagree Don't know."

The solution to this problem lies in being culturally sensitive and avoiding questions that (1) refer to socially disapproved language, attitudes, or behavior in any of the cultures involved, (2) deal with what are considered private matters in any of the cultures involved, or (3) require answers that are considered low prestige in any of the cultures involved (see previous section).

BIASED QUESTIONS

Another related issue is biased questions. These usually result from the use of stereotypes or generalizations based on race, gender, religion, nationality, age, and so forth. Such expressions of bias are usually inaccurate, may cost you your respondents' cooperation, and, in general, are unprofessional and irresponsible.

Consider the following example, which I suppose I can use because I am Pennsylvania Dutch: "The Pennsylvania Dutch make terrible language teachers (Check one): Agree Disagree Don't know." I am not sure how my brethren (and sisters) in Pennsylvania would react, but I would not be surprised if they were offended by the very existence of the question.

The solution to this problem seems obvious: Do not ever use stereotyping or generalizations based on race, ethnic group, religion, gender, nationality, age, and so forth. Also be aware that, sometimes, subtle biases can arise without the survey designer being aware of them. Such subtle biases can best be detected by asking members of any groups that might be offended to have a look at the questionnaire with that particular goal in mind.

Think about the respondents

LEVEL OF LANGUAGE

On language questionnaires, the level of the language can be very important. The problem is that the language used in questions can be overly academic or condescending to L1 respondents, or too high (or low) in terms of level of proficiency demanded of L2 learners. In short, you must find the right level of language for your respondents. On the one hand, this means that you should not use a level of language so high that the respondents feel threatened, or insecure, and thus do not understand and answer the questions. On the other hand, you should avoid language at such a low level that it comes across as simple-minded or condescending in the sense of talking down to the respondents.

Naturally, the solution to this problem is to use the correct level of wording for the respondents involved, but what constitutes the correct level will depend on many factors, such as the respondents' level of education and their language proficiency. In addition, you may sometimes want to consider using the respondents' first language; and other times, you may want to use their second language; while still other times, a combination of the two may be best. The point is that you should carefully consider the level of language proficiency of the respondents that you are targeting in your survey.

QUESTIONS RESPONDENTS ARE UNABLE TO ANSWER

Also try to avoid questions that the respondents may never have thought about, have no basis for answering, or do not have sufficient information to answer.

Consider the following examples, which might be posed to language students:

1. How important is the study of grammar compared to the study of pronunciation?
2. How much English do you know?
3. How proficient are you in English?

In all three cases, students would not have a basis or sufficient information to answer accurately – at least as these questions are phrased.

Solution? Keep the respondents for the questionnaire firmly in mind while writing the questionnaire – especially, think about their ability to answer each question. Also, have other language professionals look at the questionnaire, or try it out while making sure to ask respondents about what they were thinking or feeling as they answer each question.

NOT EVERYONE HAS AN ANSWER

A related problem is that you cannot assume that everyone has an answer to each and every question. You should also avoid giving respondents the impression that they ought to know the answer to each question.

For example: "The grammar of Russian is (circle one): very difficult relatively difficult relatively easy very easy." Perhaps some respondents have no knowledge at all about the Russian language, but, as it stands, they are required to answer.

Solution? In the instructions, allow for leaving questions blank if the respondent does not know the answer, or better, use *don't know* or *not sure* options for such closed-response questions.

QUESTIONS THAT DON'T APPLY

Making respondents answer questions that do not apply to them is a waste of their time and might be perceived by them as shoddy survey design. Either of these factors might cause the respondents to stop answering the questionnaire and carefully deposit it in the wastebasket, an outcome that you would probably like to avoid.

Consider a questionnaire that has separate questions on it about men and women. Clearly, you should avoid making all of the respondents answer all of the questions.

In general, this problem can be solved in three different ways:

1. Use two or more separate questionnaires (for instance, separate questionnaires for males and females, or different ones for teachers, students, and administrators).
2. Use multiple wording so that the respondents can pick the appropriate responses that apply to them (for example, "If you are married, does your [wife, husband] speak English?").
3. Use branching (for instance, "If your answer is NO, skip to question 50 on page three.").

IRRELEVANT QUESTIONS

To avoid wasting respondents' time, all questions should be relevant to the survey project and to the respondent. Often this problem evolves from the fact that questionnaire designers are sometimes tempted (particularly in the biodata section of a survey) to ask everything under the sun because it *might* be useful someday in analyzing the results – maybe.

Solution? Think about the purposes of the survey project as a whole and design a survey instrument that will ask all and only the questions necessary to accomplish those purposes. Why waste the respondents' time and increase the chances that they will give up and not complete the survey for information that you might not even use?

SUPERFLUOUS INFORMATION

Finally, you should avoid writing superfluous information into the questions. Extra information may be viewed as a nuisance and an imposition on the respondents' time, or it may actually confuse the respondents. In either case, such information is unnecessary and undesirable.

To avoid using superfluous information, you will need to check carefully each and every question to make sure that it contains only the information that the respondents need to have in order to answer the question.

TABLE 2.3. GUIDELINES FOR PRODUCING GOOD QUESTIONNAIRES

Write good questions (see Table 2.2)
    Think about the form.
    Think about the meaning.
    Think about the respondents.

Order the questions rationally
    Think about Gallup's quintamensional plan.
    Think about grouping questions by type, function, format, and topic.
    Think about controlling the ordering effect.

Format the questionnaire for clarity
    Think about spacing.
    Think about typefaces.
    Think about highlighting.

Write clear directions
    Think about overall directions.
    Think about specific directions.
    Think about introductions.

Edit carefully
    Think about getting others to edit.
    Think about piloting the questionnaire (think aloud).
    Think about final editing.

Guidelines for producing a polished questionnaire

Even with excellent survey questions in hand, you must still consider a number of other points to produce a good questionnaire. These concerns are listed in Table 2.3, which shows that, aside from (1) writing good questions, the main issues are (2) ordering the questions rationally, (3) formatting the questionnaire for clarity, (4) writing clear directions, and (5) editing carefully. I will address each of these issues in terms of how they affect questionnaire design, but most of them are also issues in designing an interview procedure.

Order the questions rationally

Two facts highlight the importance of ordering questions rationally: (1) jumbled-up questions (in more or less random order) may prove confusing or cause the respondent to stop answering, and (2) answering one question can affect the way subsequent questions are answered. Thus you should order questions rationally, with a view to minimizing the effects of each question on subsequent questions.

To help you make rational decisions about the ordering of questions, this section will cover (1) Gallup's quintamensional plan, (2) ideas for grouping questions by type, function, format, and topic, and (3) techniques for controlling the ordering effect.

Gallup's (1947) *quintamensional plan of question design* listed five primary elements in the opinions being tapped by a survey: awareness, general opinion, specific opinions, reasons, and intensity. He went on to suggest that the following sequence of questions would be sensible and effective:

1. Questions to find out whether the respondent is aware of (or has thought about) the issue at hand
2. Questions on the respondent's general feelings about the issue
3. Questions dealing with specific parts of the issue
4. Questions about the reasons behind the respondent's views
5. Questions about how strongly the views are held

Indeed, in many cases, questions can logically be ordered following Gallup's five points. However, you should do this only insofar as it helps to accomplish the purpose of the survey involved and it makes sense within the context of the survey as a whole.

GROUPING QUESTIONS BY TYPE, FUNCTION, FORMAT, AND TOPIC

In fact, as noted earlier in this chapter, other ways of classifying questions might be equally sensible. For instance, why not group and sequence questions using Rossett's (1982) five categories (problems, priorities, abilities, attitudes, and solutions) or Patton's (1987) six categories (behavior/experience, opinion/value, feelings, knowledge, sensory, and demographic/background)? Alternatively, why not use the various functions listed earlier in this chapter (biodata surveys, opinion surveys, self-ratings, judgments, and Q-sort)? For that matter, why not use response formats or question forms as organizational guides, or use content topics as one controlling factor in the question sequencing?

Personally, I prefer to use topic and question formats as my primary organizing units. Generally, my goal is to order the questions from those that are relatively short and easy for the respondents to answer to those that are increasingly difficult. However, within that general rule, I also apply the following five additional subrules:

1. Keep all questions of a single type together.
2. Keep all questions of a single function together.

3. Keep all questions of a single response format and question form together.
4. Keep all questions on a given topic together.
5. Because all of the above cannot be the primary organizing principle at the same time, decide on a hierarchy of importance among them, and stick with it in making ordering decisions insofar as that is possible.

An example of how these rules can be applied is fairly clear in Appendix B.

In my view, one important goal in ordering questions is to reduce the confusion that would result in the respondents' minds if they found themselves constantly switching question types, functions, formats, and topics. In other words, the less often these categories shift, the better. However, you must decide for yourself what criteria, hierarchies, and sequences will best serve your purposes.

CONTROLLING THE ORDERING EFFECT

As noted above, answering one question may affect answers on *subsequent* questions. In fact, answering one question may even affect answers on *previous* questions if the respondent chooses to go back and change answers. The following three solutions to the problem of ordering effects may prove helpful:

1. *Randomization* of the questions might take care of this effect (but would more likely create a chaotic feeling of confusion in formats and topics).
2. *Common sense* examination of questions, keeping in mind organizing principles like those discussed in the previous section (with help from colleagues and a small sample of respondents), might help.
3. *Formal study* of the effects of order (that is, trying different orders on groups of respondents and studying the effects of these different orders on the answers) might help.

Regardless of the strategy that you use, the ordering of the questions is an issue that must be carefully considered and addressed in the process of survey design.

Format the questionnaire for clarity

In addition to ordering the questions rationally, you should consider the issues involved in formatting the questionnaire for maximum clarity. You can enhance clarity by carefully using features such as spacing, typefaces, and highlighting.

SPACING

At first glance, spacing may seem like a silly concern to bring up here. However, I have found spacing to be an amazingly important issue. Remember that one of the goals in questionnaire design is to keep the questionnaire short, or at least design it so that it is perceived as short. As a result, the amount of gratuitous space left on the pages of a questionnaire should be kept to a minimum. At the same time, enough space must be left so that the pages do not look crowded and intimidating to the respondents. In other words, some perfect compromise must be reached with regard to the spacing of questions – a process that is definitely more of an art than a science. I have found that this perfect compromise is much easier to accomplish on a computer (with a word processing program) than on a typewriter.

TYPEFACES

One way to maximize the amount of material on each page is to select a relatively small typeface for the final questionnaire. Again, however, compromise is necessary. If the typeface is too large, less material can be presented on each page; but if it is too small, the respondents may find it dense and intimidating or hard to read. Because you want the readers to find the questionnaire easy to read, you should select a compromise that is compact but also pleasant and very readable.

In today's world of graphical interface computers, I feel bound to warn as well against using too many different fonts, typefaces, or type sizes on any given page. The use of these devices has become so easy that you may be tempted to use dozens on each page. Unfortunately, doing so can create pages that look more like a ransom note than a questionnaire. As a general rule, then, I advise using a tastefully small number of fonts, typefaces, and type sizes in order to avoid creating pages that have a cluttered look and a confused feel. In other words, try to strike a tasteful happy medium.

HIGHLIGHTING

One other issue worth considering is the use of highlighting. Highlighting can be done with bold-faced type, italics, different-sized type, shading, boxes, underlining, and so forth. You can tastefully use highlighting to help the reader understand the organization of the questionnaire or to emphasize certain aspects of the questionnaire. Once again, however, too much highlighting may just become confusing to the reader, so a tasteful happy medium should once again be your goal. Naturally, all of this will be much easier to accomplish with the help of a computer word processing program.

Write clear directions

Many people, especially professionals in education, are very familiar with questionnaires and how to fill them out. In language education, however, you may need to remember that some of your respondents (for instance, some international students, or EFL teachers) may be naive about questionnaires. When in doubt, you should probably try to err on the safe side by writing overly clear directions rather than directions that are not clear enough. At the same time, the length of the questionnaire is always an issue, and directions do take up space. As a rule, therefore, the directions should be as parsimonious as possible without sacrificing clarity. In addition to using a cover letter, which explains the purpose of the survey and why the respondents should fill it out (*cover letters* are explained in more detail in the next chapter), you might want to consider using three distinct types of directions within the questionnaire: overall directions, specific directions, and introductions.

OVERALL DIRECTIONS

The **overall directions** usually come at the beginning of a questionnaire (or even on a cover sheet) and should include any basic instructions necessary to complete all sections of the questionnaire. Examples of the types of information that you might want to include in the overall directions are points such as:

1. How to use the answer sheet (if applicable)
2. How to mark the answers (for example, make a dark clear mark, stay within the little boxes, and so forth)
3. The type and hardness of pencil to use
4. For open-response questions, guidelines about whether you are looking for long or short answers
5. Encouragement for the respondents to write (or not write) additional comments in the margins
. . . and so forth

In short, the overall directions should contain anything that is general enough to be pertinent to the whole questionnaire.

In the process of reviewing the specific directions for each section (see below), you may want to look for material that is being repeated in each set of directions (or at least would be applicable to all sections). Any material that is common across sections in this way should probably be presented one time only, in the overall directions at the beginning of the questionnaire.

SPECIFIC DIRECTIONS

Whenever the question type, function, format, or topic changes, you may need to supply **specific directions** so the respondents will know how to react. Naturally, the purpose of such specific directions is to facilitate answering the questions in a particular section. You should also design the specific directions so they help the respondents shift gears from one section to the next. Remember: You usually do not need to repeat information that was included in the overall directions.

In specific directions, you may need to address some or all of the following:

1. How-to-answer directions, such as "Circle the choice you prefer."
2. One or more examples of the new question type and how it should be answered.
3. Definitional directions such as "In evaluating materials, include the textbook, workbook, cassette tapes, and quizzes."
4. Procedural directions – sometimes procedural directions will appear in the specific directions; other times they might appear in parentheses among the questions themselves, as in the following example: (If yes, go to question number 21; if no, continue with next question.)

Remember, the goal of specific directions is to help the respondents understand how they are expected to react to a new set of circumstances.

INTRODUCTIONS

Particularly when frequently shifting topics in a survey, you may find it useful to use introductions for each topic. Typically, **introductions** are short introductory statements about the purpose and content of the material in each topic section. The following three examples should help to clarify the use and purpose of introductions:

1. Section A: In this section, we would like some information about you so that we can better understand the other results of this survey.
2. Section B: In this part, we are seeking your opinions about the effectiveness of the textbook that is being used in your class.
3. Section C: Here, we want your opinions about the effectiveness of the teacher of your class.

In short, the purpose of introductions is to provide a sense of organization and coherence, and to help the respondents to shift gears between different topic sections.

Edit carefully

The final stage in the survey design process is editing. In some ways, this stage is the most important, because editing allows you to pull the survey together into what I call the *CBS,* or *current best shot.* This acronym is meant to express the fact that no survey will ever be perfect, but any survey can be brought to a high level of quality if the designers give it their CBS. To get the questionnaire to this level, you may find it helpful (1) to get others to help with the editing process, (2) to try out the questionnaire with a small sample, and (3) to do final editing.

GETTING OTHERS TO HELP EDIT

At all stages of the questionnaire design process, feedback from colleagues can prove invaluable. Almost all language professionals have answered many questionnaires. Through these experiences, through their reactions to the experiences, through teacher training courses in research design, or through other professional experiences, many language professionals have developed intuitions or knowledge about what a good survey instrument should be like. You can and should use that knowledge to help you in writing a good survey.

In approaching your colleagues, you may want to supply the checklists shown in Tables 2.2 and 2.3 to help them focus on potential problems that they may find. Or, you may choose to rely on their instincts to help you find problems. To encourage comments, perhaps a draft version should provide extra space (perhaps triple-spaced, with extra-wide margins all the way around). That way, your colleagues can write down whatever pops to mind as they read through your draft survey.

In thinking about who should be included in this critiquing process, you will certainly want to use professional colleagues, but in some circumstances you might want to get help from language students, content area teachers, administrators, or anyone else involved in the issues addressed by the questionnaire – that is, anyone else who can critically examine the survey and provide useful feedback. The important point is that you should get feedback from a variety of sources.

For instance, in developing a questionnaire for midterm feedback from students to teachers in the English Language Institute at UHM, we found it surprisingly useful to get feedback from the students at our regular student representative meetings (one elected from each section of the courses in the ELI). The administrators, lead teachers, and secretaries also reviewed and discussed the questionnaire. This process of involving students, administrators, lead teachers, and secretaries in the questionnaire design had two beneficial effects: First, their comments were valuable for making the content of the questionnaire clearer and more effective; and second, by participating politically in the development of the questionnaire, these groups had a voice and stake in the questionnaire, which helped to ensure that they would accept it once it was finally put into use.

One important concern that I must mention at this point is that you may find that you have put so much personal time and effort into developing the questionnaire that it becomes "your baby." If someone is subsequently critical of it, you may find yourself reacting as if you have been personally attacked. Perhaps, rule number one in the critiquing/revision process is that the creator should never take the criticisms personally. Always remember that comments like "dumb question" or "vague" or "what?" refer to the question, not the survey designer. Remember also that it is not necessary for each and every criticism to be resolved. The critiques can be wrong too. However, you should probably consider each criticism very carefully, and, if it is sensible, you should fix the problem. Naturally, any questions about which two or more readers have made comments are more likely to be problematic.

PILOTING THE QUESTIONNAIRE

Piloting a questionnaire simply means trying it out before the actual administration to see what problems arise. The central purpose of piloting is to see what types of answers respondents produce. To that end, you should pilot it with the same types of respondents who will eventually be surveyed on the finished questionnaire. You should also pilot it under conditions similar to those that will exist during the real project. For example, if the actual project will be a mail survey with respondents filling out the questionnaire at home, then the piloting should be set up in the same way.

In addition to finding out how respondents will answer the questions, such piloting can help you spot ambiguities, confusion, or other problems in the questionnaire content. To that end, you should analyze the pilot results very carefully.

To begin your analysis, look in the margins for any respondent comments that point to unclear/ambiguous questions or vague directions. At the same time, you may want to look for places where respondents felt it necessary to clarify or qualify their answers.

You should also consider questions that everyone answers in the same way. This lack of variation may be the true state of affairs in the group, but it might also be that additional categories should be added within the question, the existing categories should be clarified, or the question should be reworded.

You may also want to examine the questions that have been left blank by large numbers of respondents and try to figure out why. Then look at the patterns of responses and consider if the data that are surfacing are useful, if there are redundancies, and if the survey will serve the purposes for which you designed it.

In short, in analyzing pilot responses, look for anything that can help to reword and refine the directions, questions, response categories, and so forth, while always keeping in mind the checklists in Tables 2.2 and 2.3.

FINAL EDITING

In the end, one person must usually take full responsibility and pull a given survey into a cogent whole. A survey made by a committee is likely to be disjointed and may never get finished. At some point, even if a committee is involved, one individual must comb through all of the drafts and feedback to pull the final product together.

Naturally, if it is you who turns out to be responsible for final editing, you should edit for spelling, grammatical, typographical, punctuation, mechanical, and other errors. Colleagues' comments and those of the respondents in the pilot survey may prove helpful in finding these relatively picky problems, but that does not relieve you from the ultimate responsibility for carefully reading and rereading the questionnaire. Colleagues' and respondents' comments about the content of the questions and directions will be even more valuable, because these individuals are likely to see the survey from different perspectives, which can help to reveal ambiguities, points of confusion, and other content problems that you would never be able to spot on your own. Put another way, colleagues' and respondents' comments can help you deal with the issues raised in the **Guidelines for Writing Good Survey Questions** section, but ultimately you must attend to all of those issues all at the same time while editing the final survey.

If there is a single truth in survey research, it is that no questionnaire is perfect. When starting out, you may find it useful to produce a first draft, give the draft to your colleagues for criticism, revise, pilot, revise, and so forth. At some point, however the process has to stop. In other words, you will eventually come to a point where you have incorporated all of the things learned from your colleagues and the pilot respondents, and where you have carefully proofread and edited the questionnaire a half-dozen times. At that point, you will simply have to let go and set about the task of administering the questionnaire. At such a point, the notion of a current best shot once again becomes important. You must realize that you have given it your CBS and go on with the work of gathering the data, as described in the next chapter.

Examples of designing a survey instrument

The examples in this chapter will include further description of the TESOL survey project as the running example, as well as a curriculum development survey project assessing the training needs of graduate teaching assistants in introductory foreign language courses at the University of Hawaii at Manoa as the rotating example.

Running example: Research survey design

Recall that the survey in this running example was developed by the TESOL Research Task Force. To refresh your memory on the background of this project, you may want to skim through the running example in Chapter 1. The discussion of the project in this chapter will center on recounting the steps involved in developing the questionnaire and describing the questionnaire itself (including how its quality was perceived by the respondents).

DEVELOPMENT STEPS

This particular questionnaire was developed in four steps: (1) brainstorming, (2) drafting a preliminary version, (3) getting feedback on the questionnaire, and (4) incorporating that feedback into a final version of the questionnaire.

The first step, brainstorming, took place on January 27 and 28, 1991, when the TESOL Research Task Force met in San Jose, California. At a certain point in the meeting, we realized that much of what we knew about members' attitudes toward research issues was based on rumor and hearsay. Because of the shaky nature of this information, we felt that we should conduct a survey to find out what the membership really felt about these research issues. We then proceeded to discuss the numbers and types of questions we wanted to include on the questionnaire, and the issues we wanted to cover. We even generated some specific questions at that meeting.

In a second step, I drafted a preliminary version of the questionnaire. I took on this task because I was the chair of the Research Task Force. Working at a word processor, I spent four full afternoons doing this task, including various combinations of drafting, revising, formatting, proofreading, printing, and photocopying. Naturally, the word processor made many of these steps much easier than they would have been on a typewriter. More important, the laser-printed result was very professional-looking, even though the questionnaire itself still had problems.

The third step was to get feedback on the draft questionnaire. Note that, at this stage, the draft questionnaire was formatted so that it had extra-wide margins, which would provide plenty of room for feedback. I sought and got feedback from TESOL colleagues all around the United States, including the members of the TESOL Research Task Force, the TESOL Executive Board, and the TESOL International Central Office, as well as current and future chairs of the Applied Linguistics and Research interest sections of TESOL International. In addition, all of my colleagues in the Department of ESL at the University of Hawaii at Manoa responded to my request for constructive criticism. Clearly, I have a wonderfully supportive group of colleagues.

The fourth step involved incorporating all of the comments and suggestions into a final, polished version of the questionnaire. Much of this work was like the word processing work described in the second step above. However, two personal observations are worth mentioning: (1) An amazing number of criticisms surfaced for what I had thought was already a very fine questionnaire, and (2) my ego was quite bruised, not only by the number of criticisms but by the blunt and sometimes patronizing ways in which they were stated. These observations are not meant as complaints but rather as warnings to prepare you for such an experience. To minimize the emotional impact of such criticisms, you should remember that they were directed at the questionnaire, not at the person who developed it. Nonetheless, you will probably find it difficult to remain dispassionate and detached given the amount of work and personal interest that you have probably invested in developing a survey instrument.

THE QUESTIONNAIRE

The resulting questionnaire (see Appendix B) included a total of 31 questions, some of which contained subparts. A variety of open-response and closed-response questions were used. Many questions were designed to obtain data about the personal, educational, and occupational characteristics of the respondents, while others were designed to explore the respondents' background in research, and still others sought their views on the *TESOL Quarterly,* the TESOL Convention, and research issues in general.

Once I had collected the questionnaire results, I discovered that the respondents were not 100 percent happy with the format, questions, topics, and so forth. In fact, no single question (closed-response or open-response) went without criticism by at least one respondent.

The closed-response questions were often criticized in the margins. For instance, the relatively simple yes–no response questions were criticized, if ever so implicitly, by those respondents who wrote words such as *sometimes* or *usually* in the margins. Other closed-response questions drew written comments, which showed that some respondents felt the questionnaire did not have enough categories to fit their opinions.

In the case of the open-response questions, the criticisms tended to be about the wording of the question. Respondents criticized some questions for being too broad to answer, and other questions for being ambiguously worded.

Several respondents made comments that showed that they were unhappy with the entire questionnaire. For example, one respondent asked, "Will this questionnaire provide relevant data?" Another similar criticism was somewhat more pointed: "*Very few* teachers will respond to this questionnaire. You should however, receive a response from every researcher. Congratulations."

Another respondent pointed out that "This questionnaire has polarised, non-polar issues, so typical of the binary thinking of some political ideologies." Indeed, in retrospect, this criticism appears to have some merit. Some of the closed-response questions did polarize the issues involved. We made two observations in the final report about this complaint. First, we provided the open-response questions to allow for the voicing of any and all points of view, and they seem to have accomplished just that (as indicated by the fact that the respondent above had the opportunity to express his opinion). Second, one purpose of the questionnaire was to discover whether such polarized views of research versus teaching existed within the organization. Ironically, the results of this survey project generally indicated that, although such polarization is a problem within the field, most respondents felt that it should be remedied.

Although the criticisms of our questionnaire were relatively few in percentage terms, we nevertheless took them quite seriously: We considered them in interpreting our results, and we discussed them in the final report on the project.

We also learned two important lessons from these criticisms: (1) Respondents will feel free to express their disdain for the design of any questionnaire they answer, and (2) their opinions on the quality of a questionnaire will vary as much as their views on anything else. Hence, you should remember from the start that no questionnaire – indeed, no single question on a questionnaire, will please all of the people all of the time.

I should also point out that for every criticism of our questionnaire, there was an opposite and equal reaction of praise. For example:

1. "Good questionnaire. I will be looking forward to reading the report of your findings in *TESOL Matters.*"
2. "I like your questionnaire – I'll be interested in reading the results. . . . Your try to tap ground feeling in TESOL is a good one."
3. "Congratulations on asking these questions! Keep up the good work, TESOL; I boost you wherever I go."

Rotating example: Curriculum survey design

The rotating example in this chapter involves a curriculum development project. As you will see, because of political considerations, the strategies involved in designing this survey were somewhat more elaborate.

Again, this survey project was one in which I was involved at the University of Hawaii at Manoa. A committee with the august title of Second Language Teaching and Curriculum Committee (SLTCC) decided to survey the coordinators of the many language courses taught at UHM to find out what the departments were doing to prepare graduate assistants for teaching introductory language courses. The eventual purpose was to design a course or materials to help prepare such graduate assistants in the future.

I foolishly volunteered to design the questionnaire, without realizing just how politically sensitive such a project could be. The strategy that I used was to set up informal interviews with key chairpersons from the various language departments to find out whom they felt I should survey (Students? Graduate assistants? Teachers? Coordinators? Chairs?) and to explore what those chairs thought the key questions were. Since this was a relatively small group of very busy individuals, the most efficient way to deal with them was in interviews. These chairs helped me to identify the coordinators in each of the departments, and provided valuable information as to the questions that were important as well as the political nuances, potential pitfalls, and personalities important to the project.

I then telephoned eight of the key coordinators (some from large departments, some from small ones) and, in the name of the SLTCC and the Dean, invited them to a meeting. At that meeting, my main purpose was to get the coordinators' views on graduate assistant training. In addition, new issues, ones they felt were important, began to surface.

On the basis of this input, I drafted a preliminary questionnaire for all language course coordinators. I then sent out copies of the draft version to each of the key coordinators and held another meeting so I could get their feedback in person. I also sought feedback from the members of the SLTCC at another special meeting of that group. The criticisms from both groups were very intense, but, because of those criticisms, I was able, after much revision, to produce a reasonably good questionnaire (see Appendix H), which I presented to the SLTCC for their approval.

Notice that, in addition to producing a sound survey instrument, I had managed to build political support for the project at each step of the process. I had interviewed key chairs for their input, and as a result they had a stake in the project; I had similarly tapped into the views of the course coordinators and the SLTCC at various meetings; and in the end, the SLTCC had given their approval to administer the final version of the questionnaire in that committee's name.

Like the rotating example in Chapter 1, this example illustrates that a combination of data-gathering techniques is much more powerful than any single instrument. In particular, this example illustrates the symbiotic nature of using interviews, meetings, and questionnaires, as well as the importance of political considerations in the survey design process.

Summary

In this chapter I covered survey instrument design issues. I began with a discussion of the types of questions that surveys can address: behavior/experience, opinion/value, feelings, knowledge, and sensory questions; as well as problems, priorities, abilities, attitudes, and solutions questions. Next I touched on the various functions of surveys, including biodata surveys, opinion surveys, self-ratings, judgments, and Q-sort. I also explored the different response and question formats by defining open- and closed-response formats, examining their pros and cons, and providing examples of specific types of open-response and closed-response questions.

Next, I provided guidelines for writing good survey questions. These guidelines, summarized in Table 2.2, centered on three main categories of suggestions: thinking about form, thinking about meaning, and thinking about the respondents. I continued with a set of guidelines for producing a polished questionnaire. These guidelines, summarized in Table 2.3, focused on four main categories of suggestions: ordering the questions rationally, formatting the questionnaire for clarity, writing clear directions, and editing carefully. Finally, to illustrate the survey design issues, I ended the chapter with two examples. In the running example, I further described the survey research that the TESOL Research Task Force conducted, and in the rotating example, I described a curriculum (needs analysis) survey project at UHM designed to determine what course coordinators thought graduate students needed in order to better teach introductory language courses.

Suggestions for further reading

Any of the following general books on survey research will cover the topic of designing survey instruments to some degree: Babbie (1973, 1975, 1990), Bailey (1982), Berdie, Anderson, and Niebuhr (1986), Fink (1995a), Fowler (1993), and Oppenheim (1966). However, for books focused on survey instrument design, see Stacey and Moyer (1982), Converse and Presser (1986), and Fink (1995c). For those particularly interested in Q-sort and Q methodology, see McKeown and Thomas (1988).

Important terms

abilities questions
alternative-answer questions
attitudes questions
behavior/experience questions
biodata surveys

checklist questions
closed responses
demographic/background
  questions
feelings questions

fill-in questions	problems questions
introductions	Q-sort
judgments	question
knowledge questions	ranking questions
Likert-scale questions	response formats
open responses	self-ratings
opinion surveys	sensory questions
opinion/value questions	short-answer questions
overall directions	solutions questions
piloting	specific directions
priorities questions	

Review questions

1. What are the six types of questions that surveys can answer (after Patton, 1987)? What are the five types described by Rossett (1982)?
2. What are the five functions of surveys that are listed in the chapter?
3. What are the two main response/question formats that are discussed in the chapter? What are the pros and cons of each?
4. In the guidelines for writing good survey questions, what are six issues involved in thinking about the form of the question?
5. According to the guidelines for writing good survey questions, what are six issues related to thinking about the meaning of the question?
6. In the guidelines for writing good survey questions, what are the six issues that should be considered in thinking about the respondents?
7. According to the guidelines for producing a polished questionnaire, what are three main issues involved in ordering the questions rationally?
8. In the guidelines for producing a polished questionnaire, what are the three main issues that should be considered in formatting the questionnaire for clarity?
9. According to the guidelines for producing a polished questionnaire, what three issues should be included in writing clear directions?
10. In the guidelines for producing a polished questionnaire, what primary issues should be included in careful editing?

Application exercises

A. Design a questionnaire using at least three of the five question types and three of the question functions discussed in the chapter. Also use as many different question formats as make sense. Preferably, this questionnaire should be for a real research or curriculum development project.

B. Get feedback on your questionnaire and analyze it using the categories in Table 2.2 to improve the questions.
C. Get feedback on your questionnaire and analyze it using the categories in Table 2.3, and polish your questionnaire. Do not leave out any steps; that is, be sure to have colleagues look at the questionnaire, pilot it (if possible) on a small group of people like the respondents that you envision for the questionnaire, and so forth.

3 Gathering and compiling survey data

This chapter will focus on the issues involved in gathering survey data and compiling those data for further analysis. I will begin by examining the importance of sampling in survey research. Next I will explore the pros and cons of using survey interviews or questionnaires. Then I will discuss the benefits of using interviews and questionnaires sequentially. I will also include separate sections covering issues related specifically to the administration of interview surveys and questionnaire surveys. Then I will explore the issues involved in compiling survey data (including the coding of closed-response questions and the transcribing of open-response questions). Finally, I will have a few comments on the messiness involved in gathering and compiling survey data. As usual, I will end the chapter with two examples: In the running example I will describe the sampling, administration, and compiling involved in the TESOL research survey, and, in the rotating example I will cover the same issues for a curriculum-related survey project for which the goal was to find out what is typically included on the syllabi of the language testing courses offered in ESL/EFL teacher training programs.

The importance of sampling

Sampling procedures are necessary in language surveys because the groups of interest in such studies are often large. Put simply, **sampling** involves selecting a smaller group of subjects from the overall population in such a way that the subgroup is representative of the larger population. Sampling is important because it can help limit the amount of effort, resources, and anguish that must go into a survey project. Thus sampling can be viewed as a way of promoting efficiency. In order to explain the issues involved in sampling, I will cover four topics: (1) the differences between populations and samples, (2) the random sampling strategy, (3) stratified random sampling strategies, and (4) the sample size necessary for adequate generalizability to the population.

Populations and samples

To understand the concept of sampling, it will help to think about the difference between a population and a sample. A **population** is the entire group of people who are of interest in a particular survey. Few language professionals have the resources to study, for example, the entire population of students studying French in American universities, or even all of the American male students studying French in France. Hence researchers find it useful to use a **sample,** that is, a subgroup of the students that is representative of the whole population. In using a sample, data can be practically, efficiently, and effectively collected. If data are properly sampled, that is, the sample is selected so that it is truly representative of the population, then the results of the survey should also be representative of results that would be obtained if the researcher studied the entire population. Two basic strategies are most often used in language surveys for selecting samples from populations. These strategies are called *random sampling* and *stratified random sampling.*

Random sampling

In **random sampling,** each individual in the population must have an equal chance of being selected. Three steps will help to ensure that each individual has an equal chance:

1. Identify clearly the population of interest in the survey.
2. Assign an identification number to each individual in the population.
3. Choose the members of the sample on the basis of a table of random numbers.

A **table of random numbers** is a list of numbers that contains no systematic patterns. Introductory statistics books usually include tables of random numbers in an appendix. Essentially, the use of a table of random numbers leaves the selection of whom the researcher will include in the sample up to a dispassionate, and random, table of numbers. Thus the researcher minimizes any personal biases (conscious or unconscious) in the results of the study. With a sufficiently large number of individuals selected randomly, the resulting **random sample** can be said to represent the population from which the researcher drew it. Researchers widely accept this assumption (that is, that random samples are representative) (for more information on random sampling, see Brown, 1988, pp. 111–113).

Researchers can also use other procedures to obtain a random sample. For example, the researcher might pull numbers out of a hat, use a deck of cards, or repeatedly throw a pair of dice in selecting a sample. Whatever procedure is used, each member of the population must have an equal chance of being selected into the sample.

Stratified random sampling

Stratified random sampling is also sometimes used in language surveys. Four steps will lead to such a sample:

1. Identify clearly the population of interest in the survey.
2. Identify the salient characteristics of the population (called **strata**).
3. Select members randomly from each of the strata in the population (using a table of random numbers or some other procedure as discussed above).
4. Examine the resulting sample to make sure that it has about the same proportions of each characteristic as the original population.

For example, in the population of all students studying Japanese at the University of Hawaii at Manoa, a researcher might identify subgroups, or strata, within the population based on the following characteristics: gender (male or female), home state, ethnic background, academic status (graduate, undergraduate, or unclassified), and major (perhaps science, humanities, or undeclared). Given correct information about the proportions of these characteristics in the population of students studying Japanese at UHM, the sample could be selected by choosing students randomly from each of the strata in proportion to those characteristics in the total population. The resulting sample would have approximately the same proportional characteristics as those of the entire population. Creating a **stratified random sample** provides a certain degree of precision to the representativeness of the resulting sample, and this may help in using the identified characteristics as variables in the analysis.

Several considerations go into deciding whether to employ random or stratified random sampling in a particular survey. First, you should employ stratified random sampling when the population in question is fairly heterogeneous in nature. Under these conditions, random sampling might not provide for selection of people from each of the strata, or subgroups, in the population. Second, you should use stratified random sampling when the samples will be small or the groupings within the study will be of unequal size. Third, you should use stratified random sampling if you want to use the strata as variables in the analysis. However, if the sample will be fairly homogeneous and reasonably large, and the population characteristics hold no specific importance in the analysis, straightforward random sampling will probably be easier to use because it eliminates the need to define the characteristics of the population and sample proportionately from each of those strata.

Sample size

One of the first questions that arises is how big a sample is big enough. I have no simple answer to this question. However, I feel safe in saying that a large sample is generally more representative of the population than a small one. For instance, common sense indicates that a sample that includes 99 percent of a population of 10,000 language students is likely to be more representative of that population than a sample containing only 1 percent of the population, or 5 percent or 10 percent. However, this commonsense notion does not truly answer the question of how big a sample is big enough. The fact is that no such answer exists because sample size decisions depend so much on the situation in the study, the size of the population, the types of survey being administered, and the sorts of statistics being applied.

Statistics teachers often give the number 28 (or sometimes 30) as a rule of thumb for the minimum sample size to use per group or per variable in a research study. This "magic number" is not necessarily bad advice. However, remember that this rule of thumb represents the *minimum number* that you would need to correctly apply the statistics that might be used in analyzing the results. I prefer to think in terms, not of minimum numbers, but rather in terms of the numbers that will be most helpful in generalizing the results to the population that you are surveying. If you are interested in surveying the students in a small language program, consider surveying all of them. Or if that is impractical because an interview procedure is involved, you might survey at least 50 randomly selected students. Such a decision will depend on (1) your purpose, (2) the importance of your results, and (3) the degree to which you want those results to generalize to the population as a whole.

The **generalizability** of a study is the degree to which the results are meaningful with regard to the entire population that the sample is supposed to represent. If random or stratified random sampling has been used, and the sample is large enough, no question should arise in the survey designer's mind about the degree to which the sample represents the population. If there is some question, then the sampling procedures should probably be modified and/or the sample sizes should be increased. (For more on sampling in language research, see Brown, 1988, or Hatch & Lazaraton, 1991).

Pros and cons of interviews and questionnaires

Having now considered the issues related to sampling, you can turn your attention to the actual administration of the survey. First, however, you must weigh the pros and cons of interviews and questionnaires so you can resolve the various problems that might arise in administering these two different types of surveys. Your purpose will be to select the most appropriate technique for a given survey project and to administer it in the most effective way possible.

Remember, in an interview, the delivery will be predominantly oral. Thus you may need to adapt certain types of questions and purposes to the oral method of communication. You may also need to consider other

TABLE 3.1. INTERVIEW VS. QUESTIONNAIRE PROCEDURES

Type of observations	Advantages	Disadvantages
Interview	High return rate Fewer incomplete answers Can involve realia Control environment Order of answering controlled Other observations can be made Relatively flexible Relatively personal Relatively rich data (written and spoken) Can be relatively complex	Time-consuming and expensive Small-scale study Never 100% anonymous Potential for subconscious bias Many other sources of potential bias Potential inconsistencies Scheduling somewhat restricted Restricted geographically
Questionnaire	Cheap and fast Large-scale study Can be anonymous Controls subconscious bias Controls other sources of bias Respondent can do in own time Standardized across respondents Can cover wide geographic area	Often low return rate Often incomplete answers Difficult to use with realia No control over environment No control over order Other observations impossible Relatively rigid Relatively artificial Relatively impersonal Relatively restricted data (and written behaviors only) Must be relatively simple

differences between interviews and questionnaires. Before deciding how you want to gather the survey data, you will probably want to think about all of the advantages and disadvantages of each of these data-gathering tools. Table 3.1 provides a summary of these pros and cons.

Beginning with interviews, one advantage, whether the interviews are done face to face or by telephone, is that they typically have a relatively high return rate in the sense that a relatively large number of those who agree to do an interview actually complete the interview. For similar reasons, the interviewer will probably not have to deal with many unanswered or incomplete answers in an interview (as compared to a questionnaire). In addition, face-to-face interviews are better for handling issues involving realia (that is, showing cards, pictures, passages to read aloud, words to pronounce, other language teaching products, lists, books, and so forth). Also, interviews, especially if they are done in an office or classroom, allow more control of the environment in which the questions are answered. This last advantage can be particularly important for avoiding noise and other distractions while the interviewee is answering the questions. The interviewer will also have control over the order in which the questions will be answered. In addition, if the interview is conducted in the homes or offices of the interviewees, the interviewers can make observations about the interviewee's environment (characteristics of the setting, interactions between people, nonverbal behaviors, attitudes, and so forth).

Interviews also allow more flexibility than questionnaires in several ways. First, the interviewer can probe for more information after a question is answered, and, second, the interviewer can change elements of the interview schedule if it is not working. Moreover, interviewees often perceive interviews as being relatively personal; that is, interviews are not as cold and mechanical as questionnaires. As a result, the interviewer may be able to build a rapport that will help to keep the interviewees interested and motivated. Furthermore, the data obtained in an interview may be relatively rich and spontaneous. Finally, because the directions can be explained and reexplained, an interview procedure can be relatively complex, at least more so than a questionnaire.

However, interviews have certain disadvantages as well. First and foremost, interviews are relatively time-consuming and expensive. Looked at another way, interviews are relatively expensive, slow, and inefficient when compared to questionnaires. In general, these logistical characteristics mean that interview procedures are typically done with relatively small numbers of subjects, which leads to relatively small-scale surveys. Whether done face to face or on the telephone, interviews can never be completely anonymous in the same way that questionnaires can. Unlike the situation with questionnaires, in interviews, interviewers may introduce subconscious biases by the way they use tone, emphasis, register, facial expression, significant pauses, appearance, accent, evident boredom, or other supralinguistic, kinesic, or sociolinguistic signals. Bias may occur in an interview because of differences (or similarities) between the interviewer and interviewee in terms of race, gender, age, social background, relative education, and so forth. Because of various forms of bias and because human beings tend to vary over time in their performance of any task, interviewers may be inconsistent in their conduct of interview after interview. In addition, scheduling of interviews is an issue that is less likely to come up when using questionnaires. Moreover, because of the expense of sending interviewers long distances, interviews tend to be more restricted geographically than questionnaires.

Similarly, questionnaires also have advantages and disadvantages, as shown in the bottom half of Table 3.1. The chief advantage to questionnaires is that they are relatively cheap, quick, and efficient. Thus they are probably better suited to large-scale surveys. In addition, assurances of anonymity can be built into questionnaires, so questionnaires are usually better for handling sensitive issues and getting the respondents' confidential views on these issues. Moreover, careful design can lead to better control over subconscious or other biases. The respondents can also fill out a questionnaire in their own time, at their own pace, and fit it into their own schedule. One implication of this time factor is that the respondents can take as much time as they like, including checking their records, schedules, or other resources if necessary. Also, because every respondent sees exactly the same wording, the data resulting from a questionnaire are more likely to be standardized, uniform, and consistent across subjects. Finally, because of the efficiency and low cost of postal services, questionnaires can be used effectively over wide geographic areas.

However, questionnaires have disadvantages, as well. The primary disadvantage, especially in mail surveys, is that there is often a very low return rate (see the Guidelines for Increasing Mail Survey Return Rates section for ways to increase the return rate). In addition, on questionnaires, respondents may skip many of the questions or only partially answer some. Relative to interviews, questionnaires are less appropriate for use with various forms of realia, as well. Moreover, researchers using questionnaires usually have little control over the environment in which the questionnaire will be filled out, or the order in which the respondents will answer the questions. Also, observations are limited to the answers to the questionnaire; that is, no other observations of the respondents' environment are possible, as is true in interviews. In addition, questionnaires are relatively rigid in that, once designed and distributed, the original design of the questionnaire and the original questions must generally be maintained throughout the survey project. Questionnaires are also relatively mechanical, artificial, and impersonal in comparison to interviews. Questionnaire data are also somewhat restricted in the sense that they include only written behaviors. Finally, questionnaires have to be simpler and clearer (especially in terms of directions), because the literacy skills among respondents may be limited or uneven and because there is no opportunity for additional clarification and explanations as would be the case in an interview.

Clearly, the choice that must be made as to whether to use an interview or a questionnaire will depend on the purposes and constraints of a particular survey project. Thinking about the advantages and disadvantages shown in Table 3.1 will help in making such a decision.

Using interviews *and* questionnaires sequentially

In all of the discussion of the advantages and disadvantages of interviews and questionnaires, I mentioned nothing about the relative strengths of the two types of surveys with regard to generating research questions for the survey project and in generating the actual survey questions for the instrument. This oversight was intentional, because the differences in generating research and survey questions are based on the aggregate advantages of each type of measure.

As I pointed out above, interviews are relatively flexible and personal, and provide for relatively rich data in written or spoken forms. The flexibility of interviews allows the interviewer to explore new avenues of opinion in ways that a questionnaire does not; thus interviews seem better suited to exploratory tasks. The personal nature of interviews may encourage interviewees to be more open and willing to express tentative or exploratory opinions, ideas, and speculation that would not come out on a questionnaire. The richness of interview data also leads to more possibilities in terms of exploring the issues involved. Taken together, these advantages of interviews (along with all of the others listed in Table 3.1) make interviews much better suited than questionnaires to the process of exploring what the issues are, what the research questions should be, and what the specific survey questions should be, as well as the relative importance of the above issues, research questions, and specific survey questions. Nonetheless, great care must be taken to deal with the disadvantages, especially that of potential biases. Weiss (1994, p. 212) suggests that:

We can guard against bias in the interview by establishing a research partnership in which the respondent understands that what we need is a full and accurate report, by obtaining detailed, concrete material rather than context-dependent generalizations, and by fashioning a substantive frame for our study that effectively captures the complexities of whatever it is we are studying.

In contrast to interviews, questionnaires may seem relatively rigid and impersonal. In addition, because questionnaires can gather only relatively limited written data, they are not particularly well suited to exploration of the basic questions involved in a project. However, questionnaires *are* well suited to gathering data once the issues, research questions, and specific survey questions have been clearly delineated. They are cheap and fast, useful for large-scale studies, and anonymous. Questionnaires also allow for controlling bias, the respondents can do them in their own time, they are standardized in format across all respondents, and they can easily cover a wide geographic area. What more could a survey designer want – once the questions are clear?

The point is that the characteristics of the two types of survey instruments are complementary in the sense that interviews are more suitable for exploring what the questions are and questionnaires are more suitable for answering those questions. Sometimes, you may want to use the strengths of both types of instruments in a single survey project. Even if you have a basic topic, or basic problem, you may not know exactly what the questions are at the outset of a survey project. In such a situation, you could use a set of interviews with the relatively open-ended goals of formulating research questions and specific survey questions. Thus the interviewer(s) would be talking with appropriate people to find out what interesting questions should be pursued in the overall project. Such exploration might usefully be combined with a search of the literature on the topic or contact with other language professionals who have already dealt with similar issues. All of the data gathered in these ways (or others) could then be synthesized into tentative but precise survey questions. Once the survey questions have crystallized, you will probably have to decide whether to follow up with a set of more structured interviews or with a large-scale questionnaire mailing. The questionnaire alternative will probably be best suited for gathering large-scale data.

I learned this strategy for effectively combining interviews and questionnaires from Chris Bernbrock, who did a master's thesis in TESL at the University of California at Los Angeles on the language learning needs of students at a Thai business college (Bernbrock, 1979). He felt that starting a needs analysis with the questions already predetermined would be arrogant. Instead, he advocated starting with a relatively open mind in an exploratory mode. To do so, Chris used interviews to find out what the appropriate questions were. Then he followed up with a number of questionnaires that he presented in the appendixes of his thesis. He reported that politeness often inhibited Thai people from giving what Westerners would call truthful answers, so he used what we jokingly referred to as the "Singha beer strategy." This strategy involved taking key respondents out to lunch to interview them, while making sure that the respondent was never lacking for Singha beer. The result of Chris's interviews was a set of very thorough questionnaires and a sound survey project. Regrettably, Chris never mentioned in his thesis the degree to which Singha beer was crucial to his particular research design.

Administering interviews

Once you have made a decision to use an interview procedure, whether alone or in combination with a questionnaire, you must consider a number of other matters if you want to administer the interviews effectively. Because interviews are relatively time-consuming, you may want to enlist a number of interviewers to help you do them. Since consistency of

TABLE 3.2A. GENERAL GUIDELINES FOR
CONDUCTING GOOD INTERVIEWS

1. Understand the general outlines of the interview.
2. Make appearance acceptable to interviewees.
3. Control personal and cultural attitudes.
4. Be familiar with the interview instrument.
5. Follow question wording exactly.
6. Record answers exactly.
7. Use follow-up questions when necessary.

results is desirable across the different interviewers, you should give all of the interviewers very clear interviewer guidelines (both general and specific guidelines) and, if possible, train them in exactly how you want them to conduct the interview.

General guidelines for conducting good interviews

General interviewer guidelines in written form will be most useful, so interviewers can absorb them at their own pace and so they can refer back to them if necessary. Following the general guidelines shown in Table 3.2a will help to make the interviews as efficient and useful as possible.

UNDERSTAND THE GENERAL OUTLINES OF THE INTERVIEW

First and foremost, the interviewers must understand the general outlines of the interview. At a minimum, they should know the purpose of the survey project and the general structure of the interview. Lynch (1997, p. 132) suggests one possible structure (with example questions):

1. *Casual, put-the-interviewee-at-ease question/comment:* "It's a little hot today, isn't it?" It may also be appropriate to explain the purpose of the interview, anonymity, etc.
2. *General questions:* "What do you think of the program?"
3. *Specific questions:* "What was it that made you feel uncomfortable about that lesson?" There will obviously be more latitude here when using less structured interviews – probes and follow-ups can be tailored to previous responses.
4. *Closing questions:* "Is there anything else you can tell me about the program?"
5. *Casual, wind-down questions/comments:* "I want to thank you, I've really learned a lot from our conversation today."

In addition, you may want to give the interviewers general guidelines and procedures for conducting the interviews. For instance, you might want to give them the guidelines listed in Tables 3.2a and 3.2b, or other guidelines of your own creation, or a list of "do's" and "don'ts," or anything else you find appropriate. You may also want to give them more detailed data on issues such as selecting respondents, giving directions to respondents, handling of realia, timing, recording techniques, and so forth.

MAKE APPEARANCE ACCEPTABLE TO INTERVIEWEES

Guidelines about the physical appearance of the interviewers may also be necessary. In general, appearance should be as inoffensive as possible from the point of view of the interviewees. In part, being inoffensive may mean dressing like the respondents. If the interviewers must dress differently from the respondents, they should probably always be different in the direction of being too clean, neat, and professional. This guideline is particularly important in settings in which the interviewers are native speakers of English and the respondents are not, because the native speakers' way of dressing casually may be viewed as "unprofessional" in many cultures. Indeed, in such a situation, the respondents may expect the interviewer to be formally dressed, and any other level of dress may hamper the interview efforts.

CONTROL PERSONAL AND CULTURAL ATTITUDES

Interviewers must also put their own attitudes and moods on hold while conducting any interview. You should instruct them to be upbeat and pleasant, and to try to get along with interviewee without being too familiar. Interviewers should always try to remain neutral, while being as aware as possible of any intercultural differences that might cause problems. For instance, in some cultures, an interviewer who comes right to the point and begins asking questions immediately may seem pushy and rude. In such a situation, the interviewer should use the appropriate cultural pattern of chatting about general topics before coming to the point and beginning to ask questions.

BE FAMILIAR WITH INTERVIEW INSTRUMENT

Interviewers must also be very familiar with the interview instrument itself. They should practice reading the questions until they are able to read them the same way every time, using a natural speed and manner. However, for some surveys, where flexibility is necessary, you may want to give the interviewers a bit more latitude and instruct them to make questions fit the situation without changing the meaning or intent.

In any case, the interviewers should be very familiar with the interview schedule.

FOLLOW QUESTION WORDING EXACTLY

In so far as it is possible, the interviewers should follow the question wording exactly. The questions have presumably been written with some care so that they will be precise. If interviewer deviates from these written questions by rephrasing them, all the effort of careful phrasing is wasted. If rephrasing occurs during the interviews, different respondents will essentially be getting different interviews. Consistency is important. That said, however, interviewers must sometimes be given leeway (as pointed out in the previous section) to make the questions fit the situation. In essence, your goal should be to make sure that the interviewers are consistent without becoming robots.

RECORD ANSWERS EXACTLY

The interviewers should also be cautioned to record the answers that they get as exactly as possible. Closed-response questions are relatively easy to record with accuracy, but you can help by having a form for each interview on which interviewers can tick off answers. For open-ended questions, verbatim transcripts are best if that is possible (sometimes with marginal comments to reflect any gestures, movement, tonal indications of attitude, and so forth). Hence, if you are planning to use numerous open-response questions in an interview, you may want to provide equipment and cassette tapes to record the interviews.

You should also give the interviewers instructions about what to do when the respondents do not cooperate. For example, given a choice, some respondents may adamantly refuse to make the choice provided by the interviewer, preferring instead to use another category or their own wording. In such a case, the interviewer should probably be told to record exactly what the respondent says.

USE FOLLOW-UP QUESTIONS WHEN NECESSARY

You may also want to provide interviewers with some latitude to probe for additional information. Such probes can be particularly useful with open-response questions, to obtain clarification or more details. However, the probes should be kept as neutral as possible, and the interviewer should avoid leading the respondent by using loaded words (as discussed in the previous chapter) that will affect the answer. In fact, when probes are anticipated, the interviewers may benefit from having several optional probes written out next to each question on the interview instrument.

TABLE 3.2B. SPECIFIC GUIDELINES TO FOLLOW DURING INTERVIEWS

Topics to avoid
1. Interviewee's nervousness
2. Gossip
3. Rumors
4. Sexist or racist comments
5. Stereotypes
6. Provocative topics

Conduct to avoid
1. Interrupting
2. Correcting grammar or pronunciation
3. Disagreeing with interviewees' views
4. Disparaging interviewees' background, training, teachers, language ability, etc.
5. Insisting on a topic or question that makes the interviewee uncomfortable
6. Looking bored or disinterested

Strategies to use
1. Start with a friendly hello and some small talk (rather than launching directly into Q/A routine)
2. Share experiences
3. Learn what to listen for
4. Have a reason for being a listener
5. Be friendly, but also professional
6. Be efficient

Specific guidelines for conducting good interviews

Specific interviewer guidelines in written form may also prove useful. Following the specific guidelines shown in Table 3.2b will help make the interviews as efficient and useful as possible.

TOPICS TO AVOID

Based on my experience and training, a number of topics seem to be best avoided altogether. These include any comments on the interviewees' nervousness. Commenting on how nervous they appear will probably only intensify it. Any form of gossip should probably also be avoided, because it is not very professional behavior in an interview setting. Passing on rumors would probably fall into the same category, as would sexist or racist remarks, or use of stereotypes. Any other provocative topics specific to the institution, city, country, or moment in history should probably also be avoided, because they can only interfere with communication and obtaining the information that you are seeking in the interview.

Also based on experience and training, I would say that it is best not to interrupt the interviewees when they are talking (or at least to do so very gently if it becomes necessary). It will probably also not be very productive to correct the second language learner interviewees' grammar or pronunciation. Doing so may alienate the interviewees and cause them to close down communication. The same is true of disagreeing with interviewees' views on any topic, or disparaging the interviewees' educational background, language training, previous teachers, language ability, or any other background characteristics. I have also found that it is not particularly productive to insist on a specific topic or question that makes the interviewee uncomfortable. Finally, looking bored or disinterested while the interviewee is talking will probably cause problems.

STRATEGIES TO USE

I have found a number of strategies useful in doing interviews, strategies that may even serve to counter the potential topic and conduct problems discussed in the previous two paragraphs. To begin with, rather than launching directly into the question-and-answer routine, start the interview with a friendly hello and some small talk. Try to share the experiences the interviewees are talking about in such a way that the interviewees will feel that you are identifying with them. After all, interviews should really just be "variants of normal conversations" (Rubin & Rubin, 1995, pp. 124–128). Also, learn what types of things to listen for in the interview process. Give yourself a good reason for being a listener. Be friendly, but also maintain a professional demeanor and always act professionally. To the best of your ability, be efficient with time. Interviews are almost always time-consuming, but they can become very time-consuming if you are inefficient.

Training interviewers

Written guidelines for conducting good interviews can be very helpful, but sometimes you will find it necessary to provide more elaborate training sessions for the interviewers. Such training sessions should be planned carefully. A number of different kinds of activities can be included in a training session that will give the interviewers some hands-on experience before they actually do the interviews.

First, you can go over the guidelines with the interviewers to make sure that they understand the basics. Discussion and questions should be encouraged at this point.

Second, you may want to provide a demonstration interview for them to watch. This interview may be done as a live demonstration or shown on videotape. Naturally, you should encourage discussion to help clarify any questions that arise during the viewing. Such discussion can also help to further elucidate the interview guidelines.

Third, if at all possible, you should provide the interviewers with some hands-on practice. They can get practice by interviewing each other in pairs or by conducting live interviews with a few real respondents that you have invited to the training session. Either way, interviewers will benefit greatly from some hands-on experience before going out into the field and doing real interviews.

One last comment on training sessions for interviews: One training session may turn out to be insufficient. If you find that the interviewers are deviating from each other or being inconsistent in other ways as the interviews progress, you may need to periodically *recalibrate* them in minisessions that provide them with review of their training and a chance to compare notes with each other.

Administering questionnaires

One of the biggest problems that survey researchers face is the possibility of low return rates on questionnaires. Even if the original sampling procedures were excellent in the sense that the researcher drew the sample either randomly or as a stratified random sample, the generalizability of a survey project's results can be severely undermined if only a small proportion of those in the sample actually return it. The problem is that the types of respondents who return questionnaires may be a specific type of "eager-beaver" or "gung-ho" respondent. Thus the results of the survey can only be generalized to "eager-beaver" or "gung-ho" people in the population rather than to the entire population. For this reason, survey designers make every effort to get a high percentage of respondents to return the questionnaire. This section will discuss a set of guidelines for increasing return rates on mail questionnaires and provide guidelines for large-group administration of questionnaires.

Guidelines for increasing mail survey return rates

Many factors may cause respondents to fail to return a questionnaire that has been mailed to them. Perhaps the questionnaire is too long and time-consuming for them to even start it. Or perhaps it requires them to put their name on it, but they want to remain anonymous. Or perhaps they are on vacation when it arrives and do not return until after the deadline for the questionnaire has passed. Many other similar factors

TABLE 3.3. GUIDELINES FOR INCREASING MAIL
SURVEY RETURN RATES

1. Use a cover letter.
2. Keep questionnaires short.
3. Offer some incentive.
4. Provide return postage.
5. Supply a self-addressed envelope.
6. Also put address somewhere on questionnaire.
7. Use follow-up letters or phone calls.
8. Time mailing carefully.

may contribute to this problem. To avoid these pitfalls, the guidelines in Table 3.3 should help.

USE A COVER LETTER

You may want to consider the importance of using a cover letter if you are mailing out a questionnaire. The overall purpose of such a letter should be to return it *immediately.* I stress the word *immediately* because you do not want your questionnaire to end up in a pile on the respondent's desk. The cover letter can foster returns by stressing the academic affiliation (or sponsorship) and credentials of those conducting the survey project, as well as by explaining the purpose of the questionnaire, the importance of that purpose, and the importance of everyone returning the questionnaire. You may also find it useful (if it fits the overall purpose of the project) to stress that the questionnaires will be kept completely anonymous. Even if the questionnaires will not be kept anonymous (that is, names and addresses are required), you can stress that the results will be kept strictly confidential. Personalizing the cover letter by filling in the respondent's name or other information somewhere in the letter may also help. Aside from being gracious, thanking the respondents for their cooperation (in advance) may also help to cajole a few more respondents into cooperating. If at all possible, you may find it useful to offer the respondents some form of incentive or reward for returning the questionnaire (see Offer Some Incentive section below). Such a reward just might tip the scale in favor of them mailing the questionnaire back to you.

A great deal of information must be included in a cover letter. At the same time, the cover letter should be short and to the point. In other words, a great deal must be accomplished in as few words as possible. Naturally, such a letter is very difficult to write, so be sure to allow enough time so you can do it well.

An example cover letter is given in Appendix G. Also, the note to the respondents at the top of the example questionnaire in Appendix B, although it is not a formal letter, is clearly performing the same function in a more compact form, which might be called a *cover note*.

KEEP QUESTIONNAIRE SHORT

The questionnaire itself should be as short as possible. However, *short* may mean several things. For instance, short can be fairly long given that, with cagey selection of type sizes and spacing, even a relatively long questionnaire can be fitted into just one or two pages. In addition, the definition of *short* may vary depending on the types of questions. For example, respondents can tolerate a relatively large number of selected-answer types of questions that they can answer quickly by circling the answers, where they might not tolerate an equal number of open-ended questions if the questions require considerable thought and extensive writing out of answers.

As an example of a questionnaire that is too long, consider the one shown in Appendix B. My feeling is that this questionnaire was far too long – largely because of the time, thought, and effort that respondents had to put into answering the open-ended questions, but also because of the large number of questions overall.

OFFER SOME INCENTIVE

As mentioned above, you should think about offering the respondents some incentive for answering the questionnaire. In one survey that I received, I found a dollar bill, which I immediately put into my greedy little pocket. I then filed the survey in the wastebasket without even looking at it. Gradually, however, I began to feel guilty, with the result that I eventually fished the questionnaire out of the basket, filled it out, and sent it back. This trick was clever, and, at least in my case, it worked. Unfortunately, most academics do not have the luxury of paying respondents even a penny.

However, you may find that you can provide several other types of incentives. For instance, as mentioned above, you may want to point out in the cover letter how valuable the project is, how important it is that everyone return the questionnaire, or where and when the respondents will be able to read the results.

Alternatively, you may want to offer to send respondents a copy of the results (or a summary of the results), or to provide them with a lecture or explanation of your results. If you decide to provide a copy of the report, you should probably put a box somewhere near the top of the questionnaire that they can check if they want a copy of that report so it can serve as an incentive, but also so you do not have to send out reports to people who do not really want them. Remember, if you make a promise to send them something, you really must remember to do it. Professional courtesy should ensure that you follow through. However, self-interest is involved as well: If you make a promise to send them a copy of the report and you break that promise, the respondents may never again co-operate on a survey.

PROVIDE RETURN POSTAGE

If at all possible, you should provide return postage so the respondents do not have to find a stamp to put on the envelope. The lack of a stamp could cost you quite a few returns. However, providing postage is not always a simple matter. For instance, in the case of the TESOL Research Task Force questionnaire shown in Appendix B, we found it very difficult to provide postage because we were mailing to many countries in addition to the United States. We considered using separate mailings, but then we would either have to provide postage for the domestic mail and not for international, or get international postal vouchers for the international respondents. In the end, because of the difficulty of doing separate mailings, because of the unfairness involved in paying for the domestic mailing but not the international, because of the complexity of using an international voucher system, and because of the expense involved, the Executive Board of TESOL settled the issue by deciding that we were not allowed to supply postage. We may have lost some returns on that basis alone, but we will never know.

SUPPLY A SELF-ADDRESSED ENVELOPE

Whether or not postage is supplied, a self-addressed envelope will make life a little easier for the respondents, and therefore encourage them to return the questionnaires. In the example immediately above, we were at least able to supply return envelopes.

ALSO PUT THE ADDRESS SOMEWHERE ON QUESTIONNAIRE

You may also want to put the address somewhere else on the questionnaire itself. The address can be included at the top in a letterhead or at the end as part of a *thank you* statement or an ". . . if there are any further questions, please do not hesitate to contact . . ." statement (as shown in Appendix B). Only if such an address is included can respondents who have misplaced the envelope return the questionnaire in an envelope that they address themselves.

USE FOLLOW-UP LETTERS OR PHONE CALLS

If the mailing is not anonymous, another useful strategy is to send out a second mailing, and/or do a series of telephone calls to those who were sent a questionnaire, but did not respond.

TIME MAILING CAREFULLY

In the academic world, the timing of the questionnaire mailing should be considered. For instance, you may want to avoid summer vacation and other vacations, as well as busy times in the academic year, because those are times when the questionnaire is most likely to get lost in the shuffle.

Guidelines for large-group administration

One way to ensure a high return rate is simply to avoid mailing questionnaires and instead administer the questionnaire to a large group of people all at one time. If you are surveying students, you might consider using a program-wide assembly to administer a questionnaire while they are a "captive audience." Or, if you are surveying teachers, you might be able to use a teachers' meeting to administer your questionnaire. For parents, a meeting at the beginning of the term, perhaps at an open house, might provide you with an opportunity to administer a survey. Regardless of the group involved and the strategy that is used to lure them into answering the questionnaire, you should consider certain important issues when doing a large-group administration. The guidelines in Table 3.4 should help in successfully administering a questionnaire to any large group of people.

ESTABLISH THE PURPOSE

First, you should make sure that the purposes for administering the questionnaire are clearly defined. Such definition should be thought of in both theoretical terms and in practical terms that the respondents will understand.

EVALUATE THE QUALITY OF THE QUESTIONNAIRE

In addition, if it has not already been done, you should evaluate the quality of the questionnaire itself. Such evaluation can be based on the guidelines provided in the previous chapter, in Tables 2.2 and 2.3.

CHECK SPACE AND TIME

Next, you should ensure that all of the essential physical conditions for the questionnaire administration have been arranged. To do so, you may need to reserve a large, well-ventilated, and quiet place to administer the questionnaire. The space should be reserved so you have enough time for some flexibility in getting the respondents into and out of that space.

PREPARE ALL PARTICIPANTS

If necessary, you should consider the necessary steps for recruiting the type and number of respondents that you will need, by calling a meeting

TABLE 3.4. GUIDELINES FOR LARGE-GROUP ADMINISTRATION

A. Establish the purpose(s)
   1. Purposes of the survey should be clear.
   2. These goals should be defined in theoretical and practical terms
B. Evaluate the quality of the questionnaire (see Tables 2.2 and 2.3)
C. Check space and time
   1. Arrange for an adequately large, well-ventilated, and quiet space.
   2. Schedule space for enough time for some flexibility.
D. Prepare all participants
   1. Respondents should be properly recruited for the project.
   2. Respondents should also be notified of the survey date and place.
   3. Consider giving the respondents precise written information.
   4. Any assistants who will help should be oriented to their duties.
   5. Crucial information should be given to assistants in writing.
E. Check logistics.
   1. Check to make sure adequate materials are on hand – including extras of all items.
   2. Get all necessary equipment, set it up, and test it – make sure backup equipment is also available.
F. Administer the questionnaire
   1. Make sure all respondents are comfortably seated.
   2. Give clear overall directions (see Chapter 2).
   3. Distribute the questionnaire in an orderly manner.
   4. Provide specific directions when necessary.
   5. Have assistants circulate so that individuals can ask questions.
   6. Time the administration.
   7. Note any problems that occur during the administration.
   8. Collect the questionnaires quickly and efficiently.
G. Thank the respondents
   1. Close the administration with profuse thanks to the respondents.
   2. If possible, provide some form of reward for the respondents.

as suggested in the introduction to this section, by contacting respondents individually to invite them to the administration, or by some other means. You may also want to make sure that the respondents have been properly notified of the date and place of the administration. In the process, you may find it helpful to provide the respondents with all necessary information in a precise written form that will anticipate any questions they might have. Where and when will the questionnaire be administered? What should they bring with them? Should they bring picture identification? This type of information prepared in advance in the form of a handout or pamphlet may save you from answering the same questions hundreds of times before the actual administration.

   You should also consider arranging a meeting of any assistants who will help you in the administration so you can orient them to their duties during the administration. These duties will vary from situation to situation, but going over the guidelines given in Table 3.4 (as they apply to the particular administration and the particular assistants) is one way to cover most of those duties. However, you may also want to provide other information, for instance, the questionnaire directions, a precise schedule of who is to be where and when, details about individual duties, and so forth. Like the respondents, you will find it useful or even necessary to give assistants the above information in writing. One stricture that I have found necessary is that assistants maintain a serious attitude and professional behavior throughout the administration. Assistants, who sometimes get bored just standing around, may tend to talk and joke among themselves. In a large-group questionnaire, such behavior can be very disturbing to those answering the questionnaire.

CHECK LOGISTICS

Before actually administering the questionnaire, you would be wise to make sure that adequate materials are on hand. Such materials might include things like the questionnaires themselves, answer sheets if needed, any necessary cassette tapes, pencils, and so forth. Perhaps it would be prudent to include a few extra copies of everything in case of unforeseen circumstances. For instance, extra copies of the questionnaire would prove useful if three of them turned out to be missing page 2, would it not? Extra cassette tapes would also be useful in case one of the cassette players accidentally destroys the first tape you try. And so forth.

You may also want to make sure that all necessary equipment is ready, available, and reserved for the administration. Such equipment might include such technological marvels as cassette players, public address systems, microphones, videotape players, and so forth, but do not forget less sophisticated equipment such as blackboards, chalk, and erasers. You would also be wise to verify that all of the equipment works by trying it out before the administration. If possible, set the equipment up in advance in the place where the administration will take place, and then test all of it. Even then, backup equipment should be kept readily available. Technology is wonderful, but remember that you are a linguist, not an engineer. Hence, Murphy's law applies particularly to the technical equipment used in large-group administrations: If something can go wrong, it probably will.

ADMINISTER THE QUESTIONNAIRE

During the actual administration of the questionnaire, you should begin by making sure that everyone is comfortably seated. Then you should give clear overall directions (see section on Overall Directions in Chapter 2),

91

including at least some information about the purpose of the survey and the amount of time the respondents will have to fill it out. After distributing the questionnaires (and any other necessary materials) in an orderly manner, more specific directions may be required for particular sections of the questionnaire. In any case, have the assistants circulate among the respondents to answer individual questions as they arise. Be sure to time the administration and note any problems that occur. Finally, collect the questionnaires quickly and efficiently.

THANK THE RESPONDENTS

You should probably close the administration by thanking the respondents profusely. Remember, the survey project might survive without you, but it will most assuredly fail without the respondents. From an even more cynical point of view, remember that you may want to use some of these same respondents in another survey project someday.

If at all possible, you should provide some form of reward for the respondents, as mentioned above. Such a reward might be something as simple as giving them a small sum of money (if you have grant money), or an offer to send them a short summary of the results. Since the point of a reward is to leave a good taste in their mouths about the whole experience, you might even consider something as simple as putting a bowl of candy at the door for them to sample on their way out.

Compiling survey data

Once you have administered a questionnaire or conducted an interview, or both, the next logical step is to compile all of the data that you have collected. The purpose of **compiling** the data is to put it into a form that will later be useful for storing, accessing, sorting, and analyzing it. Usually, you must put the data into some written form. In the case of questionnaires, the respondents have already done that work for you. In essence, the questionnaires and the answers the respondents have put on them can serve as a written record.

However, whether you did the interviews yourself or had a group of assistants doing them for you, how the written record of the interviews will look depends on what the interviewer(s) did with the information as they did the interviews. If a written interview schedule was used to record the respondents' answers in writing as the interview proceeded, then a written record already exists. If the interviews were tape-recorded and only brief notes were kept, the tapes may have to be transcribed into written form and the notes compiled so you can access them easily.

With piles of questionnaires, notes, or interview transcripts in hand, you still have much work to do. You must somehow transform and compile the information in those piles into a more useful form that you can easily store, access, sort, and analyze. In short, you will need to convert the piles of information into usable data. This process of transforming and compiling survey information into usable data is quite different for closed-response and open-response questions. For *closed-response questions,* the range of possible answers is usually fairly circumscribed and the purpose is often to analyze the data statistically. Hence, you will typically want to code the data in some statistically analyzable form. For *open-response questions,* the range of possible answers is much broader and the purpose is usually to analyze the data qualitatively. Hence, you will probably want to transcribe the data in some format that you can easily analyze qualitatively.

Coding closed-response questions

As mentioned above, because of their nature and purpose, you should code the answers to closed-response questions in some statistically analyzable form. This **coding** involves changing the information from one form to another and recording it. In the process, coding the answers from the closed-response questions in a survey project should reduce the information in the actual questionnaires or transcripts to a form that you can easily store, access, sort, and analyze. Five steps will help in this process: (1) Determine the data coding categories you want to use in advance, (2) assign numbers, letters, or code words to each category, (3) decide on a data coding approach, (4) choose a set of data coding tools, and (5) do the actual recording of the data.

DETERMINING CODING CATEGORIES

Deciding in advance on the categories to use is a crucial step that, in the long run, may save a great deal of backtracking and recoding. In other words, you will benefit from examining carefully the information that results from a set of survey results and deciding in advance how you will code each question so the data can be used easily. Hence, you should think ahead to what will eventually be done with the data when they are analyzed, which means that the information in the next chapter will also be pertinent. In addition, some statistical computer programs, which may prove useful in analyzing the data, require that the data be in one form or another, so that must be considered, as well. For example, it makes no sense to code the gender of the respondents as F and M for female and male if the statistical program can analyze only numerically coded data (as is the case with SPSS, 1999). In such a case, you will find it much more productive to code each female as a 1 and each male as a 2 from the outset. If, on the other hand, the statistical program can analyze data coded as letters and words (as is the case with ABSTAT, from Anderson-Bell, 1989), you may want to code females with the word *female* and males with *male* so the analyses will come out more clearly labeled in the printout.

Another general issue that you must consider in deciding coding categories is the scale of measurement that you will use. Recall that four scales of measurement were discussed in Chapter 1. Also recall that they became increasingly precise in the information that they provide in the following order (from least to most precise): nominal, ordinal, interval, and ratio. Remember also that you can transform scales from more precise to less precise scales as needed. As a result, you will often find that you must decide which scale to use in coding a particular question. One rule of thumb that has served me well is, when in doubt, code the data on the most precise scale available. The data can always be changed to a less precise scale later, but the reverse is not true.

ASSIGNING CODES TO DATA

If a question is on a ratio, interval, or ordinal scale, you will want to code it numerically. However, you will have more trouble assigning codes to nominal data, because you can often code them as numbers, letters, or code words for each category of the nominal scale in question. For instance, in the gender example above, the scale is clearly nominal, and you could code the responses as the numbers 1 and 2, the letters F and M, or as the words *female* and *male*. As mentioned earlier, how you decide to assign the codes will depend on the analyses that will follow and the requirements of any computer programs that you will be using.

Another issue that you must address in assigning codes to survey data is what to do with missing data. **Missing data** include any answers that the respondents left blank, or that they supplied, but in such a way that you cannot decipher them, or that you simply want to eliminate from the analysis for some legitimate reason. When in doubt, you should probably leave a blank space wherever data are missing. However, some statistical programs require you to indicate any missing data with a 99, an asterisk, or some other symbol so that the program can correctly interpret each one as a missing data point. Once again, the decisions about what to do will depend on how you will ultimately use the data, and you should decide this early in the process so you do not later find it necessary to recode the data.

One last issue that must be addressed is the collapsing of data. In the process of coding data, you may realize that the results indicate eight main categories with many responses in each and 30 other categories with only one or two responses each. In such a situation, you may find it wise to give the main categories codes from 1 through 8, and create another category 9, which is for all *others*. You can then collapse the 30 small cate-

TABLE 3.5. RECORDING DATA IN ROWS AND COLUMNS

ID	SEX	AS	NL	TOEFL	Q4	Q5	Q6	Q7	Q8	Q9	Q10	Q11
1	m	g	1	553	y	n	3	4	1	3	4	3
2	f	ug	3	507	y	n	4	4	2	3	3	3
3	f	g	5	631	n	s	3	5	1	3	4	3
4	m	ug	4	537	y	s	3	4	1	3	4	3
5	m	ug	4	515	y		2	3	2			
6	m	g	3	600	y	n	3	4	2	3	4	3
7	f	g	2	615	s	n	3	4	2	4	5	4
8	f	g	1	585	y	y	3	5	2	4	4	4
9	f	ug	4	495	n	n				3	3	4
10	f	g	4	677	y	n	5	4	2	4	4	4
11	...											

gories into this single *others* category. On other occasions, you may want to collapse data for logical reasons so the analyses will make more sense in the long run. For instance, in coding the majors of your respondents (for example, psychology, English, sociology, and so forth), two categories (say language education and applied linguistics) may turn out to make much more sense in the analysis as a single category called "applied language education" (perhaps coded ALE, or with a number). However, be cautious in making such decisions to collapse data because, once collapsed, the original categories are not easily recovered without going back to the original information and recoding everything.

DECIDING ON A DATA CODING APPROACH

Data coding for closed-response questions usually involves arranging the data in some written form into rows and columns, or records and fields, so that the data can be easily manipulated for further analysis. However, these two general approaches are very different. Therefore, you should probably decide in advance which approach is most appropriate for your particular survey project.

If you use the **rows-and-columns approach,** each row represents a respondent's answers to all the questions, while each column represents all the respondents' answers to a particular question. Table 3.5 shows a brief example of one way you can code data into rows and columns. Notice that the headings across the top of Table 3.5 begin by labeling a column for the identification numbers for each person (ID). Using this ID number as a guide, you can easily see how each of the **rows** represents the data for a single respondent. The remaining **columns** have labels for each of the questions on this short survey. Notice that biodata questions are coded on nominal scales as follows: gender (SEX) is coded *m* and *f;*

TABLE 3.6. RECORDING DATA AS RECORDS AND FIELDS

3.6a		
IDENTIFICATION NO: 1	Q4: y	Q8: 1
SEX: m	Q5: n	Q9: 3
ACADEMIC STATUS: g	Q6: 3	Q10: 4
NATIVE LANGUAGE: 1	Q7: 4	Q11: 3
TOEFL SCORE: 553		

3.6b		
ID: 2	Q4: y	Q8: 2
SEX: f	Q5: n	Q9: 3
ACADEMIC STATUS: ug	Q6: 4	Q10: 3
NATIVE LANGUAGE: 3	Q7: 4	Q11: 3
TOEFL SCORE: 507		

academic status (AS) is coded *g* for graduate students and *ug* for under-
graduates; and native language is coded 1–5 (1 = Japanese; 2 = Korean;
3 = Cantonese; 4 = Mandarin Chinese; 5 = Other). TOEFL scores, which
were taken from the students' admissions records, are coded on the original interval scale. Questions 4 and 5 (Q4 and Q5) are coded on the nominal yes (*y*), no (*n*), or sometimes (*s*) scale. The remaining six questions
are coded on a 1–5 Likert scale using the exact numbers that the respondents circled. Notice also that respondent 5 left four questions blank
and respondent 9 left three blanks. Note also that these missing data have
been coded as blanks in the appropriate columns.

Now, consider the respondent who has been assigned ID number 1.
The data in the first row of Table 3.5 are for respondent 1 and that row
indicates that respondent 1 is a male graduate student whose native language is Japanese, and who scored 553 on the TOEFL. This respondent
answered yes to Question 4, no to Question 5, and circled 3, 4, 1, 3, 4,
and 3 for Likert-scale questions 6–11, respectively.

Alternatively, the **records-and-fields approach** can be used, in which
case the respondents receive separate pages or cards (instead of rows)
called **records.** Each of the cards has spaces (instead of columns) called
fields provided for coding the questions. Tables 3.6a and 3.6b show two
example cards (or records) that illustrate how data can be coded into
records and fields. Notice that all of the information is coded for respondent 1 in Table 3.6a, and corresponding information for respondent 2 is
on a separate record in Table 3.6b. Each of the questions is then labeled
as a separate field on each of the records. Note also that the examples in
Tables 3.6a and 3.6b contain exactly the same data as the first two rows

of Table 3.5, and, to continue with this records-and-fields approach, the remaining eight rows in Table 3.5 would have to be coded on an additional eight records.

The rows-and-columns and the records-and-fields approaches are two somewhat different ways of coding data in a survey project. Each approach has advantages and disadvantages. The rows-and-columns approach is analogous to an accountant's spreadsheet and is therefore more suitable for numerical manipulation and analysis because the numbers are neatly lined up in columns. The records-and-fields approach is analogous to a card file and thus is a more familiar format to some people and may be better suited for storage and filing, because records can easily be added or removed, and they can be readily sorted.

CHOOSING DATA CODING TOOLS

Once you have decided on your approach, you are almost ready to actually record the data. However, you must make one last decision: the type of tools to use. You could conceivably use either the rows-and-columns or records-and-fields approach with simple paper-and-pencil tools. For instance, you could set up the rows-and-columns approach on clearly lined graph paper or in a ledger book like an accountant's spreadsheet. Similarly, you could use the records-and-fields approach on 3 × 5 or 6 × 8 cards in a file box. If that is all that is available, paper-and-pencil tools will work reasonably well, though they will be relatively slow and cumbersome to use.

However, if the technology is available, either approach can be used on a personal computer with great advantage. Computer **spreadsheet programs** allow for setting up rows and columns in an electronic form. Such spreadsheet programs may be fairly expensive commercial software programs such as Excel (2000), Lotus 1-2-3 (1985), or Quattro Pro (1991).

These electronic spreadsheets have the advantage of storing a tremendous amount of data in a very small amount of space. Furthermore, you can easily add or eliminate rows and columns or sort rows. Thus computer-based spreadsheets have the advantages cited above for both the rows-and-columns and records-and-fields approaches. In addition, electronic spreadsheets have functions that allow for quick and easy calculations of various kinds (including many mathematical functions and some simple statistical functions).

However, for those who prefer working in a file-card metaphor, a database program may be more suitable. Again, such **database programs** may be fairly expensive commercial software programs such as Access (2000), Paradox (1991), or dBaseIII Plus (1986). Like computer spreadsheets, electronic databases have the advantage of storing a tremendous amount of data in a very small amount of space. In addition, you can easily eliminate or add records and fields, and you can sort records quickly or select records that meet a particular requirement in any field. Databases also have mathematical functions that can be used on fields. In short, database programs have all of the primary advantages of both the rows-and-columns and the records-and-fields approaches.

The choice you make between a spreadsheet and a database program is an important one. In general, spreadsheet programs seem to be slightly better suited for manipulation of numbers, and database programs appear to be somewhat better for filing and manipulation of records, but essentially your choice will depend largely on which metaphor you like best. You should also know that many spreadsheet programs allow for transforming database files into spreadsheet files, and vice versa (see Brown, 1992b, for more discussion of spreadsheet and database programs).

One other consideration, indeed one other reason for using a computer program for data entry, is that statistical packages can make the data analysis much easier in the long run. I use three such programs on a regular basis: ABSTAT (Anderson-Bell, 1989), SPSS (1999), and SYSTAT (1999). Each of these statistical programs has its own data-entry module, so you do not have to use any other program if one of these will serve your needs. However, the data-entry modules of these three statistical programs are not as easy to use as a spreadsheet or database program.

Part of the reason that I use the three statistical programs listed above is that they allow the importation of files from other spreadsheet and database programs. In fact, because these three statistical programs have strengths and weaknesses, I use all three for different types of analyses. I particularly like these three because I can do my data manipulations and simple calculations in my spreadsheet program and then import the basic data to any one of these statistical programs for the more complex statistical analyses.

RECORDING THE DATA

Whether the actual data recording is done with a pencil on paper or at a computer keyboard, I have always found the process to be tedious and boring work – but nonetheless very important. The main problem with the boring nature of this work is that accuracy can suffer as time passes. One way to make the task more interesting and more accurate is to work with a partner. One partner can read the data out loud and the second can record it (while the first partner looks up to check the accuracy of what was recorded). The main point here is that accuracy is essential. As they say in the computer world: Garbage in, garbage out. Or, put another way, the results will never be any more accurate than the data on which they are based.

Transcribing open-response questions

Since the nature and purpose of open-response questions are quite different from those of closed-response questions, you will not be surprised to find that they are usually recorded in a different way. Instead of coding the data as is done for closed-response answers, the data from open-response questions are typically transcribed. **Transcribing** means making a copy, arrangement, or record of the data. However, in the process, transcribing the answers from the open-response questions in a survey project should reduce the information to a form that can easily be stored, accessed, sorted, and analyzed. Three steps will help in this process: (1) determine the transcribing categories to be used in advance, (2) choose a set of transcribing tools, and (3) do the actual transcribing.

DETERMINING TRANSCRIPTION CATEGORIES

In the case of open-response categories, whether working from the original questionnaires or from interview transcripts, you should probably start by simply typing the answers so that those for each question are together. For instance, you may want to type all of the open-ended responses to Question 15 in one place, Question 16 in another, and so forth. However, you may also want to plan ahead a bit and group the questionnaires on the basis of some variables that you will later want to study. For instance, if you might eventually want to compare the open-ended responses of males and females for Questions 15 and 16, you could sort the surveys in advance into two piles, one for males and one for females. Then it will be easy to type all of the answers for Question 15 in separate groups for males and females, and likewise for Question 16, or others. Later, when you decide to analyze these open-ended responses, you will be able to read through these grouped data with relative ease. Naturally, you can base such groupings or even further subgroupings on any variable you like – as long as you can sort the surveys on that variable (preferably before you begin typing the responses). Clearly, if at all possible, you will want to decide on your sorting categories (variables) in advance, so that you can do the transcribing in the correct groupings from the beginning without tedious and unnecessary false starts and retyping.

CHOOSING TRANSCRIBING TOOLS

Once you have decided on the sorting categories, you will have to decide what type of tools you want to use. You may decide to use simple paper-and-pencil tools or a typewriter to set up a filing system to record the data. For instance, you could put the answers for males answering Questions 15 and 16 on separate cards (or in separate folders) from the females' answers to the same questions. And as with closed-response questions, if paper-and-pencil or typewriter tools are all you have available, they will work reasonably well though they may prove to be relatively slow and cumbersome.

If the technology is available, you can use a personal computer to your advantage even though numerical calculations are not common in analyzing open-response answers. Computer word processing programs (for instance, Word, 2000) will allow you to type the results with relative ease, but also make it possible to sort, search for particular strings of words, move blocks of text around, shift blocks into separate files, and so forth. Once you have sorted the data into files as appropriate, other computer programs will make it possible to do lexical tallies, concordances, readability estimates, and so forth (see Chapter 5 for more details on these tools) that may help even with the qualitative analyses that you will often find yourself doing on open-ended responses.

DOING THE TRANSCRIBING

I find that the task of transcribing the open-ended responses from questionnaires, transcripts, or tapes is even more tedious, boring, and time-consuming than coding the responses from closed-response questions. Again, accuracy is important with open-ended response transcription, just as it is for closed-response coding – for exactly the same reasons. However, one problem that you may have in transcribing open-response questions (which is not an issue in coding closed-response answers from questionnaires) arises from the fact that different respondents may use different conventions for spelling, grammar, punctuation, and so forth. I have always found it best to transcribe exactly what the respondents wrote, complete with obvious errors. You can always clean up the responses later, but at least you will start with an accurate record of the respondents' actual answers. If you modify or standardize the spelling, punctuation, and so forth, of the answers as you are transcribing, you will never be able to recover the actual answers of the respondents without going back to the original data. Because you may sometimes want to quote specific responses, a record of exactly what they wrote may be important.

Technology can be helpful during the transcription process, especially if you need to transcribe taped interview data. Cassette playback machines are available with start/stop foot pedals. Using such a foot pedal allows you to keep your hands free for writing or typing your transcript, while at the same time starting and stopping the tape with your foot as necessary to match the speed of the data flow to your transcribing speed. Such machines are known as *transcribers* (for example, Sony makes two such machines, models BM77 and M1BI).

Messiness in gathering and compiling survey data

A colleague of mine tells a story of a graduate M.A.-level student in applied linguistics, who once asked her why it was that, when she (the student) did research, the research process was very messy and confusing, whereas the research reports she read in the journals were always so neat and tidy. Any experienced researcher will tell you that in real curriculum or research projects the data-gathering processes are often less than ideal. For reasons beyond the researcher's control, groups may not be randomly sampled, conditions of administration may vary on different occasions or for different groups, response rates from one group may be much higher than from another group, some people may leave a number of items blank, and so forth. This sort of messiness seems very confusing and troublesome. The only way to minimize such messiness is to plan every step of the research process carefully; but because you are doing research based on humans, you will probably never be able to avoid such messiness entirely.

You may find some comfort in knowing that messiness is a normal part of research, at least in my experience. Published reports look neat and clear because research studies are reductive in nature. As I put it in another book (Brown, 1988, p. 5):

[R]esearch can reduce the confusion of facts that language and language teaching frequently present, sometimes on a daily basis. Through doing or reading such studies, you may discover new patterns in the facts. Or through these investigations and eventual agreement among many researchers, general patterns and relationships may emerge that clarify the field as a whole.

In other words, research examines the confusions that are characteristic of language and language teaching for patterns that can help us understand what is going on. In focusing on the patterns, researchers necessarily minimize some of the confusion, and as a result, they are being reductive and presenting relatively neat and tidy reports of their research. Researchers probably do all of this because they have page limits in most of the journals and because they want to make the patterns they have found as clear as possible within those page limits.

In short, don't be surprised if your research, especially in the data-gathering and compiling stages, is somewhat messy and confusing. When you do your analyses (as explained in the next two chapters), you will begin to focus on finding patterns of useful information, which will in turn help you to see a clearer picture of what may be going on in your data.

Examples of gathering and compiling survey data

The examples in this chapter include a description of the problems I had in gathering the survey data on the TESOL survey running example, and an account of the compiling strategies I used on a curriculum survey project (Bailey & Brown, 1995), which we designed to find out what is typically included on the syllabi of language testing courses offered in ESL/EFL teacher training programs around the world.

Running example: Gathering survey data

In this section, I will focus on the sampling and mailing of the TESOL Research Task Force questionnaire, as well as on the resulting return rate and reasons for that return rate.

SAMPLING

The TESOL International Central Office mailed out a total of 1,800 questionnaires: 1,000 randomly selected from the General Membership list and 200 each selected from the Applied Linguistics, Higher Education, Research, and Teacher Education interest section lists. We sampled the 1,000 people from the General Membership in order to get the overall views of the membership. Because we believed that researchers were relatively few in number within the organization, we also took subsamples from those interest sections that we felt were likely to contain relatively larger numbers of researchers.

THE MAILING

TESOL International Central Office did the duplication and collating of questionnaires as well as the random sampling and mailing of the questionnaires. The TESOL staff selected the random samples for all groupings on an IBM-compatible computer using the TESOL International membership database. They mailed the questionnaires in April, with a deadline set for respondents of July 31, 1991. Some of the respondents pointed out that we might have gotten a better return rate if we had set a shorter deadline. However, having considered that possibility, we had decided to avoid a short deadline because such a deadline would probably have discouraged responses from members living in countries outside the United States. In truth, we ended up using any questionnaires that arrived before the TESOL Executive Board midyear meeting in October 1991.

RETURN RATE

We received a total of 607 responses. Table 3.7 shows that 334 of the responses were from the General Membership (GEN MEM), while 66 were from the Applied Linguistics (AL) interest section, 62 from Higher Education (HE), 82 from Research (RE), and 63 from Teacher Education (TE). Thus the return rates varied from a low of 31 percent for the Higher Education to a high of 41 percent for the Research interest section. The last

TABLE 3.7. TESOL RESEARCH TASK FORCE SURVEY RETURN RATES

		Interest sections				
Statistic	GEN MEM	AL	HE	RE	TE	TOTAL
Number sent out	1,000	200	200	200	200	1,800
Number returned	334	66	62	82	63	607
Return rate percent	33.4	33.0	31.0	41.0	31.5	33.7
Percent of all questionnaires	55.0	10.9	10.2	13.5	10.4	100.0

row in Table 3.7 (percent of all questionnaires) indicates that 55.0 percent of the questionnaires that we received were from the General Membership, while 10.9 percent came from the Applied Linguistics interest section, 10.2 percent from Higher Education, 13.5 from Research, and 10.4 from Teacher Education.

Table 3.7 also shows that the Research interest section had the highest return rate. Perhaps this happened because the members of this interest section are generally more interested in research issues, or because they were somewhat more sympathetic to any research efforts.

POSSIBLE REASONS FOR THE RETURN RATE

Four logistical factors might account for the relatively low overall return rate of 33.7 percent:

1. Though we provided self-addressed return envelopes, we could not supply postage. We felt it was impossible to provide postage because U.S. and international mailings were mixed and because of the extra expense involved.
2. We could not do follow-up mailings (to try to get responses from those who had not previously sent the questionnaire back) because of the extra time and cost involved.
3. The 3-page questionnaire was fairly long and complicated, with a number of open-ended questions. Some of the respondents complained about the amount of time it took to fill out the questionnaire (and they were ones who had returned it).
4. Finally, a number of people were accidentally sampled as General Members as well as members of one or more of the interest sections. Such people probably sent back only one of the questionnaires that they received.

All of these logistical factors may have contributed to the fact that only about a third of the questionnaires found their way back to us. However, such a return rate is not unusual in the social sciences, and is in fact rather high in comparison to other surveys run by TESOL International. For instance, the TESOL 1991 Membership Survey had an 11 percent response rate (12.16 percent for U.S. members, and 6.75 percent for international members). Nevertheless, a return rate as low as 33.7 percent can hardly be said to be representative. As a result, we had to interpret the results of this project very cautiously.

Rotating example: Compiling survey data

This example focuses on the compiling strategies used on a curriculum survey project. In general terms, we conducted the project to investigate how many of the ESL/EFL teacher training programs around the world offer language testing courses and what content is typically covered in those courses. More specifically, the purpose of the questionnaire was to investigate the structure, content, and student attitudes toward introductory language testing courses. Thus the questionnaire (see Appendix A) covered a variety of topics, including the instructor's background, the topics covered in the course, the types of students in the classes, as well as the students' attitudes toward language testing before and after the course. A majority of the questions were of the Likert-scale type. However, we also included open-ended questions. The questionnaire was sent to all of the active members on the Language Testing Research Colloquium mailing list during the fall semester 1990. Two months later, we sent a second mailing to those members who had not responded to the first round of mailings. We mailed the survey to approximately 400 colleagues, and a total of 177 returned their questionnaires for an overall response rate of about 44 percent. Of those who responded, 84 had taught a language testing course, and these 84 language testing teachers served as the sample in this project. (For more information on this study, see Bailey & Brown, 1995.)

I will describe the processes involved in compiling both the closed-response and open-response answers. I took primary responsibility for compiling the closed-response answers, while Bailey took charge of compiling the open-response questions.

COMPILING CLOSED-RESPONSE ANSWERS

Recall that computers can be used effectively for analyzing closed-response answers. As discussed above, the process of compiling such closed-response data for computer analysis involves coding. I will describe the coding process for the closed-response answers in the Bailey and Brown (1995) in the four stages in which it occurred: (1) deciding the data coding categories, (2) assigning numbers, letters, or code words to each category, (3) deciding on a data coding approach, and (4) choosing data coding tools.

My first task was to decide what the data coding categories for each variable would be. For instance, one variable that I needed to code was the nationality of each respondent. At first glance, nationality would seem to present no coding problems. However, difficulties did arise because respondents differed in what they called their countries. For instance, the citizens of the United States in our sample used five different responses: *American, United States, US, USA,* and the politically correct *North American.* With regard to the first four labels, I decided to use *US* to code all the responses, because *US* was the easiest to type. However, with the *North American* responses, I first had to figure out whether the respondent was from Canada or the United States, based on personal acquaintance and/or institutional affiliation and address. I had similar problems with people from the *United Kingdom, UK, GB, England, Wales,* and so forth. I am sure that some of those respondents will be less than pleased to find out that they were all coded *GB.* I also had another type of problem with the responses to a question about age. Some respondents were apparently sensitive about this issue and therefore left the question blank. As a result, I had to decide on a code for missing data. In this case, I used a blank space to represent missing data.

I also had problems in deciding on categories for the highest degrees attained by each respondent and the field of study. Part of the problem arose because different universities and different countries label degrees in different ways. Respondents held Ph.D. degrees, doctorates, Ed.D. degrees, and so forth. Furthermore, the degrees of these people were in a wide variety of fields, nearly every one of which had a different label. To help decrease potential confusion, I reduced the number of categories somewhat in the coding process to five codes for degrees, and nine codes for field of study. However, I often found myself making rather arbitrary decisions in this process. For instance, I coded the words *ESL, EFL, TESOL, TEFL,* and *Applied Linguistics* as a number 1, which I interpreted as *Applied Linguistics.*

In short, deciding on data coding categories involves deciding whether or not to reduce categories and how to do so in a standardized way, as well as what to do with missing data. Such decisions are important at the beginning of the coding process (or early in that process), because they are hard to reverse once you have complied the data and because they will affect the way the results turn out. Thus great care must be taken at this stage.

Second, I assigned numbers, letters, or code words to each category. In order to make these decisions, I first needed to decide which statistical program(s) I would use to do the analyses. Because we were planning to do the initial analyses while Bailey and I were in the same place at the same time (at the TESOL Convention, New York), and because my laptop computer at the time had no hard disk, I wanted to use a very compact statistical program. I chose the most compact program that I had at the time: ABSTAT (Anderson-Bell, 1989). This choice then shaped my decisions as to how to code the data. In this case, the statistical program could handle data in numbers, letters, or code words, so I had a fair amount of latitude in deciding what to use. However, I chose to use short, but clear, codes in all cases, because such codes are easier to type.

Third, I had to decide on a data coding approach. Because of my statistical research training, I am more comfortable with the rows-and-columns approach to data coding than with the records-and-fields approach. The rows-and-columns approach seems to me to be easier for later numerical manipulations and analyses. However, people who are more comfortable with the records-and-fields approach might disagree. Nonetheless, the rows-and-columns approach was the one that I used in this example.

Table 3.8 shows some of the rows and columns that were used in this example project. Notice the labels across the top of the spreadsheet for each column and the labels for the rows down the left side (consisting of ID numbers that were assigned to each respondent). I also wrote the ID numbers on each of the corresponding questionnaires so I would be able to get back to the original responses if I had to. The column labels are fairly cryptic in this case. That need not be the case, but these were my personal choices – perhaps resulting from a fairly cryptic personality.

Fourth, I had to choose a set of data coding tools. This decision was easy for me because I am comfortable with IBM-compatible computers and especially in using a spreadsheet program, which allows compiling in the format shown in Table 3.8. In this case, my program of choice was Quattro Pro (1991). However, other people might be more comfortable using a database program, a file-card system, or just plain pencil and paper, depending on their background, personality, abilities, training, and so forth. A person who is already comfortable with computers and certain spreadsheet or database programs will probably have simple choices to make. However, another person who is not familiar with computers and who is doing surveys on a fairly regular basis (or will have other uses for a computer) might find it worthwhile to learn how to use this new tool. Other people who have limited resources or who are doing only one survey and have no other use for a computer might find paper-and-pencil tools to be most efficient and cost-effective.

Finally, I had to do the actual recording of the data. Generally, I find this recording process to be boring and tedious. Thus, if possible, I prefer to work with a partner because, with another person, the data recording process goes faster, is more accurate and, perhaps most important, is less lonely. In this particular case, I was working alone in a hotel room in New York. Thus I often found myself doing a good deal of backtracking, and I had to take great care especially in terms of double-checking for errors.

Working questionnaire by questionnaire, I chose to enter the data from each questionnaire by moving straight across each row. In other situations, I might prefer to work through the questionnaires moving down first one column, then the next column, and so forth. I decide which way to enter the data based on the particular layout and complexity of the data I am compiling.

All in all, once I had coded the closed-response data in this example, as shown partially in Table 3.8, those data were very easy to store, access, sort, and analyze. The computer file took only 16,280 kilobytes of disk space, I could access and sort the data using my spreadsheet program, and I could use the same file in any of my statistical programs. Thus I had achieved all of my goals in compiling my closed-response data.

COMPILING OPEN-RESPONSE ANSWERS

As mentioned above, I handled the coding of the closed-response data, while Bailey took responsibility for compiling the open-response answers. We based this division of labor on our personal preferences, which were in turn based on differences in our background and training (even though we both did our graduate degrees in the same department at UCLA). I will describe her compiling of the open-response data in three stages: determining transcribing categories, choosing transcribing tools, and the actual transcribing.

First, we had to determine which transcribing categories we wanted to use. Initially, we were very ambitious: We wanted to see if there were differences in the results for different nationalities, for respondent gender, for different types of programs, and so forth. However, the magnitude of the compiling and analysis processes soon dawned on us, and we began to temper our ambitious plans. At one point, I recall that we decided to narrow the scope of the project because we felt that the only differences that would be interesting to us and to the readers of our results would be those between nationalities. However, even these contrasts fell by the wayside because of the problems that arose in coding for nationality (see discussion in the second paragraph of the section above on Compiling Closed-Response Answers) and because a number of respondents had one nationality but worked in institutions in another country. We began to wonder just what we meant by "nationality" and eventually decided to abandon the idea of contrasting different nationalities altogether. As a result, we decided not to use categories for compiling the open-response data in this project.

The point is that, had we wanted to, we could have set up separate files

TABLE 3.8. EXAMPLE CODING OF CLOSED-RESPONSE DATA

ID	SEX	AGE	NAT	DEG	MAJ	CRS	C1	C2	C3	C4…G1		G2	G3	G4…P1		P2	INT	S1	S2	S3	S4A	S4B	S4C
1	2	47	TH	3	1	4	5	2	0	5	2	5	4	1	70	30	1	1	Y	R	Y		
2	2	47	US	3	4	1	1	0	5	1	2	2	1	0	15	15	2	3	Y	O	Y	Y	
3	2	45	US	2	2	3	4	5	1	5	0	5	0	0				1		O	Y		
4	2	53	CA	2	2	2	3	0	2	3	1	1	4	1							Y	Y	
5	1	44	US	3	3	7	3	2	4	4	4	4	4	1	40	60	1	1	Y	R	Y		
6	2	41	TH	3	2	6	4	3	0	4	3	3	4	3	20	10	2	1	Y	R	Y	Y	
7	1	50	US	3	3	1	2	0	3	1	1	1	1	0	15	85	1	1	Y	R	Y		
8	1	41	AU	3	3	5	2	3	4	3	3	4	2	2				1		O	Y		
9	2	37	US	3	3	5	4	4	4	4	4	4	4	2	25	25	2	1	Y	O			
10	2	64	US	2	3	2	2	2	2	2	1	1	2	1				1		R	Y		
11	1	41	US	3	2	12	1	0	1	3	5	5	5	0	40	60	1	3	Y	O	Y		
12	1	36	US	3	3	0	1	3	3	3	4	4	4	1	60	40	1	3	Y	R			
13	2		GB	3	5	2	3	1	2	3	1	1	1	1	60	40	1	1		R	Y	Y	
14	1	41	US	3	3	6	4	2	4	4	1	1	2	2				1	Y	R	Y		
15	1	46	US	3	5	2	3	3	2	4	4	2	2	1	30	70	1	1	Y	R	Y		Y
16	1	46	US	3	6	5	3	3	3	2	1	1	2	1	20	80	2	2	Y	R	Y		Y
17	1	74	US	3	3	4	4	2	3	4	2	2	2	3	10	10	1	1	Y	O	Y		
18	2	44	US	2	5	10	4	2	3	1	5	5	4	1	40	60	2	3	Y	R	Y		
19	2	52	CH	3	3	3	3	3	3	4	1	5	4	3	90	10	1	1	Y	O	Y		
20	1	42	US	3	3	2	5	3	5	5	3	3	3	2	20	30	2	1	Y	R	Y		
21	1	46	US	3	2	3	3	4	3	4	4	4	4	0	17	17	2	3	Y	R	Y		
22	1	54	US	3	2	5	3	4	1	5	4	2	1	1	30	70	1	1	Y	O	Y		
23	1	49	US	3	3	3	5	0	1	4	3	2	2	1	20	40	2	1	Y	R	Y	Y	
24	1	44	BR	3	4	1	1	1	1	1	3	1	2	1				1	Y	O	Y	Y	
25	1	47	US	2	2	1	3	1	2	5	1	3	3	0				1	Y	O	Y		
26	1	43	NL	2	5	0	1	2	2	4	2	4	3	0	60	40	1	2	Y	O	Y		
27	1	49	SF	3	5	6	2	0	3	2	3	4	2	1	5	5	2	2	Y	R	Y		
28	2	50	CA	2	3	9	3	1	3	4	2	2	4	1				1	Y	O	Y		
29	2	40	US	3	3	4	3	3	3	4	2	3	3	2	50	50	1	1	Y	R	Y		

30	1	41	US	3	3	8	3	0	3	3	3	4	3	0	60	40	1	1	Y	O	Y		
31	1	38	GB	2		4	1	2	2	5	4	4	4	4	10	10	2	1	Y	R	Y	Y	
32	2	38	US	4	3	12	3	1	2	3	3	4	3	0	35	65	1	1	Y	R	Y		
33	1	43	US	4	3	2	5	0	1	1	1	3	2	1	15	5	2	2	Y	R	Y		
34	2	31	CA	4	5	4	5	3	3	3	3	2	1	1	10	10	2	1	Y	O	Y		
35	1		NL	3	3	0	1	1	1	4	2	2	4	1	5	15	2	1	Y	R	Y		
36	1	45	CA	3	7	3	4	1	1	2	2	3	3	1	15	5	2	1	Y	O	Y		
37	1	42	NZ	3	5	3	2	1		2	3	3	4	1				1	Y	R			
38	2	45	IS	3	3	10	3	3	3	3	2	3	3	3	80	20	1	1	Y	R			
39	2	48	NL	2	3	4	2	2	2	2	1	1	1	0				2	Y	O	Y	Y	
40	2	36	US	3	3	4	5	3	4	3	5	4	4	0	10	40	2	1	Y	R	Y		
41	2	41	US	3	5	6	3	2	2	2	1	3	3	3	25	10	2	3	Y	O	Y		
42	1		US	3	5	4	4	3	1	4	3	3	2	1	25	25	2	1	Y	R	Y		
43	1	60	US	3	5	4	2	2	2	2	3	3	2	3	25	25	2	3	Y	R	Y	Y	
44	2	48	US	3	8	4	4	3	3	4	3	3	4	2	50	50			Y	R	Y	Y	Y
45	2	44	US	2	4	10	5	4	4	4	5	5	5	2	50	50	1	1	Y	R	Y	Y	Y

Source: Bailey & Brown (1995).

TABLE 3.9. EXAMPLE COMPILING OF OPEN-RESPONSE DATA

What other types of non-course testing experience/preparation have you had?

Involvement in language test development and introduction, language test
  research, language testing conference/seminar etc.
4 years at ETS – Test Development and Research
Classroom test preparation, workshops, considerable work in outcomes
  assessment
. . .

How do your students feel about language testing before the course?

Hate it/are curious/feel guilty they don't know more/feel it gives statistics
They think it will be too technical/theoretical
Mildly interested/curious; worried about the "math"
. . .

How do your students feel about language testing after having taken the course?

Love it/accept its practicability for teaching/more confidence/more interest
They often suggest the course be required
Generally positive. Definitely more informed.
. . .

Source: Bailey & Brown (1995).

for analyzing the responses of different nationalities separately and comparing them. The fact that we did not do so does not negate the importance of thinking about compiling results into separate files before beginning the process of compiling open-responses. (For curious readers, the running example in Chapter 5 does provide an example of compiling open-response data into contrasting files.)

Second, we had to choose a set of transcribing tools. In this case, we chose to use IBM-compatible computers and the WordPerfect (Version 5.1) word processing program because we both owned IBM-compatible computers and both had and knew how to use WordPerfect (1991). Hence, this was a very easy decision. In fact, using the same computer types and word processing program also helped us in swapping files back and forth on diskettes and in writing up the final report (Bailey & Brown, 1995).

Third, we had to do the actual transcribing. As mentioned above, this sort of compiling work can be exceedingly tedious, boring, and time-consuming. At least from our perspective, these characteristics were obviated to some extent by hiring a graduate student to do the actual typing. However, Bailey had to find the institutional money to support this graduate student, which, of course, was something she had to plan in advance.

Table 3.9 provides a brief excerpt of the data as they appeared in the transcripts for three of the open-ended questions. Notice that the data are entered separately for each of three questions and are clearly labeled as such. Notice also that the data are transcribed exactly as the respondents wrote, including cryptic phrases, nonparallel structures, and so forth. This exact transcription was done so that an accurate record would exist of the actual responses.

Summary

In this chapter, I covered issues related to gathering and compiling survey data. I began with a discussion of the importance of sampling, including the relationship between populations and samples and the usefulness of random and stratified random sampling strategies. I also touched on the issues involved in deciding on an adequate sample size. Next I explored the pros and cons of interviews and questionnaires (summarized in Table 3.1). I also covered the advantages of using interviews *and* questionnaires sequentially. Then I discussed the administration of interviews, including sets of general and specific guidelines for conducting good interviews (summarized in Tables 3.2a and 3.2b), as well as ideas on what to include in training sessions for interviewers if such sessions are necessary. I also covered the actual administration of questionnaires, including guidelines for increasing mail survey return rates (see Table 3.3) and guidelines for large-group administration (Table 3.4). In the next section, I discussed compiling survey data, including the coding of closed-response questions and the transcribing of open-response questions. Finally, I continued the chapter with examples of gathering and compiling survey data and a brief discussion of the messiness involved in these processes. The running example showed the process of gathering survey data, and the rotating example illustrated potential problems in compiling both closed-response and open-response answers.

Suggestions for further reading

The general books listed in this section in Chapter 1 all cover the topic of gathering and compiling survey data. However, three other books focus exclusively on the issues related to sampling: Kalton (1983), Fox and Tracy (1986), and Fink (1995d). Other books focus on conducting certain types of surveys. For instance, for specific information on self-administered and mail surveys, see Bourque and Fielder (1995); for survey interviews, see Fowler and Mangione (1993), Frey and Oishi (1995), Rubin and Rubin (1995), Seidman (1998), or Weiss (1994); for telephone surveys, see Lavrakas (1993) or Frey and Oishi (1995); for computer-assisted interviewing, see Saris (1991). Finally, Bourque and Clark (1992) focuses on data collection and processing.

Important terms

coding
columns
compiling
database programs
fields
generalizability
missing data
population
random sample
random sampling
records

records-and-fields approach
rows
rows-and-columns approach
sample
sampling
spreadsheet programs
strata
stratified random sample
stratified random sampling
table of random numbers
transcribing

Review questions

1. Why is sampling important? What is the difference between a sample and a population?
2. How are random sampling and stratified random sampling similar and different? What issues should you consider in deciding on an adequate sample size for a given project?
3. What are the pros and cons of using interviews and questionnaires?
4. Why is it sometimes advantageous to use interviews *and* questionnaires sequentially?
5. What are some of the potential problems that might arise in administering interviews? How can you solve these problems?
6. Why are training sessions sometimes necessary for interviewers? What should you include in a training session for interviewers?
7. What steps can you take to increase mail survey return rates?
8. How can you increase the efficiency and effectiveness of large-group questionnaire administrations?
9. What are the steps necessary in coding closed-response questions?
10. What are the steps necessary in transcribing open-response questions?

Application exercises

A. Administer the survey that you created in the Application Exercises in Chapter 2 to an appropriate group of people. If you use a mail survey, follow the guidelines in Table 3.3. If you use a large-group administration follow the steps in Table 3.4.

B. Code the data for the closed-response questions in a way that will maximize your efficiency in storing, accessing, sorting, and analyzing the data later.
C. Transcribe the data from the open-response questions in a way that will maximize your efficiency in storing, accessing, sorting, and analyzing data later.

4 Analyzing survey data statistically

Once you have administered a survey and compiled the data, then comes the important task of analyzing the data you have gathered. In this chapter, I will explain some of the ways you can analyze survey data statistically. In the next chapter, I will examine some of the methods you can use to analyze your data qualitatively.

I will begin this chapter by explaining how to calculate and interpret descriptive statistics, including frequencies and percentages, graphical display of data, symmetrical and skewed distributions, as well as statistics of central tendency (the mean, mode, and median) and dispersion (range, low–high, and standard deviation). I will also provide some strategies for calculating and interpreting statistical tests for (1) examining the correlation of two sets of results, (2) comparing the means of different groupings within your results, and (3) comparing frequencies to expected frequencies. Then I will explore some of the ways you can use statistics to estimate the reliability of your survey instrument and argue for its validity. I will also include guidelines for conducting, analyzing, and reporting statistical studies. As usual, I will end the chapter with two examples: In the running example, I will describe the statistical analyses involved in the TESOL research survey. In this chapter, I will present two rotating examples: The first rotating example (from Sasaki, 1996) will illustrate issues related to analyzing survey data using means comparisons; the second rotating example (from Brown, Cunha, & Frota, in press) will illustrate correlational and factor analysis techniques.

Descriptive statistics for analyzing survey results

In survey research, the purpose of **descriptive statistics** is typically to describe, or characterize, the answers of a group of respondents to numerically coded questions. To that end, you will sometimes need to describe your results in terms of the frequencies or percentages of various answers. Alternatively, you may choose to show them in graphs or charts. At still other times, you may want to describe the central tendency of the answers or examine how the answers are dispersed, or spread out, around the central tendency. Frequencies and percentages, graphical display of data, central tendency, and dispersion will be the four topics covered in this

114

section. To wrap up this section, I will also discuss how descriptive statistics can help you understand the distributions of answers that you find in your data.

Frequencies and percentages

Frequencies are very much like what most people call tallies. Frequencies are used to count up the number of items or people in the levels of a nominal scale (defined and discussed at length in Chapter 1). For instance, if a survey study found a gender breakdown of 15 males and 25 females, 15 and 25 would be the frequencies of males and females in that study.

Frequencies can be represented as **raw frequencies** as in the previous sentence, or they can be converted to **percentages**. Obviously, percentages are calculated by dividing the total number in one category by the total number in all categories. For instance, using the example in the previous paragraph, if you wanted to know what percentage of the total group the 15 males represent, you would do the following steps.

Step 1. Figure out how many people there are total, that is, in both the male and the female categories.

$$15 + 25 = 40 \quad \text{(in the example above)}$$

Step 2. Divide the number in the male category by the total number in both the male and female categories.

$$\frac{15}{40} = 0.375$$

Step 3. Multiply the result by 100.

$$.375 \times 100 = 37.5$$

Step 4. Round to the result to two places, as is conventional in the social sciences.

$$37.50\%$$

Apparently, 37.50 percent of the participants in the example study are male, and presumably 62.50 percent are female (100% − 37.50% = 62.50%).

Percentages are sometimes easier for some readers to understand than raw frequencies, that is, for some people, being told that a study included 37.50 percent males and 62.50 percent females, as in the example, is easier to understand than being told that there were 15 males and 25 females. Consequently, I have very often found myself presenting survey results in percentage terms. However, because the raw frequencies are the basic units of analysis and because percentages sometimes obscure important information, when I have presented percentages, I have always tried to present the actual frequencies as well (for an example, see Table 4.19, later).

Graphical display of data

Yet another way of presenting frequency or percentage data is to use some of the graphing tools available in most spreadsheets. For example, as shown in Figure 4.1, you could use the Excel (2000) spreadsheet to represent the gender frequencies of 15 males and 25 females discussed in the previous two sections as a **column graph** (Figure 4.1a), or you could flip the graph on its side to create a **bar graph** (Figure 4.1b). You could also represent your results as a **pie chart** (Figure 4.1c), as a **3-D pie chart** (Figure 4.1d), or even as a **donut graph** (Figure 4.1e). You could also add percentages to any of the displays (see Figure 4.1f), or you could do a **3-D bar graph** with percentages (see Figure 4.1g).

USING GRAPHS TO UNDERSTAND DISTRIBUTIONS

One very useful aspect of graphs is that you can use them to examine the shape of the distribution of whatever numbers you are analyzing. Quite simply, the **distribution** of a set of numbers is their frequency of occurrence. For instance, the frequency of occurrence of gender in the above examples is 15 and 25, which you can see much more graphically in Figure 4.1g. With more complicated distributions, you may have more difficulty imagining the distribution without some sort of graphical representation. Consider, for instance, the following 12 answers from Question 1 on a hypothetical questionnaire: 1 5 2 4 3 2 3 3 4 3 2 4. Can you imagine what the distribution looks like? Now look at the simple column graph of the same numbers in Figure 4.2a. Not only can you visualize the distribution of the frequencies, you can also see that the distribution is **symmetrical** – that is, the distribution has the same shape on each side of the middle.

However, not all distributions are symmetrical. Some distributions are skewed. A **skewed** distribution is one that is not symmetrical because it has a few values that are very large or very small relative to the others in the distribution. Consider, for example, the following answers of 11 students to Likert-scale Question 3 on our hypothetical survey (with options from 1 to 5): 5 5 1 2 4 3 4 4 5 4 4. Again, you probably find it difficult to visualize the distribution, but a quick column graph will help. In Figure 4.2b, you can immediately see that the distribution is not symmetrical, because a few values (especially 1 and 2) are very low in frequency relative to the others. In effect, this distribution has a tail pointing in the negative direction (or in the direction of the small numbers); thus, such a distribution is called a **negatively skewed** distribution.

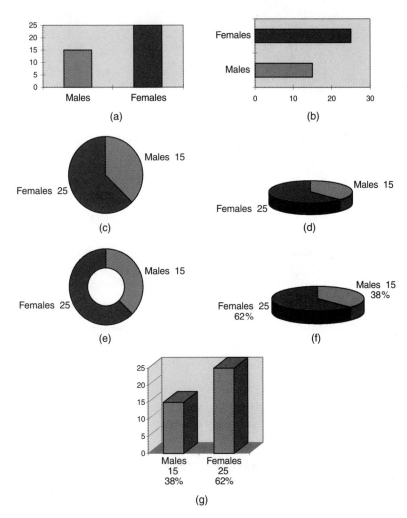

Figure 4.1 Graphical displays: (a) column graph; (b) bar graph, (c) pie chart; (d) 3-D pie chart; (e) donut graph; (f) 3-D pie chart showing percentages; (g) 3-D bar graph showing percentages.

Naturally, the opposite can occur, too, as in Question 2 on our hypothetical questionnaire, which is graphed in Figure 4.2c. Since this distribution is not symmetrical and has a tail pointing in the positive direction (or in the direction of the large numbers), such a distribution is called a **positively skewed** distribution.

Symmetrical distributions and skewed distributions (whether negative or positive) typically share one characteristic: They all have one high point

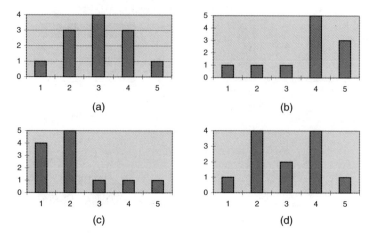

Figure 4.2 (a) Column graph for Question 1; (b) column graph for Question 3; (c) column graph for Question 2; (d) column graph for a multimodal distribution.

or peak. Distributions can also have more than one peak, as shown in Figure 4.2d. Such a distribution is referred to as **bimodal**. Naturally, more peaks could exist, creating other distributions that could be referred to as trimodal, quadrimodal, and so forth.

A CAUTION ABOUT GRAPHS

As you can see, the possibilities for graphing data are numerous and relatively easy (it took me about 10 minutes to generate all of the graphs in Figures 4.1 and 4.2). However, one problem seems to emanate from the very fact that such graphs are easy to generate in a spreadsheet and then copy into the word processor: Graphs tend to be overused in statistical reports, especially by novices. The danger in using too many graphs in a report is that you may numb your reader and make the graphs less effective. As a rule of thumb, I use graphs as much as I like to help me understand the distributions and other patterns in my results, but I use graphs in reports only when they are absolutely necessary to help readers understand key results, or when I want to emphasize a particular set of results.

Central tendency

Central tendency can be defined as the typical answer of a particular group of people. In survey research, the most commonly reported central tendency statistics are the mean, mode, and median. I will define each of these and briefly explain how they can be calculated, so you can understand them clearly. However, I will also explain how each can be obtained more easily by using a computer spreadsheet program.

MEAN

The **mean** of any set of numbers is similar to what you probably know as the arithmetic average. To calculate the mean, you add up whatever numbers are involved and divide them by the total number of numbers. I will demonstrate briefly, using the answers of the 11 students who answered Likert-scale Question 3 on the hypothetical survey (of the previous section): 5 5 1 2 4 3 4 4 5 4 4. The mean of these Likert-scale answers is calculated as follows:

Step 1. Add up all the numbers.

$$5 + 5 + 1 + 2 + 4 + 3 + 4 + 4 + 5 + 4 + 4 = 41$$

Step 2. Divide the total by the number of numbers (in this case, there are 11 numbers).

$$\frac{41}{11} = 3.7272$$

Step 3. Round the result to two places to the right of the decimal point, as is conventional in the social sciences.

$$3.7272 \approx 3.73$$

So the mean of the students' answers to the third Likert-scale question is about 3.73.

Using a formula, I would represent the steps above as follows:

$$M = \frac{\Sigma X}{N}$$

where M = mean
X = numbers
N = number of numbers

The formula indicates that the mean (M) equals the sum (Σ) of the numbers (X) divided by the number (N) of numbers involved. Using the numbers in the example above, the formula is:

$$M = \frac{\Sigma X}{N} = \frac{41}{11} = 3.7272 \approx 3.73$$

Fortunately, computer spreadsheet programs usually include a **mean function** that makes finding the mean of a set of numbers very easy. For example, in the Excel spreadsheet program commonly used on both

IBM-compatible and Macintosh computers, typing =AVERAGE and telling the program which range of numbers to consider (in parentheses) will produce the mean. For example, if the numbers you want to analyze are in the range from cell A2 to cell A12, you can calculate the mean by typing the following in any empty cell:

=AVERAGE(A2:A12)

(Note that A2:A12 is the range of answers, where A2 labels the cell in row 2 of column A, the colon signifies *to,* and A12 is the cell in row 12 of column A. In other words, the range is identified here as going from what is referred to as cell A2 to cell A12.)

MODE

The **mode** is simply the most common number. No fancy formula is needed to calculate that. Just put the numbers in order and examine them or make a graph of the numbers, and you should be able to figure out immediately which one is the most common. For instance, consider once again the 11 Likert-scale responses used as an example in explaining the mean: 5 5 1 2 4 3 4 4 5 4 4. First, put the numbers in order: 1 2 3 4 4 4 4 4 5 5 5. Second, ask yourself which number is the most common? The answer is 4, right? So, 4 is the mode.

Most computer spreadsheet programs include a **mode function** that makes finding the mode of a set of numbers even easier than simple inspection. For example, in the Excel spreadsheet program, typing =MODE and telling the program which range of numbers to consider (in parentheses) will produce the mode. For example, if the numbers you want to analyze are in the range from cell A2 to cell A12, you can calculate the mode by typing the following in any empty cell:

=MODE(A2:A12)

MEDIAN

The **median** is that number in a set of numbers which is the middle value dividing all the other numbers 50/50 (that is, so that 50 percent are above it and 50 percent are below it). Sometimes you can spot the median just by putting the numbers in order and looking at them. For instance, once again using the 11 Likert-scale responses from the explanations in the previous two sections (that is, 5 5 1 2 4 3 4 4 5 4 4), I begin by putting those responses in order: 1 2 3 4 4 *4* 4 4 5 5 5. Clearly, 4 is the median, because the sixth, or middle, case (italicized) in these 11 numbers is 4, with five numbers below it (1 2 3 4 4) and five numbers (4 4 5 5 5) above it. Finding the median in these example numbers was easy, because I created the example to work out that way. Unfortunately, real life is not always so easy.

TABLE 4.1. SELECTING THE APPROPRIATE STATISTIC FOR CENTRAL TENDENCY

	The mean *is appropriate for:*	*The* mode *is appropriate for:*	*The* median *is appropriate for:*
Focus	Average answer	Most common answer	Typical answer
	and	or	or
Distribution	Symmetrical	Bimodal	Skewed
	and	or	or
Scale	Interval/ratio	Any scale	Ordinal

Consider a situation where you have an even quantity of numbers and the two middle numbers are different. For instance, in the following set of numbers, because there is no single middle number, 5 and 6 must both be considered the middle numbers:

$$1 \ 2 \ 3 \ 4 \ 5 \ 6 \ 7 \ 8 \ 9 \ 10$$

To find the median in such a situation, the two middle numbers must be averaged; in this case,

$$\frac{5 + 6}{2} = 5.50$$

Other complications may arise as well, but fortunately, computer spreadsheet programs usually include a **median function** that makes finding the median of a set of numbers very easy. For example, in the Excel spreadsheet program, typing =MEDIAN and telling the program which range of numbers to consider in parentheses will produce the median. For example, if the numbers you want to analyze are in the range A2 to A12, you can calculate the median by typing the following in any empty cell:

$$=MEDIAN(A2:A12)$$

SELECTING INDICATORS OF CENTRAL TENDENCY

So far, we have examined three indicators of central tendency (the mean, median, and mode) and shown how they can be calculated by hand or on a computer. However, these three statistics are not all equal in meaning or usefulness in all situations. Sometimes one is appropriate, and at other times another is suitable. Table 4.1 shows the issues involved in selecting the appropriate statistic for central tendency, depending on the focus, distribution, and scale involved in a particular situation.

Notice that the *mean* is appropriate if your focus is on the average answer, if the distribution of answers is symmetrical, and if the answers are on an interval or ratio scale. The *mode* is appropriate if your focus is the most common answer or if the distribution of answers is bimodal (any scale). The *median* is appropriate if your focus is the typical answer, if the distribution is skewed (on an interval or ratio scale), or if the scale is ordinal.

Note that, for answers that are on an interval or ratio scale, it is safe to report all three statistics for central tendency. In fact, their relationship can help in understanding the degree to which the distribution is symmetrical, as follows: (1) If the mean, mode, and median are all very similar, the distribution is probably fairly symmetrical; (2) if the mode is higher than the median, which in turn is higher than the mean, the distribution is probably negatively skewed; and (3) if the mean is higher than the median, which in turn is higher than the mode, the distribution is probably positively skewed.

Dispersion

Dispersion can be defined as the degree to which the answers of the individuals in a group fluctuate around the central tendency for that group. In survey research, the most commonly reported statistics for dispersion are the range, low–high, and standard deviation. I will define each of these and briefly explain how they can be calculated. As in the previous section, I will also explain how they can be obtained more easily by using a spreadsheet program.

RANGE

The **range** of any set of numbers is the distance between the highest and lowest numbers in the set. Consider, for instance, the example used earlier of 11 students' answers to Likert-scale Question 3 on our hypothetical survey (with options from 1 to 5): 5 5 1 2 4 3 4 4 5 4 4.

The steps in finding the range of this set of numbers are as follows.

Step 1. Arrange the numbers in order.

$$1\ 2\ 3\ 4\ 4\ 4\ 4\ 4\ 5\ 5\ 5$$

Step 2. Write down the highest and lowest numbers in the set.

$$5\ 1$$

Step 3. Subtract the lowest number from the highest number and add 1 to get the range.

$$5 - 1 = 4 \qquad \text{and} \qquad 4 + 1 = 5$$

So the range of the students' answers to the Likert-scale question is 5. Using a formula, we can represent the steps as follows:

$$\text{Range} = H - L + 1$$

where H = high number
        L = low number

The formula indicates that the range equals the high number (H) minus the low number (L) plus 1. Using the numbers in the example above,

$$\text{Range} = H - L + 1 = 5 \quad 1 + 1 = 5$$

You may ask why you need to add 1 after subtracting the high from the low. Some statisticians say that you should simply subtract the low number from the high one. Others argue that, if you do not add 1, you are leaving out either the highest or the lowest number. In the example, there are five possible numbers in the range: 1 2 3 4 5. If you simply subtract, $5 - 1$, you get 4. Since there are clearly 5 numbers in the range, you have left out one of them using this method. That is why I have chosen to give you the $H - L$ +1 formula. You may find that you can report the range more clearly by simply telling your readers what the lowest and highest scores are, as in the following: "The answers for Question 1 ranged from 1 to 5."

Unfortunately, computer spreadsheet programs usually do *not* have a range function. However, you can use a calculator, or a formula in your spreadsheet program. For example, in the Excel spreadsheet program, if the numbers you want to analyze are in the range A2 to A12, you can calculate the range by using the MAX function (maximum or highest number) and MIN function (minimum number) and typing the following:

$$=\text{MAX(A2:A12)}-\text{MIN(A2:A12)}+1$$

LOW-HIGH

Because the range indicates only the distance between the highest and lowest answers, not the placement of that distance along the scale, you may also want to report the **low–high,** that is, the lowest and the highest answer in the set of answers. Consider again the example used above of students' answers to Likert-scale Question 3 on a survey: 5 5 1 2 4 3 4 4 5 4 4.

The steps in finding the low–high of this set of numbers are as follows.

Step 1. Arrange the numbers in order.

$$1\ 2\ 3\ 4\ 4\ 4\ 4\ 4\ 5\ 5\ 5$$

Step 2. Write down the lowest and highest numbers in the set as the low–high.

$$\text{Low–high} = 1 \text{ to } 5$$

The low–high is really just a simpler way of reporting range, but it has the advantage over the range of showing where in the scale the range

TABLE 4.2. CALCULATING THE STANDARD DEVIATION

① Answers		② Mean		③ Difference	④ Squared difference
5	–	3.73	=	1.27	1.6129
5	–	3.73	=	1.27	1.6129
1	–	3.73	=	–2.73	7.4529
2	–	3.73	=	–1.73	2.9929
4	–	3.73	=	0.27	0.0729
3	–	3.73	=	–0.73	0.5329
4	–	3.73	=	0.27	0.0729
4	–	3.73	=	0.27	0.0729
5	–	3.73	=	1.27	1.6129
4	–	3.73	=	0.27	0.0729
4	–	3.73	=	0.27	0.0729
		⑤	Sum	=	16.1819
		⑥	Sum/N	=	1.4711
		⑦	SqRoot	=	1.2129
		⑧	SD	=	1.21

falls. Very often both the range and low–high statistics are reported together.

STANDARD DEVIATION

The **standard deviation** (SD) of any set of numbers is a sort of average of the distance of all the answers from the mean. Basically, you subtract the mean from each number and square the results; then you add those results up for all the numbers; next you divide the resulting sum by the number of numbers and take the square root of that result.

If that seems complicated, just consider a straightforward example using the students' answers to Question 3 in our hypothetical questionnaire (the same numbers used in the explanations above). Recall that their answers were

5 5 1 2 4 3 4 4 5 4 4

The standard deviation of these Likert-scale answers is calculated as shown in Table 4.2. Notice that there are four columns in Table 4.2. Each column represents one of the first four steps. Then four more steps are listed in the lower right portion of the table. Referring to the table, the steps in calculating the standard deviation are as follows.

Step 1. List all the answers in one column.
Step 2. List the mean next to each answer.
Step 3. Subtract the mean from each answer to get the difference.
Step 4. Square each difference.
Step 5. Add up all the squared differences.
Step 6. Divide that total by the number of numbers.
Step 7. Take the square root of the result of step 6.
Step 8. Round the result of step 7 to two places to the right of the decimal point, as is conventional in the social sciences.

Following those eight steps, as indicated in Table 4.2, the standard deviation of the students' answers to the Likert-scale Question 3 is 1.21.

Using a formula, the steps above can be represented as

$$SD = \sqrt{\frac{\sum (X - M)^2}{N}}$$

where SD = standard deviation
X = numbers
M = mean of the numbers
N = number of numbers

The actual calculations for the example shown in Table 4.2 are

$$SD = \sqrt{\frac{\sum (X - M)^2}{N}}$$

$$= \sqrt{\frac{16.1819}{11}}$$

$$= \sqrt{1.4711}$$

$$= 1.2129 \approx 1.21$$

You may have noticed that, in defining the standard deviation, I wrote that it is "*a sort of* average of the distance of all the answers from the mean." The implication of the phrase *sort of* is that this calculation is not always exactly like an average of the squared deviations of the answers from the mean. If 30 or more numbers are included in the calculation, the formula given here works fine, but if 29 or fewer numbers are involved, the mean is still subtracted from each number and the results are still squared and added, but then the result is divided by the number of numbers minus 1 (for an explanation of why this is so, see Brown, 1988, pp. 118–119). In formula form (often referred to as the "*N* minus 1 formula"), the standard deviation for a set of 29 or fewer numbers is

$$SD = \sqrt{\frac{\sum (X - M)^2}{N - 1}}$$

where SD = standard deviation
     X = numbers
     M = mean of the numbers
     N = number of numbers

You may have noticed that we should have used this second formula for the first example given above for the standard deviation, because there were only 11 student answers. If so, you were right. However, I wanted both to have a small set of numbers to use in my example and to explain the simpler of the two formulas first, so I chose not to follow my own advice.

Fortunately, computer spreadsheet programs usually include a *standard deviation function* that makes finding the standard deviation of a set of numbers very easy. For example, in the Excel spreadsheet program, typing =STDEVP (for the regular formula) or =STDEV (for the N minus 1 formula) and telling the program which range of numbers to consider (in parentheses) will produce the standard deviation. For example, if the numbers you want to analyze are in the range from cell A2 to cell A12, you can calculate the standard deviation by typing the following in any empty cell:

       =STDEVP(A2:A12)   (for the regular formula)

or

       =STDEV(A2:A12)   (for the N minus 1 formula)

SELECTING INDICATORS OF DISPERSION

In this section, we have examined three indicators of dispersion: the range, low–high, and standard deviation. I have shown how they can be calculated by hand or on a computer. However, these three indicators are not exactly equal in meaning or usefulness in all situations. Sometimes one statistic is more appropriate, and at other times another is suitable. Table 4.3 shows the issues involved in selecting the appropriate statistic for dispersion, depending on the focus, distribution, and scale involved in a particular situation.

Notice that the range is appropriate if the focus is on the total extent of answers, can be applied whether the distribution of answers is skewed or symmetrical, and is useful in analyzing interval or ratio scales. The low–high is appropriate if the focus is on the upper and lower limits of answers, can be applied whether the distribution of answers is skewed or symmetrical, and is useful in analyzing interval or ratio scales. The standard deviation is appropriate if the focus is the average spread from the mean of the answers, if the distribution is symmetrical, and if the scale is either interval or ratio. Note that none of the three indicators given here

TABLE 4.3. SELECTING THE APPROPRIATE STATISTIC FOR DISPERSION

	The range *is appropriate for:*	*The* low–high *is appropriate for:*	*The* standard deviation *is appropriate for:*
Focus	Total extent of answers	Upper and lower limits of answers	Average spread from the mean of the answers
Distribution	Skewed or symmetrical	Skewed or symmetrical	Symmetrical
Scale	Interval or ratio	Interval or ratio	Interval or ratio

is particularly useful or sensible for describing the dispersion of ordinal or nominal scales. Indeed, the whole notion of dispersion makes no sense when examining nominal scales and little sense when analyzing ordinal scales. Note that for answers that are on an interval or ratio scale, it is safe, and usually appropriate, to report all three statistics for dispersion.

Descriptive statistics and distributions of answers

The descriptive statistics by themselves are not very interesting. However, when you start thinking of the various descriptive statistics in combination and start to realize how they work together to describe the distributions of responses, descriptive statistics really come alive and become useful.

Consider Table 4.4, which I worked out in my Excel spreadsheet program and then copied directly into my Word program to become part of this book. I mention the above software steps because they indicate that Table 4.4 is one relatively easy way to set up data for descriptive analysis of individual questions. Notice that I put the question labels across the top and the student identification (ID) numbers down the left-hand side in the first column. Also notice that I put the labels for the descriptive statistics below the ID numbers in the left-hand column. The next step was to enter the data for the actual answers. Notice that the answers for each student are in a row. Thus, by looking at the rows, you can see at a glance that student number 1 answered 1 2 5 3 4 5 1 2, student 2 answered 5 1 5 3 4 5 1 4, and so forth. Similarly, by looking at the columns, you can see at a glance that the answers for Question 1 (Q1) were 1 5 2 4 3 2 3 3 4 3 2 4, the answers for Q2 were 2 1 3 1 2 4 1 5 2 1 2 2, and so forth. Notice that, for student 5, I left Q3, Q4, and Q5 blank, because the student failed to answer those questions.

Once all the answers were entered into the spreadsheet, I typed in the

TABLE 4.4. LAYOUT OF DATA FOR ANALYZING DESCRIPTIVE STATISTICS

Student ID	Q1	Q2	Q3	Q4	Q5	Q6	Q7	Q8
1	1	2	5	3	4	5	1	2
2	5	1	5	3	4	5	1	4
3	2	3	1	3	2	4	1	3
4	4	1	2	2	2	4	1	2
5	3	2				4	1	3
6	2	4	4	4	4	5	1	3
7	3	1	3	3	3	4	1	4
8	3	5	4	3	4	5	2	3
9	4	2	4	3	4	5	1	2
10	3	1	5	3	4	4	1	4
11	2	2	4	3	4	5	1	1
12	4	2	4	4	4	4	1	5
Mean	3.00	2.17	3.73	3.09	3.55	4.50	1.08	3.00
Mode	3.00	2.00	4.00	3.00	4.00	5.00	1.00	3.00
Median	3.00	2.00	4.00	3.00	4.00	4.50	1.00	3.00
Min	1.00	1.00	1.00	2.00	2.00	4.00	1.00	1.00
Max	5.00	5.00	5.00	4.00	4.00	5.00	2.00	5.00
Range	5.00	5.00	5.00	3.00	3.00	2.00	2.00	5.00
SD	1.08	1.21	1.21	0.51	0.78	0.50	0.28	1.08
N	12	12	11	11	11	12	12	12

functions and formulas for the statistics for Question 1. More precisely, in the space where you now see 3.00 for the mean of Q1, I actually entered =AVERAGE(B2:B13) and the answer 3.00 appeared. (Note that B2:B13 is the range of answers for Q1, where B2 labels the cell in row 2 of column B, the colon signifies *to*, and B13 is the cell in row 13 of column B. In other words, the range is identified here as going from what is referred to as cell B2 to cell B13.) I then made similar entries for the other statistics:

Mode	=MODE(B2:B13)	
Median	=MEDIAN(B2:B13)	
Minimum score	=MIN(B2:B13)	
Maximum score	=MAX(B2:B13)	
Range	=B18-B17+1	(where B18 is MAX and B17 is MIN)
Standard deviation	=STDEVP(B2:B13)	(where STDEVP is the population SD)
Number of answers	=COUNT(B2:B13)	

TABLE 4.5. EXAMPLE TABLE OF ITEM STATISTICS

Statistic	Q1	Q2	Q3	Q4	Q5	Q6	Q7	Q8
Mean	3.00	2.17	3.73	3.09	3.55	4.50	1.08	3.00
Mode	3.00	2.00	4.00	3.00	4.00	5.00	1.00	3.00
Median	3.00	2.00	4.00	3.00	4.00	4.50	1.00	3.00
Low–High	1–5	1–5	1–5	1–5	2–4	4–5	1–2	1–5
Range	5.00	5.00	5.00	3.00	3.00	2.00	2.00	5.00
SD	1.08	1.21	1.21	0.51	0.78	0.50	0.28	1.08
N	12	12	11	11	11	12	12	12

Of course, entering all those cryptic commands was relatively laborious, but at this point you will clearly see the advantage of doing such statistics in a spreadsheet program, because my final step was to COPY all the commands for Q1 from where they are in column B across the bottom to the spaces provided for Questions Q2 through Q8; they were then automatically entered and calculated for all those other questions, too. In other words, I calculated all the same statistics for the other seven questions in one move. (Please see the spreadsheet software documentation for further information on how to copy formulas and functions.)

Table 4.5 shows the same statistics (again block-copied within my computer programs) as I might present them in an actual research report. Notice that the only thing I needed to retype was the low–high, which I had to convert by hand from the Min and Max rows.

Notice also that the three statistics of central tendency (mean, mode, and median) all indicate that Q6 had the highest answers, Q7 had the lowest, and all the other central tendencies fell somewhere in between. Notice also that the three statistics for dispersion (low–high, range, and standard deviation) indicate that Q1, Q2, Q3, and Q8 all had relatively high dispersion, while the other questions, especially Q7, had relatively low dispersion. These dispersion results simply indicate that the answers on Q1, Q2, Q3, and Q8 were relatively heterogeneous, or more spread out, than on the other questions, which were relatively homogeneous. Notice in the last row that for most of the questions, 12 students answered them; but for Q3, Q4, and Q5, only 11 students answered them. This is because student 5 did not answer those three questions. In most spreadsheet programs, blank spaces left for missing answers will not be included in the calculation of statistics. In other words, statistics such as the mean and standard deviation were calculated with student 5 completely excluded for Q3, Q4, and Q5. However, if I had entered a zero in those cells instead of leaving them blank, that zero would have been figured into the statistics and the N sizes would all have been 12.

Another way to look at such results is to think about the distributions involved. You could graph them as shown earlier in the chapter, but you can also examine the descriptive statistics and learn a great deal. For example, Q1 and Q8 appear to be fairly symmetrically distributed, as indicated by the facts that (1) all three central tendency statistics are exactly the same, (2) the values of the central tendency statistics are well centered (that is, 3.00 is exactly midway between the extreme values of 1 and 5 on this five-point scale), and (3) there is room for almost two standard deviations of 1.08 below the mean (that is, between 3 and 1 on the scale) and above the mean (that is, between 3 and 5 on the scale). Also consider Q3 and Q6, both of which appear to be negatively skewed because the means are high and there is room for only about one standard deviation above the mean. The fact that these two questions are skewed does not necessarily mean that they were bad questions. Instead, it tells me something about the pattern of responses, in much the same way that a graph would. With practice, anyone can learn to interpret the picture presented by descriptive statistics, but it does take some practice.

Statistical tests for analyzing survey results

As you saw in the first part of this chapter, descriptive statistics can be very useful for understanding the quantitative results of a survey. However, certain other statistics can help in understanding those results even further, because they help to clarify whether the results are simply chance findings or are statistically significant. **Statistical significance** indicates the probability that the results of a statistical analysis are due to chance factors. If you report that a certain statistical comparison between two means was significant at $p < .05$, this simply means that there is a 5 percent (or smaller) probability that the observed difference between the means was due to chance alone. In other words, you are 95 percent sure that the result is due to factors other than chance. Being able to say that about your results can make whatever patterns or differences you are examining in your results more convincing to yourself as well as your readers, because 95 percent represents a fairly high probability that your results are not just a random fluctuation.

Traditionally, in language studies (as in other social and behavioral sciences), we want to be 95 percent sure ($p < .05$) or 99 percent sure ($p < .01$). The choice between these options has to do with the importance of the statistical decision being made and the number of decisions being made in a particular study (I will return to these topics later, in the discussions of alpha level and Bonferroni adjustments).

Statistical tests, then, are the statistics used to estimate the probabilities discussed in the previous paragraph. In this book, I will give an overview

of three types of statistical tests: correlational statistics, means comparisons statistics, and frequency comparison statistics. The treatments given
here are necessarily brief, but they will provide the basics necessary for
using the statistical tests most commonly applied in survey research. I
strongly recommend that you also take a course or read up on these
statistics from other sources (for much more on these topics, see Brown,
1988, 1991a, 1992f; Hatch & Lazaraton, 1991).

The remainder of this section will discuss particular types of statistical
tests under headings for correlation, means comparisons, and comparing
frequencies. I will end this section by discussing the problem of multiple
comparisons and the Bonferroni adjustment.

Correlation

WHAT IS CORRELATION?

Correlation is the degree to which two sets of numbers are related. The
Pearson product–moment correlation coefficient is a numerical representation of the degree to which two sets of interval- or ratio-scale numbers
are related, or go together. It can range from 0.00 (which indicates no relationship at all) to +1.00 (which means the two sets of numbers are perfectly related) to –1.00 (which also means the two sets of numbers are
perfectly related, but in opposite directions). Naturally, all values between
0 and +1.00 can and do occur, as well as all values between 0 and –1.00.

Consider some more tangible examples. First, two sets of random numbers should produce a correlation coefficient of 0.00 or close to that value.
The two sets of numbers in Table 4.6, columns 1 and 2 (Example A),
were generated to be random numbers in my spreadsheet program, and
they do produce a correlation coefficient of 0.00 because they are completely unrelated to each other.

In contrast, the numbers shown in Example B, in columns 3 and 4 of
Table 4.6, are obviously perfectly related, and a correlation coefficient
calculated for them would turn out to be +1.00 (I know this to be true,
because I just used the =CORREL function in my spreadsheet to calculate one).

Notice that the sets of numbers shown in Example C, in columns 5 and
6 in Table 4.6 (where the numbers in column 6 are considerably larger
than those in column 5), as well as those shown in Example D, in columns
7 and 8 (where the numbers in column 8 are considerably smaller than
those in column 7), are also perfectly correlated at +1.00. Clearly, then,
the degree of correlation is not directly affected by the relative magnitudes
of the two sets of numbers involved.

As mentioned above, a perfect negative correlation of –1.00 occurs
when two sets of numbers are perfectly related but in opposite directions.

131

TABLE 4.6. EXAMPLES OF POSITIVELY CORRELATED NUMBERS

Example A		Example B		Example C		Example D	
Column 1	Column 2	Column 3	Column 4	Column 5	Column 6	Column 7	Column 8
3.96	3.34	1	1	1	9	1	0.09
9.61	1.61	2	2	2	10	2	0.10
1.57	1.40	3	3	3	11	3	0.11
3.25	7.90	4	4	4	12	4	0.12
8.52	4.63	5	5	5	13	5	0.13
1.90	6.18	6	6	6	14	6	0.14
4.92	1.14	7	7	7	15	7	0.15
7.18	3.57	8	8	8	16	8	0.16
7.46	8.84	9	9	9	17	9	0.17
8.32	5.18	10	10	10	18	10	0.18

TABLE 4.7. EXAMPLES OF NEGATIVELY CORRELATED NUMBERS

Example E		*Example F*		*Example G*	
Column 9	*Column 10*	*Column 11*	*Column 12*	*Column 13*	*Column 14*
1	10	10	9	10	0.09
2	9	9	10	9	0.10
3	8	8	11	8	0.11
4	7	7	12	7	0.12
5	6	6	13	6	0.13
6	5	5	14	5	0.14
7	4	4	15	4	0.15
8	3	3	16	3	0.16
9	2	2	17	2	0.17
10	1	1	18	1	0.18

Examples of sets of numbers that are negatively correlated are shown in Table 4.7. Notice in Examples E, F, and G in Table 4.7 that, in each case, as one set of numbers goes up, the other goes down, which is what I mean when I say that the numbers are related in opposite directions. These are all examples of how negative correlations might look. Examples F and G also illustrate that negative correlations are not directly affected by the relative magnitude of the two sets of numbers, any more than the positive correlations in Table 4.6 were.

HOW ARE CORRELATION COEFFICIENTS CALCULATED?

To calculate a Pearson product–moment correlation coefficient, simply follow these seven steps:

Step 1. Line up the two sets of numbers so they are in pairs for each participant.

Step 2. Calculate the mean and standard deviation for each of the two sets.

Step 3. Subtract the mean of each set from each number in that set.

Step 4. Multiply the results of the subtractions for the two sets pair by pair.

Step 5. Add up the results of these cross-multiplications.

Step 6. Separately, multiply the number of pairs times the standard deviation of the first set times the standard deviation of the second set.

Step 7. Divide the result of step 5 by the result of step 6.

Table 4.8 shows the calculations for the two sets of numbers shown in Example D (in Table 4.6).

TABLE 4.8. PRELIMINARY STEPS IN CALCULATING A PEARSON
PRODUCT–MOMENT CORRELATION COEFFICIENT

Col. 1 X	Col. 2 M_X		Col. 3 $X - M_X$	Col. 4 Y	Col. 5 M_Y		Col. 6 $Y - M_Y$	Col. 7 $(X - M_X)(Y - M_Y)$
1	− 5.50	=	−4.50	0.09	− 0.135	=	−0.05	0.2025
2	− 5.50	=	−3.50	0.10	− 0.135	=	−0.04	0.1225
3	− 5.50	=	−2.50	0.11	− 0.135	=	−0.03	0.0625
4	− 5.50	=	−1.50	0.12	− 0.135	=	−0.02	0.0225
5	− 5.50	=	−0.50	0.13	− 0.135	=	−0.01	0.0025
6	− 5.50	=	0.50	0.14	− 0.135	=	0.01	0.0025
7	− 5.50	=	1.50	0.15	− 0.135	=	0.02	0.0225
8	− 5.50	=	2.50	0.16	− 0.135	=	0.03	0.0625
9	− 5.50	=	3.50	0.17	− 0.135	=	0.04	0.1225
10	− 5.50	=	4.50	0.18	− 0.135	=	0.05	0.2025

M_X = 5.500000 M_Y = 0.135000   Sum = 0.8250
SD = 2.872281   SD = 0.028723 $NS_X S_Y$ = 0.8250

Step 1. Notice that column 1 and column 4 contain the two sets of numbers labeled X and Y. These numbers should be arranged such that the two numbers in each pair are in the same row. For example, the numbers in Table 4.8 for the first person are 1 and 0.09, for the second person 2 and 0.10, and so forth.

Step 2. Notice also that the means and standard deviations for the two sets of numbers X and Y were calculated and put at the bottom of the table.

Step 3. Then, the means for the X numbers (M_X) were put in column 2 and the means for the Y numbers (M_Y) were put in column 5 so that the mean for the appropriate set of numbers could be subtracted from the numbers. The results of these subtractions were then put in columns 3 and 6 for the X and Y numbers, respectively.

Step 4. Next, the results in columns 3 and 6 were cross-multiplied for each pair and the new results were placed in column 7.

Step 5. Finally, the results of the cross-multiplications were added to yield a value of 0.8250.

Step 6. Then, separately, the number of pairs (N = 10) was multiplied times the standard deviation of the first set of numbers (S_X = 2.872281) times the standard deviation of the second set (S_Y = 0.028723) and the result [$NS_X S_Y$ = 10(2.872281)(0.028723) = 0.8250] was put at the bottom of column 7.

Step 7. Finally, the result of step 5 was divided by the result of step 6, 0.8250/0.8250 = 1.00, which is exactly the result I reported earlier for those two sets of numbers.

Two things should be noted about the calculations above: (1) For the sake of accuracy, the numbers were kept at six places throughout the calculations until the very last step; and (2) the population standard deviation was used (that is, the N formula was used rather than the $N-1$ formula), even though the sample size is small.

Using a formula, the steps above can be represented as

$$r_{XY} = \frac{\sum(X - M_X)(Y - M_Y)}{N S_X S_Y}$$

where r_{XY} = Pearson product–moment correlation coefficient
  X = first set of numbers
  Y = second set of numbers
  M_X = mean of the first set of numbers
  M_Y = mean of the second set of numbers
  S_X = standard deviation of the first set of numbers
  S_Y = standard deviation of the second set of numbers
  N = number pairs of numbers

Calculations for the example shown in Table 4.8 are

$$r_{XY} = \frac{\sum(X - M_X)(Y - M_Y)}{N S_X S_Y}$$

$$= \frac{0.8250}{10(2.872281)(0.028723)}$$

$$= \frac{0.8250}{0.8250} = 1.00$$

The explanations above should help in understanding the correlation coefficient and how it is calculated. However, all of these calculations can be avoided by learning to use a spreadsheet program, in which you only need to enter the numbers and then use a function like the =CORREL in my Excel program to calculate the Pearson product–moment correlation coefficient. In this case, you will need to indicate the two ranges of numbers involved in the correlation coefficient; for example, if the two ranges were A2 to A13 and B2 to B13, the function would be typed as follows:

=CORREL(A2:A13,B2:B13)

HOW IS THE STATISTICAL SIGNIFICANCE OF A CORRELATION
COEFFICIENT DETERMINED?

In Table 4.6, Example A, I showed two sets of random numbers that were correlated at 0.00. The truth of the matter is that I had to try many sets of random numbers before I got a result that was exactly 0.00. For the

135

TABLE 4.9. CORRELATION COEFFICIENTS RESULTING FROM REPEATED TRIALS
USING RANDOM NUMBERS

Trial	N = 100	N = 50	N = 30	N = 10	N = 5
1	−0.130	0.159	−0.111	−0.434	−0.752
2	−0.104	0.063	−0.079	0.032	0.219
3	0.008	0.091	0.106	−0.220	−0.124
4	−0.038	−0.185	0.240	0.141	0.979
5	0.014	0.103	0.201	−0.291	−0.254
6	−0.113	−0.041	−0.001	−0.338	−0.236
7	−0.037	−0.114	−0.090	0.042	−0.751
8	−0.001	−0.090	0.245	0.169	0.614
9	0.102	−0.060	−0.025	0.036	−0.672
10	0.078	0.078	0.218	0.298	0.659

purposes of explanation, I felt that I needed to show you an example in which random numbers correlated at zero. Reality is a little different. By chance alone, sets of random numbers produce correlation coefficients that vary by chance away from zero to some degree in either a positive or negative direction. In fact, random numbers seldom produce coefficients of exactly zero. Consider the correlation coefficients shown in Table 4.9, which are all based on sets of random numbers. Notice in the first column of Table 4.9 that there are a total of 10 trials and across the top that there are 10 trials for sets of 100 random numbers, 50 random numbers, 30 such numbers, 10 numbers, and 5 numbers. Since all of correlation coefficients are based on numbers generated as random numbers, the sets would be expected to correlate at zero, but in fact, none of them correlate at exactly zero. They produced some correlation, positive or negative, just by chance. In the relatively large samples of 100, the correlations are close to zero, but in the smaller samples, the chance correlations fluctuate much more (in fact, up into the 0.90s). So clearly, the sample size has something to do with how much the correlation coefficients will vary by chance alone.

In doing survey research, you may sometimes want to know the degree to which a correlation coefficient that you have calculated is a chance finding like those shown in Table 4.9. This is why I am explaining how to determine the statistical significance of your results. Recall that statistical significance was defined above as indicating "the probability that the results of a statistical analysis are due to chance factors." In the case of correlation coefficients, statistical significance indicates the probability that an observed correlation coefficient (that is, one you have calculated) is due to chance factors. Traditionally, determining the significance of a correlation coefficient has required making two preliminary decisions about: (1) your alpha decision level and (2) whether you are interested in a one-tailed or two-tailed decision.

The **alpha decision level,** or just **alpha level,** is the probability level that you think will be acceptable for deciding whether an observed correlation coefficient is due to chance alone. In social sciences research, alpha is typically set at either .01 or .05, depending on the importance of the decisions involved. The following guidelines should help you make that decision.

1. Use .01 if you want to be relatively sure of your results and are therefore only willing to accept a probability of less than 1 percent that the findings are chance results. Put another way, use .01 if you want to be at least 99 percent sure that your results are due to factors other than chance.
2. Use .05 if you are exploring your data and willing to accept a probability of less than 5 percent that the findings are chance results; that is, you are willing to accept being 95 percent sure that the results are due to factors other than chance.

Once you have decided whether to use a .01 or .05 alpha level, you should include that information somewhere in the report of your results, probably somewhere near your research questions or discussion of the design or analysis in your project. Note that alpha is sometimes written as $\alpha < .01$ or $\alpha < .05$ (for alphas of less than .01 or .05, respectively). Later, when you are reporting your actual results and the associated statistical tests, the actual probabilities that you find for any statistics should be referred to as $p < .01$ or $p < .05$ (for probabilities of less that .01 or .05, respectively).

The next step in determining the significance of a correlation coefficient is to decide whether your decision is one-tailed or two-tailed. You should use a **one-tailed decision** when, before calculating the coefficient, you have a reasonable theoretical or common-sense reason for suspecting that the correlation coefficient will be either positive or negative. For instance, I would reasonably expect two similarly worded Likert-scale questions designed to measure the same thing (where respondents are required to read statements and circle 1, 2, 3, 4, or 5 along a continuum from strongly disagree to strongly agree) to be positively correlated. Conversely, I would expect two Likert-scale questions where respondents are required to judge opposite statements (with one of them stated as the negative of the other) to be negatively correlated. Both of those would be reasonable expectations, based on theory and common-sense experience. Hence, I would be justified in using a one-tailed decision.

You should use a **two-tailed decision** when you have no theoretical or commonsense reason for believing that a correlation coefficient will be either negative or positive. I most often find myself using two-tailed decisions when I am just "fishing around" or exploring my data to see what relationships of interest may exist. In such cases, I have no justification for expecting the direction of any of my correlations, so I take the conservative route (that is, I lessen the chance of finding a significant difference) by making the decision two-tailed. When fishing around, I often find myself making multiple significance tests, in which case it is advisable to make adjustments in the alpha level, as will be explained later in the section entitled The Problem of Multiple Comparisons and the Bonferroni Adjustment.

Once you have decided on an alpha level and determined whether you are making a one-tailed or two-tailed decision, you need only refer to a table like the one shown in Table 4.10 to find out whether a particular observed correlation coefficient that you have calculated is significant. For instance, the first correlation coefficient in the upper left corner of Table 4.9 is $r = -.130$.

The N size for that correlation coefficient was 100.[1] Let's say I want to be 95 percent sure that my results are due to factors other than chance, so I set the alpha level at $\alpha < .05$, and I decide that a two-tailed decision is appropriate because I have no idea whether the correlation coefficient will be positive or negative when I am using random numbers, as was the case in Table 4.9. To determine whether the observed correlation coefficient of −.130 is statistically significant, enter Table 4.10 at the top and look for the two columns that represent two-tailed decisions. Those would be the two columns farthest to the right, correct? Then decide which of those two columns represents the 95 percent probability level (or $p < .05$). The appropriate column for this significance test is the second one from the right. Finally, look down the left-hand side of the table until you find the point where N is 100. For this significance test, the appropriate row turns out to be the second-to-last row. Where the second-to-last row and the second column from the right intersect, you will find what is called the **critical value,** or value equal to or above which the observed correlation coefficient must be in order to be significant. In this case the critical value is .2050. Since the magnitude of the observed correlation (regardless of sign) of .130 is not equal to or higher than .2050, this observed correlation coefficient is not statistically significant. Such a result would be expected, because the observed coefficient was based on random numbers.

However, if you were to find in your survey project that you got a coefficient of .21 and you had exactly the same situation as in the previous

1 Note that sometimes the exact value of N representing your sample will not be listed in the left-hand column of Table 4.10. In such a case, you should move down to the nearest row below your N size. For example, if your N size were 65, you would move down to the nearest row below 65, which is the row for 62, and use those critical values in making your statistical decisions.

TABLE 4.10. CRITICAL VALUES FOR THE PEARSON PRODUCT-MOMENT
CORRELATION COEFFICIENT

(N)	One-tailed decision: Reasons to expect either a negative or a positive correlation		Two-tailed decision: No idea about direction of correlation	
	95% Certainty $p < .05$	99% Certainty $p < .01$	95% Certainty $p < .05$	99% Certainty $p < .01$
3	.9877	.9995	.9969	1.0000
4	.9000	.9800	.9500	.9900
5	.8054	.9343	.8783	.9587
6	.7293	.8822	.8114	.9172
7	.6694	.8329	.7545	.8745
8	.6215	.7887	.7067	.8343
9	.5822	.7498	.6664	.7977
10	.5494	.7155	.6319	.7646
11	.5214	.6851	.6021	.7348
12	.4973	.6581	.5760	.7079
13	.4762	.6339	.5529	.6835
14	.4575	.6120	.5324	.6614
15	.4409	.5923	.5139	.6411
16	.4259	.5742	.4973	.6226
17	.4124	.5577	.4821	.6055
22	.3598	.4921	.4227	.5368
27	.3233	.4451	.3809	.4869
32	.2960	.4093	.3494	.4487
37	.2746	.3810	.3246	.4182
42	.2573	.3578	.3044	.3932
47	.2428	.3384	.2875	.3721
52	.2306	.3218	.2732	.3541
62	.2108	.2948	.2500	.3248
72	.1954	.2737	.2319	.3017
82	.1829	.2565	.2172	.2830
92	.1726	.2422	.2050	.2673
102	.1638	.2301	.1946	.2540

Source: Adapted from Fisher and Yates, 1963.

example (that is, 100 respondents, an alpha level of .05, and a two-tailed
decision), then the result would be significant in that your observed correlation of .21 would be higher than the critical value of .2050. So you
would be able to say that your result was significant (at $p < .05$). Remember, such a significant result simply means that it has only a 5 percent probability of having occurred for chance reasons, or that you are

139

95 percent sure that it is not due to chance alone. Significance does not mean that the result is meaningful or interesting. Meaningfulness is a judgment call that you must make on the basis of the magnitude of the correlation coefficient itself (for much more detailed explanations of how to make such judgment calls, and for other pitfalls of correlational analysis, see Brown, 1988, 1996, or Hatch & Lazaraton, 1991).

ASSUMPTIONS OF THE PEARSON PRODUCT–MOMENT
CORRELATION COEFFICIENT

The Pearson product–moment correlation coefficient is a very useful statistic, but it will work well only as an indicator of the degree of relationship between two sets of numbers if certain assumptions are met. The assumptions of the Pearson product–moment correlation coefficient are: (1) Both sets of numbers are interval or ratio scales, (2) the numbers within each set are independent of one another, (3) both distributions are symmetrical, and (4) a linear relationship exists between the two sets of numbers. If all three assumptions are met, the resulting coefficient can reasonably be interpreted as the degree to which the two sets of numbers are related. If one or more assumptions are violated, the resulting coefficient may overestimate or underestimate the actual state of affairs to an unknown degree.

Checking assumptions 1 and 2 can be done by using common sense. (1) To check the scales, you need only think about them: If both sets of numbers are interval or ratio scales as defined in Chapter 1, assumption (1) is met. (2) To check the **independence** of the numbers within each set of numbers, you simply need to examine them to make sure that the same student did not appear twice in the data (that is, did not produce two pairs of scores) and that the subjects did not cheat or otherwise cooperate with each other. (3) You can check the symmetry of the distributions by examining the descriptive statistics for each set of numbers to see if the mean, median, and mode are similar and to see whether there is room for at least two standard deviations on each side of the mean within the range of scores. You should also graph each set of numbers in a column or bar graph and decide whether it looks more or less symmetrical. (4) Finally, you can check the linearity of the relationship between the two sets of numbers by plotting the two sets of numbers against each other in a scatterplot and examining them.

For instance, if we were to plot the numbers in Example D in Table 4.6, which served as the basis of the demonstration calculations for the correlation coefficient (the ones that turned out to be 1.00), the **scatterplot** shown in Figure 4.3 would result. Notice that each pair of numbers is represented by a diamond: 1 and .09, 2 and .10, 3 and .11, 4 and .12, etc. Notice also that the diamonds are in a straight line. This straight line is

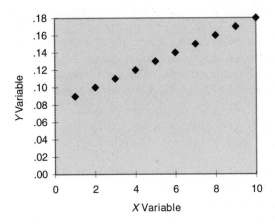

Figure 4.3 Scatterplot of a perfectly linear relationship.

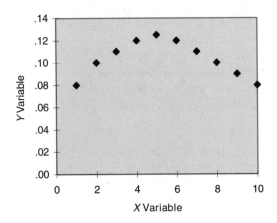

Figure 4.4 Scatterplot of a curvilinear relationship.

what I meant by **linearity**. In real data, such an obvious linear relationship seldom occurs.

In part, when checking the linearity of your data, you are checking to ensure that the two sets of numbers are not in a curvilinear relationship like that shown in the scatterplot in Figure 4.4. If such a curve appears in your plot, you will have trouble interpreting whatever correlation coefficient is involved (the numbers, incidentally, in the example, are correlated at a nonsignificant −.17). You would have similar problems interpreting numbers that were in a curvilinear relationship in the other direction, like those shown in Figure 4.5 (which are correlated at a nonsignificant −.32).

141

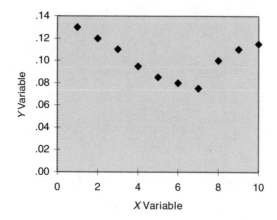

Figure 4.5 Scatterplot of another, different curvilinear relationship.

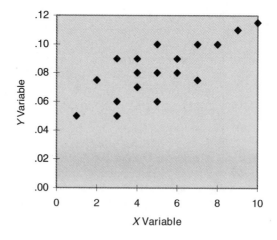

Figure 4.6 Scatterplot of a fairly realistic linear relationship (where $r = .76$).

Many types of curvilinear relationships can appear in your numbers, and I cannot begin to illustrate all of them. However, the chief characteristic of a **curvilinear relationship** is, as the name implies, that the points in a scatterplot will observably curve one or more times. To ensure that you have met the assumption of linearity, you should be looking for a **linear relationship,** one where drawing a line straight through the data in one direction or another makes sense.

One last example should illustrate what I mean. The scatterplot shown in Figure 4.6 is based on 18 pairs of numbers that are not in a perfect linear relationship, but nonetheless are in a reasonable linear relationship, not a curvilinear one. Incidentally, the numbers shown in Figure 4.6 correlate at .76, which is significant for $n = 18$ at $p < .01$ (two-tailed).

Clearly then, deciding whether the assumption of linearity has been met can be a judgment call. However, if you do not see a clear linear relationship in the scatterplot, you should seriously consider the possibility that your correlation coefficient is uninterpretable. (For more information and examples related to the assumptions of correlational analysis, see Brown, 1988, 1996, or Hatch & Lazaraton, 1991.)

OTHER FORMS OF CORRELATIONAL ANALYSIS

Before leaving the topic of correlation, I must point out that the foregoing discussion focuses only on the Pearson product–moment correlation coefficient, which is appropriate only if your numbers are on interval or ratio scales. Other correlation coefficients exist for calculating the degree of relationship between two sets of numbers on other scales. For instance, if you have two sets of ordinal scale numbers, you can use the **Spearman rho (ρ) correlation coefficient.** If you have two sets of numbers that are on dichotomous nominal scales, you can use (1) the **phi coefficient** (if they are true dichotomies, that is, they are naturally occurring dichotomies) or (2) the **tetrachoric coefficient** (if the dichotomies were artificially created from interval or ratio scales). If one set of numbers is interval or ratio and the other set is a dichotomous nominal scale, you can use the **point-biserial correlation coefficient** (if the dichotomy is a true, naturally occurring dichotomy) or the **biserial coefficient** (if the dichotomy was artificially created from an interval or ratio scale).

Explaining the calculation and interpretation of all of these coefficients would take many pages that I would rather use to cover other survey design issues. Consequently, I will refer you to Brown (1988, 1996) and Hatch and Lazaraton (1991) for further information on these alternative correlation coefficients. I must say, though, that interpreting all of these alternative coefficients is similar to interpreting the Pearson product–moment correlation coefficient.

Comparing means

WHAT ARE MEANS COMPARISONS?

Table 4.11 shows 15 sets of 30 random numbers that I generated in my spreadsheet program. Notice along the bottom of the table that I also used the spreadsheet to calculate means and standard deviations for each set of random numbers. The reason I went through these steps was to illustrate how means can differ by chance alone. For instance, notice in

TABLE 4.11. MEANS AND STANDARD DEVIATIONS FOR 15 SETS OF RANDOM NUMBERS

Var1	Var2	Var3	Var4	Var5	Var6	Var7	Var8	Var9	Var10	Var11	Var12	Var13	Var14	Var15
17	19	60	31	6	37	36	52	85	45	90	10	51	97	0
92	19	97	69	32	99	68	97	90	29	81	33	59	61	48
27	93	27	54	27	45	50	82	11	18	67	48	39	36	0
39	86	6	81	63	8	34	53	83	90	55	19	72	0	26
72	1	49	77	44	95	47	79	90	32	90	13	68	79	48
81	87	19	95	34	77	68	28	24	67	94	29	9	23	52
86	92	89	30	49	76	55	26	26	86	34	97	90	50	14
30	21	85	28	50	90	55	21	15	76	91	56	16	60	49
91	82	98	14	78	14	8	69	24	36	39	30	52	77	52
18	2	31	35	1	29	10	56	19	51	13	53	29	65	57
70	60	76	56	53	49	5	24	19	9	45	54	33	94	14
47	27	68	40	44	5	71	39	90	41	10	97	8	97	29
79	15	20	53	11	1	40	18	99	49	81	80	40	80	40
25	81	27	87	19	49	62	44	81	29	52	65	78	73	97
44	18	79	86	79	86	73	27	27	98	66	89	25	49	57
92	52	97	73	80	61	74	55	59	99	22	90	15	54	58
55	71	40	15	6	17	99	27	61	93	43	70	13	60	66
52	43	41	22	57	36	35	85	38	63	77	96	24	19	14
7	13	65	78	67	86	13	61	37	66	9	2	54	33	49
37	81	46	93	56	8	12	47	83	84	92	70	93	23	86
0	74	22	8	76	51	54	97	64	85	39	81	81	49	51
96	29	88	93	75	73	3	86	49	85	40	74	46	44	63
89	77	90	44	30	2	45	38	63	27	57	21	73	57	15
68	67	94	54	81	23	28	64	50	88	76	32	87	17	49

26	13	13	91	63	5	46	64	23	24	43	71	0	24	84
27	86	37	27	13	27	2	91	78	97	86	51	41	44	39
16	64	57	62	67	40	66	42	16	9	27	23	67	25	18
45	25	7	40	28	84	40	30	85	33	32	39	26	80	75
37	0	77	8	36	12	77	65	36	98	0	89	37	15	85
91	92	73	56	73	76	13	73	93	29	88	80	26	16	44
M 51.87	49.67	55.93	53.33	46.60	45.37	42.97	54.67	53.93	57.87	54.63	55.40	45.07	50.03	45.97
SD 29.19	32.26	29.69	27.34	24.74	31.71	25.69	23.78	28.89	29.65	28.36	28.61	26.41	26.53	25.19

Chapter 4

Table 4.11 how none of the means turned out to be exactly the same. In fact, some of the means are very different. Consider variables 6 and 10, which have means of 45.37 and 57.87, respectively. The difference of 12.5 points between these two means seems very large, yet because the numbers in these sets were randomly generated, I can only conclude that the difference of 12.5 points occurred by chance alone.

Means comparison statistics are designed to determine the probability that differences between means that are observed in studies have occurred by chance alone, as they did in the example in the previous paragraph. The simplest of these statistics is called the *t*-test. The *t*-test can be used to compare two means to determine the probability that the difference is statistically significant at a certain probability level.

Consider some tangible examples. First, two sets of random numbers should produce means that are different only at chance levels. In fact, when I perform a *t*-test using my Excel spreadsheet and the =TTEST function, I find that the two sets of random numbers in variables 6 and 10 (in Table 4.11) miss being significant even at $p < .05$. Thus, I can only interpret the observed difference of 12.5 points between the two means as due to chance alone, which in fact was the case because the numbers were generated randomly.

In most real studies, however, the numbers are not random. In the case of survey research, I might ask two groups of language teachers to estimate the amount of work time they spend doing paperwork (Question 37 in our hypothetical survey). Perhaps I want to compare those estimates for a group of 10 language teachers at public high schools with 10 language teachers in private high schools. Table 4.12 shows some numbers that I made up to represent the answers of these two groups of teachers.

Notice in Table 4.12 that I have used one column for the group variable (assigning an A to identify each teacher in the private school group and a B to identify those teachers in the public school group) and a second column for their estimates of the amount of time spent doing paperwork. This arrangement of columns (note that each person gets his or her own row) is typical of comparisons of groups that are made up of different people. Such comparisons, where the sets of numbers being compared were generated by different people, are referred to as **independent,** and you should use one type of *t*-test, known as an **independent *t*-test** in such situations.

If, instead, I wanted to compare the answers of a single group of 30 private school language teachers before and after a paperwork reduction policy was put into place, the situation would be somewhat different, as shown in Table 4.13. This arrangement of columns and rows (note that here, too, each person gets his or her own row) is typical of comparisons in which questions are repeated over time. Such comparisons, in which the sets of numbers being compared were produced by the same people, are referred to as **paired** (they are also sometimes labeled *matched, de-*

146

TABLE 4.12. EXAMPLE OF
INDEPENDENT-GROUPS
MEAN COMPARISON

Group[a]	Q37
A	10
A	8
A	5
A	5
A	10
A	20
A	25
A	10
A	5
A	10
B	20
B	15
B	35
B	20
B	15
B	20
B	15
B	15
B	20
B	30

M_A	=	10.80	M_B	=	20.50
SD_A	=	6.31	SD_B	=	6.50
N_A	=	10.00	N_B	=	10.00

[a]Group A = private school; group B = public school.

pendent, or *repeated*), and you should use a special type of *t*-test, known as a **paired *t*-test** in such situations.

As I will explain in the next two sections, independent and paired *t*-tests are calculated differently.

HOW ARE INDEPENDENT MEAN COMPARISONS CALCULATED?

To calculate an independent *t*-test, follow these seven steps.

Step 1. Calculate the mean and standard deviation for each of the two sets of numbers.

Step 2. Subtract the mean for one group from the mean for the other group.

Step 3. Square the standard deviation for one group and divide it by the number of people in that group.

TABLE 4.13. EXAMPLE OF PAIRED GROUPS
MEAN COMPARISON

Statistic		Before	After	Diff.
		10	10	0
		8	5	3
		5	5	0
		5	5	0
		10	5	5
		20	10	10
		25	10	15
		10	10	0
		5	5	0
		10	5	5
		25	10	15
		10	5	5
		5	5	0
		10	5	5
		5	5	0
		5	5	0
		5	5	0
		10	5	5
		20	10	10
		25	10	15
		25	20	5
		10	5	5
		5	5	0
		10	5	5
		25	10	15
		10	5	5
		5	5	0
		10	5	5
		10	5	5
		15	5	10
M	=	11.77	6.83	4.93
SD	=	7.04	3.29	5.01
N	=	30.00	30.00	30.00

Step 4. Square the standard deviation for the other group and divide it by the number of people in that group.
Step 5. Add up the results of step 3 and step 4.
Step 6. Take the square root of the results of step 5.
Step 7. Divide the result of step 2 by the result of step 6.

Using a formula, the steps above can be represented as

$$t_{\text{obsAB}} = \frac{M_A - M_B}{\sqrt{(SD_A{}^2/N_A) + (SD_B{}^2/N_B)}}$$

where t_{obsAB} = t-test observed for the difference in means for groups A
        and B
        M_A = mean for group A
        M_B = mean for group B
        SD_A = standard deviation for group A
        SD_B = standard deviation for group B
        N_A = number of people in group A
        N_B = number of people in group B

An example of actual calculations might help here. I will use the results
shown in Table 4.12, which were based on independent responses (estimating the amount of time they spend doing paperwork) from private
school teachers (group A) and public school teachers (group B). Recall
that the descriptive statistics were as follows:

$$M_A = 10.80 \qquad M_B = 20.50$$

$$SD_A = 6.31 \qquad SD_B = 6.50$$

$$N_A = 10.00 \qquad N_B = 10.00$$

To calculate an independent t-test for the difference in these two means,
I apply the formula as follows:

$$
\begin{aligned}
t_{\text{obsAB}} &= \frac{M_A - M_B}{\sqrt{(S_A{}^2/N_A) + (S_B{}^2/N_B)}} \\[2mm]
&= \frac{10.80 - 20.50}{\sqrt{(6.31^2/10) + (6.50^2/10)}} \\[2mm]
&= \frac{-9.70}{\sqrt{(39.8161/10) + (42.25/10)}} \\[2mm]
&= \frac{-9.70}{\sqrt{3.98161 + 4.225}} \\[2mm]
&= \frac{-9.70}{\sqrt{8.20661}} \\[2mm]
&= \frac{-9.70}{2.8647181} \\[2mm]
&= -3.3860225 \approx -3.39
\end{aligned}
$$

Note that you need not worry about which mean comes first in the subtraction in the numerator of the formula, because negative and positive *t*-values are treated the same. In other words, *t* is interpreted regardless of sign.

HOW ARE PAIRED MEAN COMPARISONS CALCULATED?

To calculate a paired *t*-test, simply follow these five steps:

Step 1. Line up the two sets of numbers so that each set is a column and each pair is a row.
Step 2. Calculate the difference between the numbers in each pair by subtracting one from the other.
Step 3. Calculate the mean and standard deviation for the differences.
Step 4. Divide the standard deviation of the differences by the square root of the number of pairs.
Step 5. Divide the mean of the differences by the result of step 4.

The formula is

$$t_{obsD} = \frac{M_D}{SD_D/\sqrt{N}}$$

where t_{obsD} = *t*-test observed for the difference in paired means
M_D = mean of the differences
SD_D = standard deviation of the differences
N = number of pairs

An example of actual calculations might help here. I will use the results shown in Table 4.13, which were based on the paired answers of a single group of 30 private school language teachers (estimating the amount of time they spend doing paperwork) before and after a paperwork reduction policy was put into place. Notice that in the column farthest to the right in Table 4.13, I have recorded the differences between the two percentages (before and after) for each pair. Then, at the bottom of the table, to the right, I have calculated and recorded the mean, standard deviation, and number of pairs. Based on these descriptive statistics for the differences, I can then apply the formula as follows:

$$t_{obsD} = \frac{M_D}{SD_D/\sqrt{N}}$$

$$= \frac{4.93}{5.01/\sqrt{30}}$$

$$= \frac{4.93}{5.01/5.4772}$$

$$= \frac{4.93}{5.01/5.4772}$$

$$= \frac{4.93}{0.9147}$$

$$= \frac{4.93}{0.9147} = 5.3897452 \approx 5.39$$

These explanations should help in understanding how you should calculate the independent and paired *t*-tests. However, all of these calculations can be avoided entirely by learning to use a spreadsheet program, in which you need only to enter the numbers and then use a function like the =TTEST function in my Excel program to calculate either type of *t*-test.

HOW IS THE STATISTICAL SIGNIFICANCE OF A MEAN
COMPARISON DETERMINED?

As I pointed out above and showed in Table 4.11, even random numbers can produce some very large differences between means. Obviously, we would like to know the degree to which a difference between two means that we have calculated is a chance difference. This is why we study the statistical significance of our results. Recall that I defined *statistical significance* as indicating "the probability that the results of a statistical analysis are due to chance factors." In the case of mean comparisons, statistical significance simply indicates the probability that a difference between two observed means is due to chance factors.

Traditionally, in order to determine the significance of a mean comparison, researchers have begun by setting an alpha level and deciding whether they are interested in a one-tailed or a two-tailed decision. As with correlation coefficients, the alpha level is simply the probability level that you think will be acceptable for deciding if a particular observed mean difference is or is not due to chance alone, and the alpha level is typically set at .01 or .05.

The next step in determining the significance of a mean comparison is to decide whether it is a one-tailed or two-tailed decision. You should use a *one-tailed decision* when, before calculating the *t*-test, you have a reasonable theoretical or commonsense basis for suspecting that one mean will be higher than the other, or vice versa. You should use a *two-tailed decision* when you have no theoretical or commonsense reason for believing that one mean or the other will be higher. As explained in the discussion on correlation coefficients, I most often use two-tailed decisions when I am just exploring my data to see what relationships of interest, if any, may exist. Having no justification for expecting any particular direction in any of my means comparisons, I take a conservative stance by making the decision two-tailed. In such a situation, I am usually making multiple significance tests for more than one means comparison, and I must make adjustments in the alpha level, as explained later in the chapter in the section on Bonferroni adjustment.

Once you have decided on an alpha level and whether you want to use a one-tailed or two-tailed decision, you can use either the independent or the paired t-test to determine the t-statistic. Then, to determine whether the difference between your two independent or paired means is statistically significant at a certain probability level, you can refer to a table like the one shown in Table 4.14. To make all of that clear, I will provide three tangible examples.

Example 1. In this example, I will use two sets of 30 randomly generated numbers, which should produce means that are only different at chance levels. In this case, I will use the rather large difference between means of randomly generated numbers that I discussed above, that is, the randomly generated variables 6 and 10 in Table 4.11 ($M_6 = 45.37$ and $M_{10} = 57.87$; and $SD_6 = 31.71$ and $SD_{10} = 29.65$). Because they are based on randomly generated numbers, the difference should fail to be significant even at $p < .05$. Treating them as independent groups, I apply the appropriate t-test as follows:

$$t_{\text{obsAB}} = \frac{M_A - M_B}{\sqrt{(SD_A^2/N_A) + (SD_B^2/N_B)}}$$

$$= \frac{45.37 - 57.87}{\sqrt{(31.71^2/30) + (29.65^2/30)}}$$

$$= \frac{-12.5}{\sqrt{(1005.5241/30) + (879.1225/30)}}$$

$$= \frac{-12.5}{\sqrt{33.5175 + 29.304}}$$

$$= \frac{-12.50}{\sqrt{62.8215}}$$

$$= \frac{-12.50}{7.926}$$

$$= 1.577088 \approx 1.58$$

Because I am dealing with random numbers, I am inclined to set the alpha level at a liberal .05 (to increase the chances of finding a statistically significant difference as much as is permissible given traditional alpha

TABLE 4.14. CRITICAL VALUES OF *t*

One-tailed →	0.05	0.025	0.01	0.005
Two-tailed →	0.10	0.05	0.02	0.01
df				
1	6.314	12.706	31.821	63.657
2	2.920	4.303	6.965	9.925
3	2.353	3.182	4.541	5.841
4	2.132	2.776	3.747	4.604
5	2.015	2.571	3.365	4.032
6	1.943	2.447	3.143	3.707
7	1.895	2.365	2.998	3.499
8	1.860	2.306	2.896	3.355
9	1.833	2.262	2.821	3.250
10	1.812	2.228	2.764	3.169
11	1.796	2.201	2.718	3.106
12	1.782	2.179	2.681	3.055
13	1.771	2.160	2.650	3.012
14	1.761	2.145	2.624	2.977
15	1.753	2.131	2.602	2.927
16	1.746	2.120	2.583	2.921
17	1.740	2.110	2.567	2.898
18	1.734	2.101	2.552	2.878
19	1.729	2.093	2.539	2.861
20	1.725	2.086	2.528	2.845
21	1.721	2.080	2.518	2.831
22	1.717	2.074	2.508	2.819
23	1.714	2.069	2.500	2.807
24	1.711	2.064	2.492	2.797
25	1.708	2.060	2.485	2.787
26	1.706	2.056	2.479	2.779
27	1.703	2.052	2.473	2.771
28	1.701	2.048	2.467	2.763
29	1.699	2.045	2.462	2.756
30	1.697	2.042	2.457	2.750
40	1.684	2.021	2.423	2.704
60	1.671	2.000	2.390	2.660
120	1.658	1.980	2.358	2.617
∞	1.645	1.960	2.326	2.576

Source: Adapted from Fisher & Yates, 1963.

levels in the social sciences). Also, because neither of the two variables under examination has any theoretical or commonsense rationale for being higher or lower than the other, I will make the comparison two-tailed. The only other piece of information I need in order to determine whether or not a *t* value of 1.58 observed is significant is the number of *degrees of freedom* (df), which, in the case of an independent *t*-test, is the total number of subjects minus 2 (df = $N_A + N_B - 2$). In this particular example, that means that df = $30 + 30 - 2 = 58$.

To find the critical value for *t* for this example, you must look at Table 4.14. First locate the row across the top that corresponds to a two-tailed decision. Then, locate the column within that row that is designated for the .05 alpha level. That turns out to be the third column from either side. Next, go down the column until you find the row that corresponds to 58 degrees of freedom. Since no row corresponds directly to df = 58, you need to move down to the closest number below 58 – in this case, it turns out to be 40. The critical value of *t* in that column and row turns out to be 2.021. Since the observed value was 1.58 and it does not exceed the critical value of 2.021, I can only say that *p* > .05. In other words, the probability is greater than the traditional 5 percent level, so I cannot say that the difference between the two means was significant. Since the means were based on random numbers, this result makes sense.

Example 2. In this example, I will use the two independent groups of 10 that I presented for the example calculations for the independent *t*-test, as shown in Table 4.12 ($M_A = 10.80$ and $M_B = 20.50$; and $SD_A = 6.31$ and $SD_B = 6.50$). In the example calculations above, it turned out that $t_{obsAB} = -3.39$.

Because the decision involved is not a particularly important one, I would be inclined to set the alpha level at a liberal .05 (to maximize the chances of finding a statistically significant difference within the traditional framework of permissible alpha levels). Also, because I do not have any particular theoretical or commonsense reason to assume that public school teachers do more paperwork than private school teachers or vice versa, I will make the comparison two-tailed. The only other piece of information I need in order to determine whether or not a value of −3.39 observed is significant, is the number of *degrees of freedom* (df), which, in the case of an independent *t*-test, is the total number of subjects minus two (df = $N_A + N_B - 2$). In this particular example, this means that df = $10 + 10 - 2 = 18$.

To find the critical value for *t* in Table 4.14, first locate the row across the top that corresponds to a two-tailed decision. Then, locate the column within that row that is designated for the alpha .05 level. That again turns out to be the third column from either side. Next, go down the column until you find the row that corresponds to 18 degrees of freedom.

In this case, that turns out to be the 18th row from the top of the critical values. The critical value of t in that column and row turns out to be 2.101. Since the observed value was -3.39, and its absolute value (ignoring the sign) does exceed the critical value of 2.101, I can say that $p < .05$. In other words, the probability is less than the traditional 5 percent level, so I can say that there is less than a 5 percent probability that the observed difference in means was due to chance factors. Conversely, I can say that I am 95 percent sure that the observed difference was due to factors other than chance.

Example 3. For the last example, I will use the paired means for 30 students that I presented in the example calculations for the paired t-test, as shown in Table 4.13. In the example calculations above, it turned out that $t_{obsD} = 5.39$.

Assume, in this case that I want to set my alpha level at .01 because the result will be used for a relatively important political decision. Let's assume that the estimates of amounts of paperwork were being compared before and after a workshop on paperwork reduction. Common sense tells me that if there is any difference, it will be in the direction of a reduction in the amount of paperwork being done before and after the workshop, so I make the comparison a one-tailed decision. The only other piece of information I need in order to determine whether a t-value of 5.39 observed is significant is the number of *degrees of freedom* (df), which, in the case of a paired t-test, is the number of pairs minus 1 (df $= N - 1$). In this particular example, this means that df $= 30 - 1 = 29$.

To find the critical value for t in Table 4.14, first locate the row across the top that corresponds to a one-tailed decision. Then, locate the column within that row that is designated for the .01 alpha level. That turns out to be the second column from the right side. Next, go down the column until you find the row that corresponds to 29 degrees of freedom. In this case, that turns out to be the 29th row from the top (or sixth from the bottom) of the critical values. The critical value of t in that column and row turns out to be 2.462. Since the observed value was 5.39, and its absolute value (regardless of sign) does exceed the critical value of 2.462, I can say that $p < .01$. In other words, the probability is less than the traditional (and conservative, or relatively safe) 1 percent level, so I can say that there is less than a 1 percent probability that the observed difference in means was due to chance factors. Conversely, I can be 99 percent sure that the observed difference was due to factors other than chance.

Remember, each time you say that your result is significant (at $p < .05$, or at $p < .01$), it simply means that the result has only a 5 percent (or 1 percent) probability of having occurred for chance reasons, or that you are 95 percent (or 99 percent) sure that it is not due to chance alone. Significance does not mean that the result is meaningful or interesting. That is

155

a judgment call that you must make on the basis of the magnitude of the actual difference between the means in the given context (for much more detailed explanations of how to make such judgment calls, and for other pitfalls of mean comparisons analyses, see Brown, 1988, or Hatch & Lazaraton, 1991).

ASSUMPTIONS OF THE *t*-TEST

The *t*-test is a very useful statistic, but it is only a reasonable indicator of the significance of the difference between two means if certain assumptions are met. The assumptions of the *t*-test are: (1) The scale is interval or ratio, (2) the numbers in each set are independent of one another (for independent *t*-tests), (3) both distributions are symmetrical, and (4) the variances are equal. If all of those assumptions are met, then the resulting *t*-test can reasonably be interpreted as the probability that the means are significantly different. If one or more assumptions is violated, the resulting *t*-test may overestimate or underestimate the actual state of affairs. Assumptions 1 and 2 can be checked by using common sense. (1) To check the scale, you simply need to think about it. If it is an interval or ratio scale as defined in Chapter 1, assumption 1 is met. (2) To check the independence of the numbers in each set (a requirement only for the independent *t*-test), you simply need to examine them to make sure that the same student did not appear twice in the data (that is, no student produced two scores) and that the students did not cheat or otherwise cooperate in their work. If it turns out that the data are not independent – that is, that the numbers on both sets were produced by the same people – you may want to apply the paired *t*-test instead of the independent one. (3) You can check the symmetry of the distributions by examining the descriptive statistics for each set of numbers to see if the mean, median, and mode are similar and to see if there is room for at least two standard deviations on each side of the mean within the range of scores. You should also graph each of the sets of numbers in a column or bar graph and decide if it looks more or less symmetrical. (4) Finally, if the sample sizes are the same for the two groups involved, the *t*-test is *robust* to violations of the assumption of equal variances. Consequently, you may want to randomly select subjects to eliminate from the larger sample until the two groups are equal. Or if the group sizes are different in size, you may decide to check the equality of the variances by conducting an F_{max} test or other similar procedure. While a full explanation of the F_{max} test is beyond the scope of this book, a brief explanation is probably in order. Calculating the F_{max} test simply involves forming a ratio of the two standard deviations squared, as follows:

$$F_{max} = \frac{SD^2_{large}}{SD^2_{large}}$$

Notice that the larger standard deviation is placed in the numerator. According to Tabachnick and Fiddell (1996), "If sample sizes are relatively equal (within a ratio of 4 to 1 or less for the largest to smallest cell size), an F_{max} value as great as 10 is probably acceptable" (p. 80). If the ratio is greater than 4 to 1, you should check for the significance of F_{max} using the steps explained for interpreting the significance of any F ratio in Hatch and Lazaraton (1991, pp. 316–317, 599–601).

OTHER FORMS OF MEANS COMPARISONS

Before leaving the topic of means comparisons, I must point out that the forgoing discussion focuses on only the two most commonly used forms of *t*-tests. Other forms of *t*-tests exist for samples with unequal variances. In addition, the *t*-test is designed for comparing one and only one pair of means. As a result, a whole family of statistics, generally referred to as analysis of variance (ANOVA), exists for making multiple comparisons (also see the discussion of the Bonferroni adjustment below). Furthermore, comparisons for the medians of ordinal scales are also possible using a family of statistics called non-parametrics. Explaining the calculation and interpretation of all of these statistics would take many pages that I would rather use to cover other survey design issues. Consequently, I will refer you to Brown (1988, 1996) and Hatch and Lazaraton (1991) for further information on these alternate forms of means and medians comparisons. However, I must add that interpreting all of those statistics is similar to interpreting the *t*-test.

Comparing frequencies

WHAT ARE FREQUENCY COMPARISON STATISTICS?

As I pointed out in the section on descriptive statistics, frequencies are essentially tallies. Recall that I showed how correlation coefficients based on random numbers can vary by chance alone (in Table 4.9), and how means based on randomly generated numbers can vary by chance alone (in Table 4.11). Similarly, frequencies observed in any population can vary by chance alone, and as with correlation coefficients and means, statistical tests can be used to determine the probability that a certain pattern of frequencies occurred by chance alone.

Consider the example shown in Table 4.15 (from Brown, 1991b). In a questionnaire that was part of that study, English department and ESL department teachers were asked to select the best and worst features (from among the following six possibilities: cohesion, content, mechanics, organization, syntax, and vocabulary) after they had read and rated each of a series of compositions written by English department and ESL

TABLE 4.15. OVERALL *BEST* FEATURES IDENTIFIED BY ENGLISH
(ENG) AND ESL FACULTIES

Best feature	ENG Raters	ESL Raters
Cohesion	55	26
Content	71	86
Mechanics	21	24
Organization	32	65
Syntax	29	6
Vocabulary	16	17

Source: Adapted from Brown, 1991b.

department students. Table 4.15 shows the frequencies of times the raters in each department selected each feature as the compositions' best features. For instance, in the first row, you will see that English department raters selected *cohesion* as the best feature 55 times and ESL raters selected that feature 26 times. Examining the rest of the table, you will notice that, in some cases, English department raters selected a particular feature more frequently than ESL raters, and vice versa. Unfortunately, given that frequencies can vary by chance alone, you have no way of knowing whether the differences you see in that table are chance fluctuations or interesting patterns worth interpreting.

Frequency comparison statistics are designed to solve that problem by helping to determine the probability that frequencies depart from what would be expected in a given table. The simplest of these statistics is called the **chi-square** (or χ^2) statistic. The χ^2 statistic can be used to compare two or more frequencies to determine the probability that the departure from what would be expected by chance alone is statistically significant at a certain probability level. As you will see below, the chi-square statistic can be used to test the significance in one-way or two-way χ^2 analyses.

One-way χ^2 designs are those in which frequencies are being compared for one variable at a time. Hence, a simple comparison of the frequencies for the English department and ESL department raters to expected frequencies in cohesion would be a one-way χ^2 analysis that would look like the following:

FREQUENCY OF TIMES COHESION WAS
SELECTED AS THE BEST FEATURE

English dept.	ESL dept.
55	26

Three departments or four departments could equally well be involved. As long as the variable, departments, constitutes one nominal-scale variable for which the frequencies are being compared to expected frequencies, the analysis is considered one-way.

Two-way χ^2 designs are typically those in which frequencies are being compared for two nominal scale variables at the same time. For instance, in Table 4.15, frequencies are separated out for two departments (English and ESL) and six features (cohesion, content, mechanics, organization, syntax, and vocabulary). This is an example of a two-way χ^2 analysis for which an overall χ^2 value could be calculated. If that overall value turns out to be significant at an acceptable level, then you might want to follow up with any interesting one-way χ^2 analyses inside that two-way table. (Note that these analyses can also be *n*-**way** χ^2 **designs**, that is, they can be three-way, four-way, etc., if more variables are involved.) To explain how the χ^2 statistic works, I will first have to explain the general case.

CALCULATING χ^2, THE GENERAL CASE

To calculate a χ^2 statistic, simply follow these six steps.

Step 1. Line up the observed frequencies.
Step 2. Determine what the appropriate expected frequency is for each observed frequency.
Step 3. Subtract the expected frequency from the observed frequency in each case.
Step 4. Square each of the results of step 3.
Step 5. Divide each of the squared values obtained in step 4 by the expected frequency.
Step 6. To get the observed value of χ^2, add the results of step 5.

Using a formula, the basic chi-square statistic is

$$\chi^2 = \sum \frac{(f_{obs} - f_{exp})^2}{f_{exp}}$$

where χ^2 = chi-square statistic
f_{obs} = observed frequency
f_{exp} = expected frequency

CALCULATING χ^2 IN ONE-WAY ANALYSES

The primary difference between calculating χ^2 for one-way and two-way (or *n*-way) analyses is in how the expected frequencies are determined. For one-way analyses, you calculate the expected frequencies by adding the observed frequencies and dividing by the number of cells (for example, see step 2 below). So the steps in calculating the χ^2 value for a one-way analysis using the cohesion example discussed twice above are as follows.

Step 1. Line up the observed frequencies:

$$55 \qquad 26$$

Step 2. Determine what the appropriate expected frequency is for each observed frequency (add up the frequencies and divide by the number of cells):

$$\frac{55 + 26}{2} = \frac{81}{2} = 40.50$$

Step 3. Subtract the expected frequency from the observed frequency in each case:

$$55 - 40.50 = 14.50 \qquad \text{and} \qquad 26 - 40.50 = 14.50$$

Step 4. Square each of the results of step 3:

$$14.5^2 = 210.25 \qquad \text{and} \qquad 14.5^2 = 210.25$$

Step 5. Divide each of the squared values obtained in step 4 by the expected frequency:

$$\frac{210.25}{40.50} = 5.1914 \qquad \text{and} \qquad \frac{210.25}{40.50} = 5.1914$$

Step 6. To get the observed value of χ^2, add the results of step 5.

$$5.1914 + 5.1914 = 10.3828 \text{ or about } 10.38$$

Using a formula, the basic chi-square statistic for a one-way analysis (with two cells) is

$$
\begin{aligned}
\chi^2 &= \frac{(f_{obs1} - f_{exp})^2}{f_{exp}} + \frac{(f_{obs2} - f_{exp})^2}{f_{exp}} \\
&= \frac{(55 - 40.50)^2}{40.50} + \frac{(26 - 40.50)^2}{40.50} \\
&= \frac{210.25}{40.50} + \frac{210.25}{40.50} \\
&= 5.1914 + 5.1914 \\
&= 10.3828 \approx 10.38
\end{aligned}
$$

Naturally, if the one-way analysis had three, four, five, or more cells, the expected frequencies would be different, and the formula would have to be expanded to fit the added number of cells.

TABLE 4.16. OVERALL *BEST* FEATURES IDENTIFIED BY ENGLISH (ENG) AND ESL
FACULTIES – WITH MARGINALS (ROW AND COLUMN TOTALS)

Best feature	ENG raters	ESL raters	Row marginals (totals)
Cohesion	55	26	81
Content	71	86	157
Mechanics	21	24	45
Organization	32	65	97
Syntax	29	6	35
Vocabulary	16	17	33
Column marginals (totals)	224	224	448

Source: Adapted from Brown, 1991b.

CALCULATING χ^2 IN TWO-WAY ANALYSES

As noted above, the primary difference between calculating χ^2 for one-way and two-way analyses is in how the expected frequencies are determined. For two-way analyses, the expected frequencies for each cell are determined by multiplying the total row frequency times the total column frequency and dividing that result by the total of all the frequencies in the analysis (for example, see step 2 below). So the steps in calculating the χ^2 value for the two-way analysis shown in Table 4.15 are as follows.

Step 1. Line up the observed frequencies as well as their **marginals** (row and column totals) as shown in the first three columns of Table 4.16.
Step 2. Determine what the appropriate expected frequency is for each observed frequency (multiply the appropriate row and column marginals and divide the result by the overall total). For instance, for the upper left cell of Table 4.16, the expected frequency would be the first column (ENG RATERS) marginal times the first row (COHESION) marginal, divided by the overall total in the bottom right corner of the table, or $(224 \times 81)/448 = 18144/448 = 40.50$. Table 4.17a shows the calculations for all the expected frequencies in Table 4.16. Notice that these calculations are not difficult, but they are repetitive and boring. For that reason, I did them in my spreadsheet program.
Step 3. Subtract the expected frequency from the observed frequency in each case, as shown in the first, second, and fourth columns of numbers in Table 4.17b.
Step 4. Square each of the results of step 3, as shown in the third column of numbers from the right in Table 4.17b.
Step 5. Divide each of the squared values obtained in step 4 by the expected frequency, as shown in the three columns farthest to the right.

TABLE 4.17A. OVERALL *BEST* FEATURES IDENTIFIED BY ENGLISH (ENG) AND ESL FACULTIES – CALCULATING EXPECTED FREQUENCIES

Raters	Best feature	Observed frequency (f_{obs})	(Col. × Row) / total	=	Overall total	(Col. × Row) / total	=	Overall total	=	Expected frequency (f_{exp})
Eng	Cohesion	55	(224 × 81)	/	448.00	18,144	/	448.00	=	40.5
	Content	71	(224 × 157)	/	448.00	35,168	/	448.00	=	78.5
	Mechanics	21	(224 × 45)	/	448.00	10,080	/	448.00	=	22.5
	Organization	32	(224 × 97)	/	448.00	21,728	/	448.00	=	48.5
	Syntax	29	(224 × 35)	/	448.00	7,840	/	448.00	=	17.5
	Vocabulary	16	(224 × 33)	/	448.00	7,392	/	448.00	=	16.5
ESL	Cohesion	26	(224 × 81)	/	448.00	18,144	/	448.00	=	40.5
	Content	86	(224 × 157)	/	448.00	35,168	/	448.00	=	78.5
	Mechanics	24	(224 × 45)	/	448.00	10,080	/	448.00	=	22.5
	Organization	65	(224 × 97)	/	448.00	21,728	/	448.00	=	48.5
	Syntax	6	(224 × 35)	/	448.00	7,840	/	448.00	=	17.5
	Vocabulary	17	(224 × 33)	/	448.00	7,392	/	448.00	=	16.5

TABLE 4.17B. OVERALL *BEST* FEATURES IDENTIFIED BY ENGLISH (ENG) AND ESL FACULTIES – CALCULATING CHI SQUARE IN TWO-WAY DESIGNS

Raters	Best feature	$(f_{obs} - f_{exp})^2$	$/ f_{exp}$	=	$(f_{obs} - f_{exp})^2$	$/ f_{exp}$	=	$(f_{obs} - f_{exp})^2$	$/ f_{exp}$	=	Sub-result
ENG	Cohesion	$(55 - 40.50)^2$	/ 40.50	=	14.50^2	/ 40.50	=	210.25	/ 40.50	=	5.1914
	Content	$(71 - 78.50)^2$	/ 78.50	=	-7.50^2	/ 78.50	=	56.25	/ 78.50	=	0.7166
	Mechanics	$(21 - 22.50)^2$	/ 22.50	=	-1.50^2	/ 22.50	=	2.25	/ 22.50	=	0.1000
	Organization	$(32 - 48.50)^2$	/ 48.50	=	-16.50^2	/ 48.50	=	272.25	/ 48.50	=	5.6134
	Syntax	$(29 - 17.50)^2$	/ 17.50	=	11.50^2	/ 17.50	=	132.25	/ 17.50	=	7.5571
	Vocabulary	$(16 - 16.50)^2$	/ 16.50	=	-0.50^2	/ 16.50	=	0.25	/ 16.50	=	0.0152
ESL	Cohesion	$(26 - 40.50)^2$	/ 40.50	=	-14.50^2	/ 40.50	=	210.25	/ 40.50	=	5.1914
	Content	$(86 - 78.50)^2$	/ 78.50	=	7.50^2	/ 78.50	=	56.25	/ 78.50	=	0.7166
	Mechanics	$(24 - 22.50)^2$	/ 22.50	=	1.50^2	/ 22.50	=	2.25	/ 22.50	=	0.1000
	Organization	$(65 - 48.50)^2$	/ 48.50	=	16.50^2	/ 48.50	=	272.25	/ 48.50	=	5.6134
	Syntax	$(6 - 17.50)^2$	/ 17.50	=	-11.50^2	/ 17.50	=	132.25	/ 17.50	=	7.5571
	Vocabulary	$(17 - 16.50)^2$	/ 16.50	=	0.50^2	/ 16.50	=	0.25	/ 16.50	=	0.0152
								Sum	=	χ^2 =	38.3872

Step 6. To get the observed value of χ^2, add the results of step 5, as shown in the bottom right corner of Table 4.17b.

Using a formula, the χ^2 statistic for the two-way analysis (2×6 cells = 12 cells in total) explained in Tables 4.15–4.17 is

$$
\begin{aligned}
\chi^2 = {} & \frac{(f_{obs} - f_{exp})^2}{f_{exp}} + \frac{(f_{obs} - f_{exp})^2}{f_{exp}} + \frac{(f_{obs} - f_{exp})^2}{f_{exp}} \\
& + \frac{(f_{obs} - f_{exp})^2}{f_{exp}} + \frac{(f_{obs} - f_{exp})^2}{f_{exp}} + \frac{(f_{obs} - f_{exp})^2}{f_{exp}} \\
& + \frac{(f_{obs} - f_{exp})^2}{f_{exp}} + \frac{(f_{obs} - f_{exp})^2}{f_{exp}} + \frac{(f_{obs} - f_{exp})^2}{f_{exp}} \\
& + \frac{(f_{obs} - f_{exp})^2}{f_{exp}} + \frac{(f_{obs} - f_{exp})^2}{f_{exp}} + \frac{(f_{obs} - f_{exp})^2}{f_{exp}}
\end{aligned}
$$

$$
\begin{aligned}
= {} & \frac{(55 - 40.50)^2}{40.50} + \frac{(71 - 78.50)^2}{78.50} + \frac{(21 - 22.50)^2}{22.50} + \frac{(32 - 48.50)^2}{48.50} \\
& + \frac{(29 - 17.50)^2}{17.50} + \frac{(16 - 16.50)^2}{16.50} + \frac{(26 - 40.50)^2}{40.50} + \frac{(86 - 78.50)^2}{78.50} \\
& + \frac{(24 - 22.50)^2}{22.50} + \frac{(65 - 48.50)^2}{48.50} + \frac{(6 - 17.50)^2}{17.50} + \frac{(17 - 16.50)^2}{16.50}
\end{aligned}
$$

$$
\begin{aligned}
= {} & \frac{210.25}{40.50} + \frac{56.25}{78.50} + \frac{2.25}{22.50} + \frac{272.25}{48.50} + \frac{132.25}{17.50} + \frac{0.25}{16.50} \\
& + \frac{210.25}{40.50} + \frac{56.25}{78.50} + \frac{2.25}{22.50} + \frac{272.25}{48.50} + \frac{132.25}{17.50} + \frac{0.25}{16.50}
\end{aligned}
$$

$$
= 5.1914 + 0.7166 + 0.1000 + 5.6134 + 7.5571 + 0.0152
$$
$$
+ 5.1914 + 0.7166 + 0.1000 + 5.6134 + 7.5571 + 0.0152
$$
$$
= 38.3872 \approx 38.39
$$

Notice that the formulaic approach is exactly parallel to the spreadsheet approach shown in Tables 4.17a and 4.17b. Naturally, if the analysis had a different number of cells, the formula would have to be expanded or reduced to fit the appropriate number of cells.

The explanations above should help in understanding how you should calculate the χ^2 statistic for one-way and two-way analyses. However, all of these calculations could be avoided by learning to use a spreadsheet program, in which you only need to enter the observed and expected frequencies and then use the =CHITEST function in a spreadsheet like Excel to calculate either type of χ^2.

164

HOW IS THE STATISTICAL SIGNIFICANCE OF A χ^2 COMPARISON DETERMINED?

As I pointed out earlier, even randomly generated frequencies can produce some very large differences from each other and from expected frequencies. Obviously, we would like to know the degree to which such differences between frequencies and expected frequencies that we have calculated are chance differences. This is why we study the statistical significance of our results. Recall that *statistical significance* was defined as indicating "the probability that the results of a statistical analysis are due to chance factors." In the case of frequency comparisons, statistical significance simply indicates the probability that a difference between frequencies and expected frequencies that we have calculated are due to chance factors.

Traditionally, in order to determine the significance of a frequency comparison, researchers have first had to set an alpha level. Recall that the alpha level is simply the probability level that you think will be acceptable for deciding if a particular observed mean difference is or is not due to chance alone. The alpha level is typically set at .01 or .05.

Once you have decided on an alpha level, you must think through your analysis to figure out whether it is one-way, or two-way, or *n*-way. Then, you can calculate the appropriate χ^2 observed statistic. To determine whether the differences between your observed frequencies and the expected frequencies are statistically significant at a certain probability level, you will then need to refer to a table like the one shown in Table 4.18.

COMBINING TWO-WAY AND ONE-WAY ANALYSES

When you are working with a two-way analysis, finding the overall χ^2 statistic and whether it is significant is only the first step. Usually, you will also want to proceed to do further, more detailed analyses. If the overall χ^2 is not significant, that indicates that it is probably not worth your while to proceed to do more detailed analyses of individual groups of cells. However, if the overall χ^2 is significant, you can take that result to mean that something significant exists in the analysis; you essentially have reason to believe that you will not be wasting your time if you use one-way analyses or additional smaller two-way analyses to further explore the results in your larger two-way table.

For instance, in the actual analyses reported in Brown (1991b) for the example discussed with regard to Tables 4.15–4.17, I combined both an overall two-way analysis with six one-way analyses in trying to understand the results of that table. The full set of analyses is shown in Table 4.19. Notice in Table 4.19 that the overall χ^2 of 38.39 is shown in the bottom right corner and that footnote *c* below the table (*c*Overall chi square,

TABLE 4.18. CRITICAL VALUES OF χ^2

df	0.050	0.025	0.010	0.005	0.001
1	3.842	5.024	6.635	7.879	10.828
2	5.992	7.378	9.210	10.600	13.816
3	7.815	9.348	11.345	12.838	16.266
4	9.490	11.143	13.277	14.860	18.467
5	11.071	12.833	15.086	16.750	20.515
6	12.592	14.449	16.812	18.548	22.458
7	14.067	16.013	18.473	20.278	24.322
8	15.507	17.535	20.090	21.955	26.125
9	16.919	19.023	21.666	23.589	27.877
10	18.307	20.483	23.209	25.188	29.588
11	19.675	21.920	24.725	26.757	31.264
12	21.026	23.337	26.217	28.300	32.909
13	22.362	24.736	27.688	29.819	34.528
14	23.685	26.119	29.141	31.319	36.123
15	24.996	27.488	30.578	32.801	37.697
16	26.296	28.845	32.000	34.267	39.252
17	27.587	30.191	33.409	35.719	40.790
18	28.869	31.526	34.805	37.156	42.312
19	30.144	32.852	36.191	38.582	43.820
20	31.410	34.170	37.566	39.997	45.315
21	32.671	35.479	38.932	41.401	46.797
22	33.924	36.781	40.289	42.796	48.268
23	35.173	38.076	41.638	44.181	49.728
24	36.415	39.364	42.980	45.559	51.179
25	37.653	40.647	44.314	46.928	52.620
26	38.885	41.923	45.642	48.290	54.052
27	40.113	43.194	46.963	49.645	55.476
28	41.337	44.461	48.278	50.993	56.892
29	42.557	45.722	49.588	52.356	58.302
30	43.773	46.979	50.892	53.672	59.703
40	55.759	59.342	63.691	66.766	73.402
50	67.505	71.420	76.154	79.490	86.661
60	79.082	83.298	88.379	91.952	99.607
70	90.531	95.023	100.425	104.215	112.317
80	101.879	106.629	112.329	116.321	124.839
90	113.145	118.136	124.116	128.299	137.208
100	124.342	129.561	135.807	140.169	149.449

Source: Adapted from Pearson and Hartley, 1963.

TABLE 4.19. OVERALL *BEST* FEATURES IDENTIFIED BY ENGLISH (ENG)
AND ESL FACULTIES[a]

Best feature	ENG raters	ESL raters	Total	χ^2
Cohesion	55	26	81	10.38[b]
% col.	24.60%	11.60%	18.10%	
Content	71	86	157	1.43
% col.	31.70%	38.40%	35.00%	
Mechanics	21	24	45	0.20
% col.	9.40%	10.70%	10.00%	
Organization	32	65	97	11.23[b]
% col.	14.30%	29.00%	21.70%	
Syntax	29	6	35	15.11[b]
% col.	12.90%	2.70%	7.80%	
Vocabulary	16	17	33	0.03
% col.	7.10%	7.60%	7.40%	
Total	224	224	448	38.39[c]

[a]In some of these tables, the column percentages do not add up to exactly
100% because of rounding. In no case are the totals off by more than 0.1%.
[b]$p < .05$ (df = 1).
[c]Overall chi square, 38.39; df = 5, $p < .05$.
Source: From Brown, 1991b.

38.39; df = 5, $p < .05$) emphasizes that: (1) this particular χ^2 statistic is for
the overall two-way analysis, (2) the analysis was for 5 degrees of freedom (in two-way analyses, df = [rows − 1] [columns −1] = [2 − 1][6 −1]
= 1 × 5 = 5), and (3) the χ^2 statistic is significant at the predetermined $p <$
.05 probability level.

Notice also that the column farthest to the right contains other χ^2
statistics. These are all one-way analyses for the row in which they are
found. So, for instance, the observed χ^2 of 10.38 in the upper right corner of the table is for the two English and ESL rater cells involved in
cohesion (55 and 26). Since the χ^2 is part of a one-way analysis and is
based on the same two numbers used in the example above for one-way
analyses, the results are exactly the same. Notice also that footnote *b*
[[b]$p < .05$ (df = 1)] for this χ^2 (and two others of the one-way χ^2 statistics) explains that the observed χ^2 is significant at the .05 probability
level and is based on 1 degree of freedom (in one-way analyses, df = 2
cells −1 = 1).

In doing such calculations, you should pay attention to the fact that
the expected frequencies used in the one-way analyses are based only on
the frequencies involved in each case and *not* on the expected frequencies already used in conducting the overall two-way χ^2 analysis.

ASSUMPTIONS OF χ^2

Note that the χ^2 statistic is only a reasonable indicator of the significance of the difference between observed and expected frequencies if certain assumptions are met. The assumptions of the χ^2 statistic are that: (1) the scale is nominal (that is, it is based on frequencies), (2) each observation is independent of all others, and (3) the expected frequencies are equal to or greater than 10 for df = 1 analyses, or 5 for all other analyses. If all of those assumptions are met, then the resulting χ^2 statistic can reasonably be interpreted as the probability that the observed frequencies are significantly different from the expected frequencies. If one or more assumptions is violated, the resulting χ^2 statistic may provide an overestimate or underestimate of the actual state of affairs.

Assumptions 1 and 2 can be checked by using common sense. (1) To check the scale, you simply need to think about it. If it is a nominal scale (that is, it is based on frequencies) as defined earlier in the chapter, assumption (1) is met. (2) To check the independence of the frequencies in each cell, you simply need to examine and think about those frequencies to make sure that the closely related frequencies (produced by the same person, from the same sentence, etc.) are not represented in more than one cell and that no cheating or other types of cooperation resulted in the creation of frequencies within any cell. If it turns out that the data are not independent, you may want to apply the McNemar test, categorical modeling, or other statistics for nonindependent analyses that are well beyond the scope of this book (see Hatch & Lazaraton, 1991, pp. 417–419, 517–520). If you think about it, the assumption of independence is not entirely satisfied in the study shown in Table 4.19. The two groups of people (English and ESL department raters) are independent because they are entirely different people, but the frequencies found in the different features (cohesion, content, mechanics, organization, syntax, and vocabulary) were assigned by the same raters in a way that was not predictable. Thus, the frequencies across these categories are not entirely independent. In planning the overall χ^2 analysis, I should have realized that the cells were not independent and accounted for it by using different statistics. However, in the one-way analyses conducted successively for cohesion, content, mechanics, organization, syntax, and vocabulary as shown in Table 4.19, the assumption of independence (for the English and ESL raters) is met.

Unfortunately, those analyses create another problem, which I could have accounted for (as explained in the next section). Although these violations of assumptions are not usually considered as serious as similar violations for means comparisons statistics, I should nonetheless have dealt with them, either by avoiding the problems altogether by using different forms of analysis or at least by discussing the potential effects of such violations on my results. I did neither and I regret the oversight, because that not only weakens the study in question, it also contributes to an overall tendency in language studies to be cavalier in the use of statistical analyses. *Mea culpa.*

(3) You can check the assumption that expected frequencies are equal to or greater than 10 for df = 1 analyses, or 5 for all other analyses, by examining the expected frequencies. If you find that this assumption is not met in one or more cells, you might consider gathering more data so that your overall sample size is larger, or consider combining some of your categories so that the expected frequencies are larger. This assumption was met in the study reported in Table 4.19.

The problem of multiple comparisons and the Bonferroni adjustment

When making statistical comparisons of correlation coefficients to zero, or means to each other, or observed frequencies to expected frequencies in testing for statistical significance, you may often find yourself in the position of wanting or needing to make multiple comparisons within the same data set. The problem with such multiple comparisons is that, for reasons I explained in Brown (1990) for multiple *t*-tests, as a second or third or fourth comparison is made, the chances of finding a spuriously significant difference by chance alone increases.

Consider an extreme example. Using my spreadsheet program, I generated 100 columns of 60 random numbers each. I then randomly created another column that contained 30 ones and 30 twos to represent two groups of students. Using the statistical program, SPSS for Windows (SPSS, 1999), I then calculated independent *t*-tests for the two groups on each of the 100 sets of random numbers. The results indicated that there were five statistically significant differences at $p < .05$ and two such differences at $p < .01$. That is almost exactly what I would expect. Even if I were to make 100 such comparisons with real data, I would have difficulty interpreting the results. For example, consider a set of results from 100 *t*-test comparisons wherein five (that is, 5 percent) turned out to be significant at $p < .05$. How could I interpret such results as anything other than chance findings, given that I got similar results with random numbers? (Believe it or not, such things have been done in language research; for example, see Politzer & McGroarty, 1985).

If it turned out with real data that seven of the multiple *t*-tests were significant at $p < .05$, I would know that about five of the *t*-tests were probably spuriously significant, while two were significant for other than chance reasons. However, I would not know which two *t*-tests were the significant ones and which five were the spuriously significant ones. Hence, I would not be able to interpret any of the results as statistically significant.

When I make one mean comparison with real data using a t-test $\alpha < .05$, that statistic indicates the probability that my result is a chance finding at $p < .05$. As explained earlier, when I make 100 comparisons, the results are uninterpretable. Everything in between two comparisons and 100 is just a matter of degrees.

A less than 100 percent satisfying strategy for accounting for this problem is to use a Bonferroni adjustment to alpha (as advocated in SYSTAT, 1996, p.106 and elsewhere). The **Bonferroni adjustment** is simple: Just divide the alpha level you set for the study by the number of comparisons being made. For instance, in Table 4.19, I used multiple χ^2 statistics, one two-way analysis, and six one-way analyses, for a total of seven. In the entire study associated with that table, I used a total of 38 two-way and one-way χ^2 statistics, of which 10 were found to be statistically significant. Since in fact I used a total of 38 χ^2 statistics in the study associated with Table 4.19, the Bonferroni adjustment would be $\alpha/38 = .05/38 = .001923 \approx .001$ to be conservative. If I had made that Bonferroni adjustment in the study reported in Table 4.19, I could have used that conservative .001 alpha level, which would have dictated using different critical values in making my statistical decisions. For instance, for the two-cell one-way analyses in that study, the 10.828 χ^2 critical value (shown in the upper right corner of Table 4.18 for df = 1 and a .001 significance level) would have been appropriate; for the three-cell one-way analyses in that study, the 13.816 χ^2 critical value (shown one row down in Table 4.18 for df = 2 and a .001 significance level) would have been appropriate; and for the two-way analyses in that study, the 20.515 critical χ^2 critical value (shown in the fifth row in Table 4.18 for df = 5 and a .001 significance level) would have been appropriate.

Reexamining the results of the study in question, I find that in the study as it was reported (without Bonferroni adjustments), 15 of the 38 χ^2 statistics were reported to be significant at .05. Using the Bonferroni adjustment, only seven of those 15 would have been significant at $p < .001$, or $p < .05$ for the study as a whole. Thus, I interpreted as significant eight differences that were probably spurious. The Bonferroni adjustment would not only have helped me to interpret the correct number of significant differences, it would also have told me which were significant. For example, with the Bonferroni adjustment in Table 4.19, the overall two-way χ^2 statistic would have been significant at .001, but only two of the one-way χ^2 statistics (organization and syntax) would have been significant at that level. Hence, the significant difference for cohesion that I reported could only have been considered spurious.

Because it is an approximation, the Bonferroni adjustment is not always the best solution to the problem of multiple comparisons. However, if no other solution exists, the Bonferroni adjustment is better than doing nothing. The Bonferroni adjustment can also be used for multiple correlation coefficients or for multiple *t*-tests. For instance, recall that in Table 4.9, a number of correlation coefficients were calculated from various numbers of random numbers, yet even though they were based on random numbers, the coefficient in the row for trial 4 and column for $N = 5$ would have been spuriously significant (one-tailed $p < .05$). However, if a Bonferroni adjustment had been used, that coefficient would not have been significant. As another example, recall the 100 *t*-tests that I calculated based on 100 columns of random numbers. Remember also that five of those *t*-tests were significant at .05 and two were significant at .01. However, if I had used the Bonferroni adjustment, none of those spuriously significant differences would have resulted.

Thus, when doing multiple significance tests, whether using correlation, mean comparisons, or frequency comparisons, you should definitely use the appropriate statistics to avoid making multiple comparisons. However, if no such statistics exist or it is not possible to use them, you should at minimum use the approximation offered by the Bonferroni adjustment and then stick to the level that the adjustment suggests.

Checking survey reliability statistically

Whenever you use any instrument for measurement, you want it to measure consistently and to measure the right thing. For instance, if you use a scale to measure weight, you would like it to show the same value every time you measure the same object. That notion of consistency is also known as **reliability.**

Survey reliability is the consistency with which a survey (or a subtest of a survey) measures whatever it is measuring. If you have both quantitative and qualitative questions on your survey, you should be concerned about the survey reliability of both types of questions, but you may have to address them separately. In the following discussion, I will explain how to estimate the reliability of quantitative answers, and I will also cover ways to analyze the reliability of qualitative answers in the next chapter.

Methods for estimating reliability of quantitative answers

A number of methods exist for estimating survey reliability of quantitative answers, including the repeated-surveys method, the equivalent-surveys method, and the internal-consistency method.

REPEATED-SURVEYS RELIABILITY

The **repeated-surveys method** (like what language testers call *test–retest reliability*) is one way of examining and estimating the reliability of a

171

survey instrument. To use this strategy, you will need to administer a particular survey instrument two times to the same group of respondents. You will need to administer the instruments far enough apart in time so that respondents do not remember their exact answers on the first administration when answering the second one, and close enough together in time so that respondents have not changed their views substantially. You would then need to compare the results of the two administrations for agreement or correlation of the answers.

The **agreement** of answers is the percentage of answers that were the same on both occasions. This figure is also sometimes called the **percent of agreement** (or the **agreement coefficient**). To calculate the agreement of answers, you need to count up the number of answers across all respondents that were exactly the same on both administrations and divide that number by the total number of answers (the number of respondents times the number of questions).

In situations where a total score on a survey (or subsection of a survey) makes sense, you may also want to examine the *correlation* (the degree of relationship) of those answers for the total scores on the two administrations. A **correlation coefficient** shows the degree to which two sets of numbers are related or go together. As explained above, you can calculate the correlation of two sets of scores generated by the same people on two administrations of a survey by lining up the scores of the two administrations in a spreadsheet and using the correlation function (=CORR in Excel), or by using a statistics program to do the same thing (for further explanation of the correlation coefficient and its many variants, see Brown, 1988, 1996).

EQUIVALENT-SURVEYS RELIABILITY

The **equivalent-surveys method** (like what language testers call *equivalent forms reliability*) is another way of examining and estimating the reliability of a survey instrument. This strategy requires that you develop two survey instruments that are equivalent, or parallel, in structure. Thus you would have to create, for example, Forms A and B of a survey instrument, each of which asks equivalent but different questions. These surveys could then be administered to a group of respondents on two different occasions and the results compared for agreement or correlation of the answers.

You could then examine the agreement of the answers by calculating the percentage of agreement of the answers on the two forms in exactly the same way as explained for the repeated-surveys method. The agreement coefficient would provide an estimate of the amount of agreement in answers between the two forms.

When a total score on a survey (or subsection of a survey) makes sense, you could also examine the correlation coefficient for the total scores on the two forms. Again, you could do this by lining up the scores of the two administrations in a spreadsheet and using the correlation function (=CORR in Excel), or by using a statistics program to do the same thing.

The correlation coefficient for the total scores on the two forms would tell you the reliability in percentage terms of those total scores on either of the forms (that is, a correlation coefficient of .87 would indicate that either form of the survey was 87 percent reliable and, by extension, 13 percent unreliable).

INTERNAL-CONSISTENCY RELIABILITY

The **internal-consistency method** (called the same thing by language testers) examines the consistency of the answers to questions within a single form of a survey administered on a single occasion. So, from a practical point of view, this method is much easier to use than either the repeated-surveys or the equivalent-surveys method. However, internal consistency is all this method will tell you about. If you are interested in the consistency of your survey over time, you should use the repeated-surveys method. If you are interested in the consistency of your survey across two equivalent forms of that survey, you should use the equivalent-surveys method.

The most commonly reported internal-consistency reliability in survey research is Cronbach alpha. **Cronbach alpha** (α) provides an accurate internal-consistency estimate, and it can be used with answers that are coded dichotomously (right or wrong; yes or no) or are on a scale (such as a Likert scale). This last characteristic makes Cronbach alpha relatively flexible compared to other methods for estimating survey internal-consistency reliability, and that fact probably explains why it is the most commonly reported reliability statistic.

One relatively easy way to calculate Cronbach alpha involves scoring the answers for the odd-numbered questions separately from the even-numbered questions. An example is shown in Table 4.20. These example questions are taken from one subsection of a hypothetical questionnaire, a subsection that stretches from Question 11 to Question 20. Notice that the three columns in Table 4.20 on the right represent the first three steps, that is, putting each student's score on the odd-numbered items in one column, their score on the even-numbered items in a second column, and their total score in yet a third column. Thus, each of these three columns represents one step. Then two more steps are listed in the lower right portion of the table. Referring to the table, the steps in calculating Cronbach alpha are given on page 175.

TABLE 4.20. CALCULATING THE CRONBACH ALPHA

ID	Q11	Q12	Q13	Q14	Q15	Q16	Q17	Q18	Q19	Q20	1 Odd	2 Even	3 Total
101	5	4	3	4	4	3	4	4	4	5	20	20	40
102	5	5	3	4	4	3	3	4	4	4	19	20	39
103	3	2	3	3	3	4	4	3	3	1	16	13	29
104	2	1	2	2	2	1	2	2	1	2	9	8	17
105	1	1	1	2	1	1	2	1	1	1	6	6	12
106	1	2	1	2	1	1	1	2	1	1	1	12	13
107	5	5	4	5	5	4	5	5	5	5	24	24	48
108	5	4	3	4	4	4	4	4	4	5	20	21	41
109	5	5	3	4	4	3	3	4	4	4	19	20	39
110	3	2	3	3	3	4	4	3	3	1	16	13	29
111	2	1	2	2	1	1	2	2	1	2	8	8	16
112	1	1	1	2	1	1	1	1	1	1	8	6	11
113	1	2	1	1	1	1	1	2	1	1	5	7	12
114	5	5	4	5	5	5	5	5	5	5	24	25	49
115	5	4	3	4	3	3	4	4	4	5	19	20	39
116	5	5	4	4	4	3	3	4	4	4	20	20	40
117	3	2	3	4	3	4	4	3	3	1	16	14	30
118	2	1	2	2	2	1	2	2	1	2	9	8	17
119	1	1	1	2	1	1	2	1	1	1	6	6	12
120	1	2	1	1	2	1	1	2	1	1	6	7	13

4 SD = 7.0597   6.5338   13.3233

5 SD² = 49.8400   42.6900   177.5100

Step 1. Score the odd-numbered questions (1, 3, 5, 7, 9, 11, etc.) for each student and put the result in a column of its own.

Step 2. Score the even-numbered questions (2, 4, 6, 8, 10, etc.) for each student and put the result in a second column.

Step 3. Calculate and put the total scores for all the questions in a third column.

Step 4. Use a spreadsheet or manually calculate the standard deviation for each of the three columns.

Step 5. Square all three of the standard deviations.

Step 6. Use the following formula:

$$\alpha = 2\left(1 - \frac{S^2_{odd} + S^2_{even}}{S^2_{total}}\right)$$

Step 7. Enter the squared values of the three standard deviations in the appropriate places in the formula.

$$\alpha = 2\left(1 - \frac{49.84 + 42.69}{177.51}\right)$$

Step 8. Perform the necessary calculations.

$$\alpha = 2\left(1 - \frac{92.53}{177.51}\right)$$

$$= 2(1 - 0.5213)$$

$$= 2(0.4787)$$

$$= 0.9574 \approx .96$$

So, the Cronbach alpha internal-consistency reliability estimate for the example 10-item Likert scale turns out to be .96. In other words, these questions are about 96 percent reliable and about 4 percent unreliable.

A caution about survey reliability

One aspect of survey reliability that is particularly important to think about is that it simply indicates that the respondents were answering consistently. Hence, if a survey is designed with subsections that measure distinctly different things, the fact that high reliability is found for the whole survey may be bad news. Such a result would mean that the respondents were answering the same way across all the subsections. If indeed those subsections were designed to measure distinctly different things, respondents should not be answering the same way across all the subsections. Thus, high reliability for the whole survey could indicate that the subsections might not be as different as the survey designer initially thought, or alternatively, might indicate that the respondents (or a substantial number of them) were being lazy or not paying any attention to the actual questions, and were consistently answering one way or another.

In short, for survey instruments that have distinct subsections, examining the reliability of each of the subsections is much more important than calculating the reliability for the survey instrument as a whole (for more information on reliability as it applies to language tests, see Brown, 1996, pp. 185–230; for more information on survey reliability, see Bohrnstedt, 1983, pp. 79–96, or Litwin, 1995, pp. 5–31).

Survey validity

In addition to being reliable, you want the scale to measure the right thing. In the example used for reliability, yes, you would like a scale for measuring weight to be consistent, or reliable, but you would also like that scale to be measuring weight, not length, density, speed, humidity, or some combination of those factors. In other words, you would like it to be measuring what it is intended to measure, weight. This notion is known as **validity**.

The essence of the idea of **survey validity** is that it is the degree to which a survey (or a subtest of a survey) is measuring what it claims to be measuring. Establishing the validity of a survey instrument involves demonstrating that it is measuring what it was intended to measure by using one or more of the following validity strategies: face validity, criterion-related validity, content validity, construct validity, and decision validity. Naturally, the more strategies are used and the more persuasive the arguments presented, the more readers will view your survey instrument as valid. I will now discuss each of these validity strategies in more depth, though the treatment will necessarily be brief.

Face validity

Face validity is the degree to which a survey instrument looks valid to untrained people. From a political point of view, people are not likely to cooperate in a survey study if the instrument does not look valid. Typically, the face validity of a survey instrument is assessed by asking a group (similar to those who will eventually be the respondents) to look at the instrument or go through the process of answering the questions, and then make a judgment about the degree to which the instrument seems valid. Although this is certainly the least scientific approach for establishing survey validity, and produces the least convincing argument for the validity of a survey instrument, you might be surprised at the quality of the feedback you can get from naïve judges like this. Virtually all educated people in many countries have answered questionnaires in one form or another. Hence, they are likely to have some insights and opinions about how a survey should look generally, or about which types of survey questions work best for which purposes. So it is probably a good idea at least to think about face validity and perhaps to get some feedback on the issue before using the other, more powerful validity arguments presented in the sections that follow. One danger is that some people confuse face validity with content validity. You should avoid doing that at all costs. Face and content validity arguments are distinctly different, as you will see by comparing the description immediately above with the material in the next section on content validity.

Content validity

Content validity is the degree to which the survey content matches the theoretical content of whatever you are trying to measure. After carefully designing your questions on the basis of theory, you may want to take one or both of the following approaches: the descriptive approach and/or the expert ratings approach.

THE DESCRIPTIVE APPROACH TO CONTENT VALIDITY

One effective way to ensure content validity is to plan your survey instrument very carefully (preferably on the basis of strong theoretical arguments). Then, one way to defend the content validity of your items is to explain how you planned the questions. To do so, you will probably want to use the literature on whatever constructs are involved and simply show why and how you defined the construct and wrote the questions as you did, somehow describing the questions in the process (and probably appending the survey instrument to the report or article). For example, in Brown, Robson, and Rosenkjar (1996), after describing the extensive literature on each of the constructs measured in our study, we discuss the actual instruments as they were adapted for our study. For instance, the instrument used to measure the motivation construct was described as follows:

Motivation was measured with the *Attitude/Motivation Test Battery* (A/MTB). Gardner and Smythe (1981, p. 511) put together a list of constructs that attempted to measure all of the attitudinal factors related to second language acquisition of French in Canada. They later developed the eleven sections of the *Attitudes/Motivation Test Battery* from that list (Skehan, 1989, p. 55). The assessment format for most of the constructs was a Likert scale; although a short section measuring motivational intensity and desire to learn French used a multiple-choice format, and the evaluative reactions to French courses and French teachers employed a semantic differential technique.

The version of the A/MTB used in this study was adapted to the Japanese situation by Robson. Questions dealing with attitudes toward French Canadians and attitudes toward European French in particular were changed to ones asking for attitudes toward English-speaking Americans in Japan and English-speaking Americans in the United States, respectively, because these groups were identified as the target culture for these particular students.

The first section contained 64 items and asked for information about the following topics: attitudes toward English-speaking Americans in Japan (ten items); interest in foreign languages (ten items); attitudes toward English-speaking Americans in the United States (ten items); attitudes toward learning English (five positively worded items and five negatively worded items); integrative orientation (four items); instrumental orientation (four items), English class anxiety (five items); and parental encouragement (ten items). Each item was scored using a seven-point Likert scale with a score of one for strongly disagree, a score of four for neutral and a score of seven for strongly agree, unless the question was negatively worded resulting in reverse scoring.

The second section contained twenty multiple-choice questions dealing with motivational intensity (ten items) and desire to learn English (ten items). Very little adaptation was necessary in this section. Negatively worded choices are scored one, more neutral items are scored two, and positively worded choices are scored three. An additional item called an orientation index has two integrative orientation choices scored two points and two instrumental orientation choices scored one point for responses to the question "I am studying English because. . . ."

The third and final section had two semantic differential assessments. Under the headings *My English Teacher* and *My English Course*, two rows of twenty-five descriptors each were provided with seven blanks in between. A mark next to a positively worded descriptor was scored seven and a mark next to a negatively worded descriptor was scored one with a score of four for a mark in the middle. No adaptation was necessary in this section except for changing the word French to English wherever it occurred.

Following the adaptation, the A/MTB was translated into Japanese by two native-speaking Japanese instructors of EFL. The two translators cross-checked each other's work, after which the questionnaire was piloted, producing Cronbach alpha coefficients ranging from a low of .82 to a high of .85. The questionnaire was then re-checked by three other Japanese native speakers (also EFL instructors) resulting in the correction of several Kanji errors and the re-wording of a few items. The final questionnaire had a total of 134 items for a total possible score of 853 (pp. 40–41).

The goal of such a description is, of course, to explain to your readers just exactly what you did and what the result was in such a way and in such detail that they will be convinced of the content validity of your survey instrument. Naturally, you will never convince all readers completely. However, you may find it helpful in convincing readers to also use the expert ratings approach to content validity that I explain next.

TABLE 4.21. CONTENT VALIDITY EXPERT FORM

#	Question	No match					Perfect match
1	Volunteer to answer teacher's questions	0	1	2	3	4	5
2	Readily volunteer to share opinions	0	1	2	3	4	5
3	Seek clarification from teacher	0	1	2	3	4	5
4	Verbally indicate not understanding	0	1	2	3	4	5
5	Wait to be called on before speaking	0	1	2	3	4	5
6	Listen quietly when teacher speaks	0	1	2	3	4	5
7	Listen quietly to classmates	0	1	2	3	4	5
8	Do assigned homework	0	1	2	3	4	5
9	Arrive over 15 minutes tardy	0	1	2	3	4	5
10	Speak audibly in English	0	1	2	3	4	5

Source: Based on questions from Sasaki, 1996.

EXPERT RATINGS APPROACH TO CONTENT VALIDITY

Another approach you might want to use in studying and defending the construct validity of your survey instrument is to use **experts,** who are by definition people who know a lot about whatever area of psychology, education, linguistics, or language teaching your construct belongs to. Once you have convinced such experts to help you by begging them, trading services with them, or even paying them, you should do the following.

1. Write more questions than you think you will need for each construct you want to measure in your survey (as a rule of thumb, you might want to write 50 percent more than you will ultimately need; so if you want to end up with 10 questions, you might want to start with 15).
2. Have the experts examine your theoretical rationale and definitions for the constructs being measured.
3. Have them examine the survey questions themselves one by one.
4. Have the experts rate the degree to which the survey questions match the constructs as you have defined them. You may want to work out in advance some forms that they can look at to rate the questions and some sort of scale for them to select their rating (see Table 4.21 for an example form based on questions taken from Sasaki, 1996).
5. Once you have the experts' ratings, you should select those questions that are rated the highest by the experts, which of course means eliminating the weakest questions. If you started with 50 percent extra, say 15 questions, when you pare the number back to the best 10 questions, you should be left with a reasonably good questionnaire and you will

still have the expert ratings for those items to use in defending the content validity of your test. If, in the process, you need to revise or replace some of the questions, you should probably turn back to the experts and have those new or revised items rated as well.

Ultimately, many of the readers of whatever report you write will probably want to look at the questions themselves. Hence, you should probably consider appending the actual survey instrument to whatever report you produce in the end. Openly and honestly making the questions available to readers may turn out to be one of your strongest content validity arguments – unless, of course, the questions were not written very well or do not match very well with the constructs in question, in which case you should not be making any arguments for their validity.

Criterion-related validity

Criterion-related validity is the degree to which the survey is related to another well-established measure of whatever you are trying to measure. Criterion-related validity evidence can be either concurrent or predictive in nature.

CONCURRENT VALIDITY

Concurrent criterion-related validity is the correct label if the data for the new survey (the one you are trying to validate) and the well-established criterion survey are gathered at the same time. Because the data were gathered at approximately the same time, concurrent criterion-related validity may be the preferred strategy in situations where respondents' views are likely to change considerably over time. For example, in Brown et al. (1996), part of our discussion of the instrument we used to measure personality traits was as follows.

The *Y/G Personality Inventory* assesses twelve traits: social extraversion, ascendance, thinking extraversion, rhathymia, general activity, lack of agreeableness, lack of cooperativeness, lack of objectivity, nervousness, inferiority feelings, cyclic tendencies, and depression. The twelve traits in this inventory have been shown (see Robson, 1992) to consistently fall into two categories: neuroticism and extraversion (in the list above, the first six represent extraversion and the next six represent neuroticism). In Robson (1992), the *Y/G Personality Inventory* was also shown to have a good level of concurrent validity with the *Maudsley Personality Inventory* (MPI) (Eysenck, 1959, 1990). Generally, the six extraversion and six neuroticism traits had correlations from .60 to .80 with MPI extraversion and neuroticism and factored into the same two groups. This instrument can thus be said to have a high degree of construct and criterion-related validity, and despite its age, it is still regarded as an appropriate measure by leading researchers in the field (see Angleitner, 1991) (pp. 39–40).

Notice in the quote above that we say that Robson (1992) had shown that the the *Y/G Personality Inventory* had a good level of concurrent validity with the *Maudsley Personality Inventory* (MPI) and that the six extraversion and six neuroticism scales had correlations ranging from .60 to .80 with MPI extraversion and neuroticism scales. In this way, we were arguing that the survey instrument we were using had a moderate to strong relationship with a previously well-established measure of the same construct, the MPI.

PREDICTIVE VALIDITY

Predictive criterion-related validity is the correct label if the nature of the information being gathered is predictive of some later-occurring characteristics. For instance, if a questionnaire on motivation is designed to measure (at the beginning of a course) the chances of a student finishing a particular course of language study, it could be validated by administering the questionnaire at the beginning of the course (one that has a high dropout rate), then keeping track of who drops out and who stays to the end of the course. The analysis that would help build a predictive validity argument would simply involve calculating a point-biserial correlation coefficient (see Brown, 1996, pp. 176–178) to examine the degree of relationship between the scores on the questionnaire and the fact that the students stayed in the course or dropped out. If the correlation coefficient turned out to be significant (at, say, $p < .01$) and was reasonably high (at, say, .80), that would constitute an argument for the predictive criterion-related validity of the questionnaire.

Construct validity

Construct validity is the degree to which the survey can be shown experimentally to be measuring whatever construct you are trying to measure. As I pointed out in Chapter 1, constructs (sometimes also called psychological constructs) are psychological traits or characteristics that are operating in participants' brains. The examples that I give in Chapter 1 were language aptitude, cultural attitudes, aggressiveness, motivation, anxiety, personality characteristics, preferred learning styles and strategies, and so forth. Establishing construct validity involves setting up some sort of experiment to demonstrate that indeed the survey instrument under development is measuring the construct it is supposed to measure. Construct validity experiments come in three basic forms: differential-groups validity study, intervention validity study, and convergent/divergent studies.

Differential-groups validity studies use groups of people who naturally have and do not have the construct being measured and compare their performances on whatever instrument is being analyzed for validity. For example, in analyzing the validity of the *Attitude/Motivation Test Battery* (A/MTB) discussed in an earlier section, Brown et al. (1996) might identify two groups for comparison: one made up of students who are known (either through observation or based on other motivation scales) to be highly motivated and another group known (through the same procedures) to have low motivation. In other words, they would be comparing one group that has a high level of the motivation construct with one that has a low level.

They could then administer the A/MTB and, if the results showed that the high-motivation students scored significantly higher on all the subtests than the low-motivation students (for example, using a statistic like the *t*-test with the alpha level adjusted using the Bonferroni procedure), that result would constitute evidence for the construct validity of the A/MTB. If, on the other hand, some of the subscales did not turn out to differentiate among such groups, that result would raise questions about the validity of those subscales of the instrument, at least for those types of students. In that case, the authors could (1) investigate why the results turned out as they did and explain away the results (usually not a very satisfactory solution), (2) eliminate the subtests that did not prove to be valid and use the instrument without them, or (3) revise those subscales that did not prove to be valid and administer them to similar students under the same conditions to see if their validity had been improved.

Intervention validity studies also use groups of people who have and do not have the trait being measured, but the groups are made up of the same people before they have the trait and after they have gained it. This strategy works best with constructs that can be taught or changed in individuals. If, for instance, I was trying to measure self-esteem, I might set up an intervention study, wherein I would begin by administering my self-esteem instrument to a group of people with low self-esteem. I would then give them a treatment that raises their self-esteem; that is, I would teach them things that are presumed to raise their self-esteem. I could then administer the self-esteem instrument again after the treatment and compare the results on the instrument before and after the treatment. If the results showed that the students scored significantly higher after the treatment than before the treatment (again using a statistic such as the *t*-test with the alpha level adjusted using the Bonferroni procedure), that would constitute evidence for the construct validity of my self-esteem instrument. If, on the other hand, no such significant difference occurred, interpretation of the result might be difficult because they could mean that: (1) the instrument is not valid, (2) the treatment does not work, (3) self-esteem can not be taught, or (4) all three. Naturally, if there are subscales and some of them did not turn out to differentiate between the before and after treatment conditions, that would raise questions about the validity of those subscales of the instrument, at least for the types of students in the study. In such a case, I could (1) investigate why the results turned out as they did and try to explain away the results (usually not a very satisfactory solution), (2) eliminate the subtests that did not prove to be valid and use the instrument without them, or (3) revise those subscales that did not prove to be valid and administer them again to similar students under the same conditions to see if their validity had been improved.

Convergent/discriminate validity studies work best for instruments that have distinct subscales, or groups of instruments that can be considered subscales in a larger study. Convergent/divergent validity studies are usually based on some form of correlational analysis; all of the questions on all of the subscales must be administered to a group of respondents who are presumed to vary on all of the subscales involved – that is, who are not homogeneous with regard to the scales being measured. **Convergent validity** is demonstrated when all the questions on scales measuring the same construct are more highly correlated with each other than with the questions on scales measuring other constructs. **Discriminate validity** is demonstrated when all the questions on scales measuring different constructs are less highly correlated with each other than the questions on scales measuring the same constructs. Notice that these two definitions are more or less mirror images of each other. As a result, these two forms of validity can really form a strong argument for the validity of the scales involved only when they are used together.

For example, in its most basic form, convergent/discriminate validity analysis involves examining the correlations of the scores for all questions with the scores of all other questions. If it turns out that the questions within subscales (as originally designed based on theory) correlate highly (that is, converge) and they correlate low with the items of all other subscales (that is they discriminate), then that would constitute one argument for the convergent/discriminate validity of the scales individually and as a group. Remember that convergent validity and discriminate validity form a much stronger argument for the validity of the scales involved when taken together than either does when considered separately and alone.

Unfortunately, such a clear picture seldom emerges from a simple matrix of the correlations of all survey questions with each other. For instance, as you will see in second rotating example later in this chapter, the correlation matrices shown in Tables 4.31 and 4.32 are not very helpful for discerning convergent or discriminate validity patterns. Fortunately, alternative forms of correlational analysis can help you explore the patterns in your correlation coefficients. By far the most commonly used analyses for examining the convergent/discriminate validity of survey instruments are principal components and factor analysis strategies, explained in the next section and shown in the second rotating example of this chapter as well. I would also like to suggest that under certain circumstances the multitrait-multimethod strategy can be used to explore the convergent/discriminate validity of survey questions and scales.

Factor analysis is a set of statistical procedures used to explore the underlying variance structure of a set of correlation coefficients. Thus, factor analysis is useful for exploring and verifying the patterns in a set of correlation coefficients like those found between pairs of items or subsections on a survey instrument. Most often in survey research, factor analysis is used to analyze all of the variance accounted for by the correlation coefficients, ignoring the variance (called **error variance**) that the correlation coefficients do not account for. (Note that in some situations you may want to analyze all of the variance including the error variance, in which case you should be using **principal components analysis.** For a reasonably short treatment of both factor and principal components analyses, see Tabachnick & Fidell, 1996; for more involved coverage, see Gorsuch, 1983, or McDonald, 1985.)

I will cover only factor analysis (rather than principal components analysis) here, because that is the type of analysis used most commonly in survey research. Because my purpose is simply to give you a brief idea of the sorts of things that you can do with factor analysis, I will not be able to give the details of the statistical analyses or show how it can be done by hand. Although it is possible to do factor analysis by hand, it would be very inefficient to do so because computers make the process vastly easier. I typically use a statistics program such as SPSS for Windows (SPSS, 1999) or SYSTAT (1999) to do the analysis in just a few minutes.

In analyzing your survey instrument for validity, you may be interested in exploring how subsections on a series of survey instruments converge and discriminate in patterns that make sense within each instrument, or you may be interested in studying how the individual questions in subsections of a particular survey instrument converge and discriminate. In this section, I will show how factor analysis can be applied to demonstrate the convergent and discriminate validity of a series of instruments analyzed together. In the second rotating example later in the chapter, I will provide an example of how the same strategy can be used to explore the patterns in individual questions in subsections of a particular survey instrument.

Turning to the case where factor analysis is used to explore the convergent and discriminate structures of subsections of a series of survey instruments, I will use the analyses in Brown et al. (1996) to illustrate the processes involved in such interpretations. Those results are shown in Table 4.22, which presents their factor analysis results after what is called a varimax rotation of those results.

While conducting this factor analysis, one intermediary step was to decide how many factors to examine in the analysis. In this case, the authors first checked the eigenvalues; eight of them were over 1.00 (a traditional cut-point for eigenvalues). *Eigenvalues* show the amount of total variation in the group of variables that was accounted for by each variable. Second, examination of the scree plot confirmed that an eight-factor solution was appropriate. These eight factors accounted for 66.2 percent of the variance in the correlation coefficients in this study. The **loadings** (that is, the correlations of each of the variables in the study with each of the factors) on the eight factors are shown in Table 4.22. The asterisks indicate loadings of .30 or higher, and the boldface type indicates the highest loading for each variable. Farthest to the right, Brown et al. (1996) presented a column of **communalities** (h^2), which indicate the total proportion of variance that the eight factors account for in each variable. For instance, the eight factors account for 67.9 percent of the total variance in Social Extraversion and 67.1 percent of the total variance in Ascendance, but only 46.6 percent of the variance in Thinking Extraversion. At the bottom of the table, the row of figures in italics gives the proportion of variance in the overall solution accounted for by each factor. For example, the first factor accounts for 21.9 percent of the variance in this solution, whereas the second factor accounts for 12.8 percent, and so forth.

Toward the bottom of the table, notice that all the subscales of the SILL loaded most heavily on factor 2 and that the FLCAS loaded most heavily on factor 5. Notice also that the proficiency measures (Michigan structure and Cloze) loaded on factor 7. The remaining interpretation becomes somewhat more complex. As the authors put it:

The two other measures, the A/MTB and the Y/GPI, present more complex patterns of loadings. Eight of the subscales of the A/MTB load fairly heavily on factor three, and two subscales, English Class Anxiety and Motivational Intensity, load most heavily on factor five with the FLCAS. This pattern makes sense because all three of the variables loading on factor five can be viewed as being related to anxiety. This is obvious for the FLCAS and the English class Anxiety scale, but Motivational Intensity may be related to anxiety because of the types of items in this scale: many of its items deal with classroom behaviors such as speaking out, volunteering, or asking for assistance that could be negatively affected by anxiety.

If a scale, like the SILL, has patterns of loadings on one factor that indicate its various subscales are convergent, or homogeneous and measuring the same sorts of things (in that the loadings of the component subscales load together on one factor), and yet discriminate, or are divergent from the other scales (in that no other subscales load heavily on the same factor), factor analysis can constitute an argument for the validity of the scales involved. In the above example, the validity of the SILL, FLCAS, Michigan, and Cloze seem to be supported in this way. In addition, with the

TABLE 4.22. FACTOR LOADINGS AFTER VARIMAX ROTATION

Measure Subscale	Factors 1	2	3	4	5	6	7	8	h^2
Y/GPI (Personality)									
Social Extraversion	-.369*	.216	.121	.580*	.295	.139	-.197	-.018	.679
Ascendance	-.381*	.146	.077	.591*	.350	.143	-.082	-.016	.671
Thinking Extraversion	-.567*	-.203	-.001	.164	-.243	-.060	-.063	.100	.466
Rhathymia	.064	.070	.170	.823*	-.042	-.033	-.082	.010	.724
General Activity	-.370*	.248	.157	.592*	.128	.136	-.003	-.144	.629
Agreeableness (Lack)	.211	.158	.038	.750*	.152	-.082	.034	.081	.670
Cooperation (Lack)	.685*	-.021	-.102	.051	-.043	-.106	-.043	-.132	.515
Objectivity (Lack)	.738*	.049	-.054	.243	-.149	.081	-.129	.088	.662
Nervousness	.826*	-.062	-.076	-.160	-.083	-.034	.018	.037	.727
Inferiority Feelings	.697*	-.070	-.037	-.366*	-.358*	-.020	-.126	.060	.774
Cyclic Tendencies	.769*	-.127	.052	.196	-.099	-.033	-.042	.014	.661
Depression	.828*	-.033	-.054	-.173	-.186	-.049	-.106	.084	.775
A/MTB (Motivation)									
Att Amer in Japan	-.020	.076	.755*	-.005	-.134	.251	-.067	-.141	.681
Interest Foreign Lang	-.047	.189	.720*	.071	.107	-.044	.128	.244	.651
Att Amer in General	-.130	.085	.667*	-.022	-.070	.329*	-.101	-.093	.602
Att Learning English	-.118	.148	.671*	.102	.225	.063	.054	.153	.578
Integrative Orient'n	.023	.115	.775*	.159	-.062	.061	.019	-.049	.651
Instrumental Orient'n	.005	-.001	.483*	.127	-.015	-.232	-.043	-.558*	.616
English Class Anxiety	-.178	.023	-.080	.118	.824*	.011	.022	.013	.732
Parent Encouragement	-.011	.147	.527*	.105	-.080	.153	-.211	-.087	.392
Motiv'l Intensity	-.023	.359*	.226	.073	.554*	.135	-.036	.105	.523
Desire to Lrn English	-.065	.296	.585*	.039	.338*	-.013	.034	.221	.599

Orientation	.024	-.071	.140	.048	-.003	-.026	.027	.812*	.688
Att English Teacher	.018	-.003	.249	-.030	.082	.842*	.068	.053	.787
Att English Class	-.107	.036	.215	.096	.011	.829*	.107	.021	.768
FLCAS (Anxiety)	-.335*	.129	-.044	.248	.690*	-.037	.073	-.092	.683
SILL (Strategies)									
Remembering	-.049	.755*	.075	.099	.033	.033	-.022	-.061	.595
Mental Processes	.001	.872*	.139	.102	.127	-.003	.049	.054	.811
Compensating	-.024	.764*	.125	.033	.096	-.079	.010	-.005	.616
Organizing and Eval	-.060	.842*	.242	.034	.100	.023	.065	.029	.788
Managing Emotions	.094	.743*	.065	.136	-.098	.054	-.233	-.125	.666
Learning with Others	-.076	.782*	.136	.157	.133	.059	.051	.004	.685
Michigan	-.117	.031	-.013	-.155	.032	.079	.809*	-.049	.703
Cloze	-.082	-.047	-.064	.030	.005	.073	.837*	.095	.728
Proportion of Variance	.219	.128	.087	0.68	.052	.040	.035	.033	.662

* = Loadings over .30; **bold** = highest loading for each variable.
Source: Brown et al., 1996, Table 2.

exception of the Thinking Extraversion subscale, the validity of the Y/GPI scale seems to be supported in that the subscales load predominantly on two factors in a way that corresponds to the two categories of subscales that were built into the Y/GPI: extraversion and neuroticism. The pattern for the A/MTB is least clear because the loadings of the subscales are spread over four factors. Nonetheless, eight of the 13 subscales load fairly heavily on factor 3. (For much more information on factor analysis, see Gorsuch, 1983, McDonald, 1985, or Tabachnick & Fidell, 1995.)

MULTITRAIT-MULTIMETHOD STRATEGY

The **multitrait-multimethod** (M-M) strategy is a way of designing and carrying out a validity study so that multiple constructs (hence, multi-trait) are being measured and multiple methods (multimethod) are being used to do so. The M-M strategy was first proposed and explained by Campbell and Fiske (1959). This strategy involves carefully planning the types of constructs being tested and the methods used to test them, so that the correlation coefficients among them can be examined for convergent and discriminate validity.

One precondition to such an M-M study is that the constructs must be very different from each other so they do not themselves correlate highly. Perhaps the three constructs shown for the fictitious study in Table 4.23 would work: motivation, anxiety, and extroversion. Of course, if they do turn out to be highly correlated, the M-M strategy may not work at all. Hence, careful planning must be used to make sure you use very different constructs.

A second precondition for M-M studies is that the methods of measuring the constructs must be very different from each other so that they do not themselves correlate highly. This means that using three paper-and-pencil questionnaire-type scales (for example, Likert scales, yes/no judgments, and agree/disagree dichotomies) for such a validity study will probably not work very well, because they are similar methods that are more likely to be highly correlated with each other, even when measuring different constructs. Hence, truly different methods should be selected, perhaps like those shown for the fictitious study in Table 4.23: face-to-face interviews, questionnaires, and classroom observations.

Notice that the example M-M study shown in Table 4.23 is not complicated, but rather is simply a special and systematically designed arrangement of correlation coefficients. Notice also that Table 4.23 contains three triangles (labeled *a, b,* and *c*) and three rectangles (labeled *X, Y,* and *Z*). The three triangles, *a, b,* and *c,* run diagonally across and down the middle of the table, and they show the correlations between instruments measuring different traits using the same method. Triangle *a* shows the correlations among all interview instruments for the three traits (motivation, anx-

TABLE 4.23. A HYPOTHETICAL MULTITRAIT-MULTIMETHOD MATRIX FOR VALIDATING MEASURES OF MOTIVATION (M), ANXIETY (A), AND EXTROVERSION (E) USING INTERVIEWS, QUESTIONNAIRES, AND OBSERVATIONS

Methods	Interviews			Questionnaires			Observations		
Constructs	M	A	E	M	A	E	M	A	E
Interviews									
Motivation (M)	—		*a*						
Anxiety (A)	0.26	—							
Extroversion (E)	0.35	0.33	—						
Questionnaires (X)									
Motivation (M)	0.65	0.24	0.33	—		*b*			
Anxiety (A)	0.19	0.71	0.17	0.41	—				
Extroversion (E)	0.16	0.21	0.57	0.34	0.44	—			
Observations (Y, Z)									
Motivation (M)	0.61	0.21	0.19	0.76	0.19	0.23	—		*c*
Anxiety (A)	0.11	0.69	0.15	0.31	0.69	0.20	0.39	—	
Extroversion (E)	0.19	0.12	0.63	0.23	0.19	0.77	0.45	0.40	—

iety, and extroversion). Triangle *b* contains all three questionnaire instruments, and the triangle *c* holds all three observation instruments.

Now consider the correlations in the rectangles. Notice that some are in boldface type and others are not. Those coefficients that are not in boldface type are the correlations between different traits and different methods. Those coefficients that are in boldface type running diagonally across and down each rectangle are for the same trait but different methods. A convergent validity argument for the instruments involved requires that the boldface coefficients (the ones measuring the same traits with different methods) be high in magnitude. A discriminate validity argument for the instruments involved requires that the coefficients in regular typeface (that is, the correlations for different traits and different methods) be lower than the boldface coefficients (the ones measuring the same traits with different methods) and that the values in triangles *a, b,* and *c* be lower than the reliability of the instruments. If those conditions exist, you have run a successful M-M validity study. If those conditions do not exist, the validity of the measures must be carefully examined from other perspectives.

M-M validity studies have seldom actually been used by language professionals, probably because it is rare to chance upon a situation in which the constructs and traits are so systematically different and intentionally designing such a study is difficult. There is one notable exception that has little to do with survey design, a language testing study by Bachman and Palmer (1983). Nonetheless, the multitrait-multimethod strategy for establishing the validity of survey instruments could prove useful under the right conditions, so it is worth knowing about.

Decision validity

Decision validity is the degree to which a survey instrument is being used to make decisions in the intended manner. Particularly when survey instruments are being used to make decisions about peoples' lives (say, in important research projects that may have field-wide ramifications or curriculum projects that will have program-level impact), their decision validity must be considered from two perspectives: the value implications of the survey, and its social consequences (after Messick, 1988, who made these arguments for tests).

The **value implications in decision validity** require analysis of the political and contextual ramifications of instrument interpretation and use in a particular setting. For a survey instrument, the very act of taking a survey may have certain political and personal implications that must be taken into consideration. You may also find that the values assigned to different issues, questions, topics, and so on, are not the same for all groups in a particular setting. This may be particularly true in settings where the various participants come from different cultures. Any such value implications should be considered carefully (through interviews, meetings, or other information-gathering techniques) when using a survey instrument for making research- or curriculum-related decisions.

The **social consequences in decision validity** require analysis of the potential social consequences of the proposed use of the instrument, or the actual social consequences of its use in a particular setting. For a survey instrument, that means carefully considering what will happen because the instrument is being used. What are any social purposes of administering the instrument? How will people react to its being administered? How will the results be used? How will teachers, students, parents, and so on, react to the results if they turn out one way? Or another way?

For more information on validity as it is applied to language tests, see Brown (1996, pp. 231–267); for more information on survey validity, see Bohrnstedt (1983, pp. 97–114) or Litwin (1995, pp. 33–45).

General guidelines for statistical studies

Although the following guidelines are available elsewhere (that is, in the back of any issue of *TESOL Quarterly*), I present them here because they are of crucial importance to anybody who wants to publish their survey research, or who just wants to do a professional job of conducting, analyzing, and reporting their study. Also, although I recognize that the *TESOL Quarterly* is only one of many journals in applied linguistics and language teaching, it is the only journal in our field (to my knowledge) that provides such clear-cut guidelines for statistical research. The particular guidelines shown here were taken from TESOL (2000a) but, as I pointed out earlier, they are published at the back of each issue. The guidelines that follow are organized into three sections: reporting the study, conducting the study, and interpreting the results:

Statistical guidelines*

Because of the educational role the [*TESOL*] *Quarterly* plays modeling research in the field, it is of particular concern that published research articles meet high statistical standards. In order to support this goal, the following guidelines are provided.

REPORTING THE STUDY

Studies submitted to the [*TESOL*] *Quarterly* should be explained clearly and in enough detail that it would be possible to replicate the design of the study on the basis of the information provided in the article. Likewise, the study should include sufficient information to allow readers to evaluate the claims made by the author. In order to accommodate both of these requirements, authors of statistical studies should present the following.

*© TESOL. Reprinted with permission.

1. A clear statement of the research questions and hypotheses that are being examined.
2. Descriptive statistics, including the means, standard deviations, and sample sizes, necessary for the reader to correctly interpret and evaluate any inferential statistics.
3. Appropriate types of reliability and validity of any tests, ratings, questionnaires, and so on.
4. Graphs and charts that help explain the results.
5. Clear and careful descriptions of the instruments used and the types of intervention employed in the study.
6. Explicit identifications of dependent, independent, moderator, intervening, and control variables.
7. Complete source tables for statistical tests.
8. Discussions of how the assumptions underlying the research design were met, assumptions such as random selection and assignment of subjects, sufficiently large sample sizes so that the results are stable, etc.
9. Tests of the assumptions of any statistical tests, when appropriate.
10. Realistic interpretations of the statistical significance of the results keeping in mind that the meaningfulness of the results is a separate and important issue, especially for correlation.

CONDUCTING THE ANALYSES

Quantitative studies submitted to the *TESOL Quarterly* should reflect a concern for controlling Type I and Type II error. Thus, studies should avoid multiple *t*-tests, multiple ANOVAs, etc. However, in the very few instances in which multiple tests might be employed, the author should explain the effects of such use on the probability values in the results. In reporting statistical analyses, authors should choose one significance level (usually .05) and report all results in terms of that level. Likewise, studies should report effect size through such strength of association measures as omega-squared or eta-squared along with beta (the possibility of Type II error) whenever this may be important to interpreting the significance of the results.

INTERPRETING THE RESULTS

The results should be explained clearly and the implications discussed such that readers without extensive training in the use of statistics can understand them. Care should be taken in making causal inferences from statistical results, and these should be avoided with correlational studies. Results of the study should not be overinterpreted or overgeneralized. Finally, alternative explanations of the results should be discussed.

Examples of analyzing survey data statistically

The running example in this chapter will, naturally, be the TESOL survey project. The first rotating example will be based on a study conducted in Japan by Sasaki (1996), which examined the differences between teachers' perceptions of students' classroom behaviors and their preferences in those behaviors, and a second rotating example will be based on a study conducted in Brazil by Brown, Cunha, and Frota (in press) to investigate the relationship between various types of motivation.

Running example: Analyzing survey data statistically

Recall that the survey being used in this running example was developed by the TESOL Research Task Force. To refresh your memory on this project, you may want to skim through the running example sections of the previous three chapters. In this section, I will focus on how we (Brown, Knowles, Murray, Neu, & Violand-Hainer, 1992a) explained the results of the TESOL Research Task Force questionnaire using different types of descriptive statistics for different types of questions.

To give you some idea of the types of categories and quantity of statistics reported by the TESOL Research Task Force, I provide a simple list of the tables included:

Table 1: Personal Characteristics of Groups Sampled
Table 2: Questionnaires Returned
Table 3: Educational Characteristics of Groups
Table 4: Occupational Characteristics of Groups Sampled
Table 5: Research Background Characteristics of Groups Sampled
Table 6: Views on *TESOL Quarterly*
Table 7: Average Ratings (1–5) for TESOL Publications
Table 8: Average Ratings (1–5) of TESOL Convention Components
Table 9: Views on Sessions at TESOL
Table 10: Views on Research

Notice that the tables move from describing the sample (Tables 1 to 5) to describing the results in terms of the participants' views (Tables 6, 9, and 10) or their average ratings (Tables 7 and 8). The previous sentence makes the reporting of results seem too simple.

To give you an idea of how many different types of questions we used and how many different ways we used descriptive statistics, I will begin by considering the statistics shown in Table 4.24 (which was Table 1 in the original report). Notice in Table 4.24 that the five groups are labeled across the top, including the General Membership (Gen Mem), as well as four interest sections: Applied Linguistics (AL), Higher Education (HE), Research (RE), and Teacher Education (TE). Notice that the variables being described are listed down the left-hand side of the table, including gender, nationality, first language, and average age. The first three variables are described using simple percentages, and the last variable is described with an average (mean).

TABLE 4.24. PERSONAL CHARACTERISTICS OF GROUPS SAMPLED

		Interest Section				
Characteristic	*Gen Mem*	*AL*	*HE*	*RE*	*TE*	*Total*
Gender (%)						
Female	72.1	72.7	82.3	62.5	62.9	71.0
Male	27.9	27.3	17.7	37.5	37.1	29.0
Nationality (%)						
US	89.6	72.7	98.4	79.0	84.1	86.7
Other	10.4	27.3	1.6	21.0	15.9	13.3
First Language (%)						
English	89.7	83.3	96.8	90.1	88.9	89.7
Latin Language	5.8	4.5	1.6	3.7	6.3	5.0
Germanic	0.9	4.5	1.6	2.5	0.0	1.5
Sino-Tibet	2.7	6.1	0.0	2.5	3.2	2.8
Semitic	0.3	0.0	0.0	1.2	0.0	0.3
Other	0.6	1.5	0.0	0.0	1.6	0.7
Average Age	44.7	41.9	45.0	42.6	45.3	44.2

Our comments in the original paper on the statistics in Table 4.24 might be of interest:

In general, the groups appear to be fairly similar, with several notable exceptions: 1. Higher Education appears to have a larger proportion of females, while Research and Teacher Education have generally lower proportions, 2. Higher Education has a considerably larger proportion of people with US nationality than the other groups with a correspondingly higher percentage of first language speakers of English, 3. Applied Linguistics and Research groups are several years younger on average than the other groups.

Table 4.25 (Table 2 in the original report) is not so much about the subjects themselves but rather about the way the sampling went on a mail questionnaire. Notice, first of all, that Table 4.25 is exactly the same across the top in terms of the column labels. In fact, all 10 tables have the same layout across the top. That is not an accident. I did it so that the tables would be easier for readers to read and understand.

Then, notice in Table 4.25 that the number of questionnaires sent out and the number returned are shown in frequencies. Then they are shown as both column percentages and row percentages. In the third row is a column percentage where we gave the return rate, which is the number of questionnaires returned (the second figure in each column) divided by the total number of questionnaires sent out (the first figure in each column). In the fourth row are row percentages, where we divided the total number returned in each group by the total number returned (for example, for

TABLE 4.25. QUESTIONNAIRES RETURNED

Characteristic	Gen Mem	Interest sections				Total
		AL	HE	RE	TE	
Number sent out	1,000	200	200	200	200	1,800
Number returned	334	66	62	82	63	607
Return rate percent	33.4	33.0	31.0	41.0	31.5	33.7
Percent of all questionnaires	55.0	10.9	10.2	13.5	10.4	100.0

AL, the percentage is 66/607 = 0.1087, or about 10.9 percent). The following is what we said about Table 4.25 in the original report:

A total of 607 questionnaires were returned. According to Table 2 [Table 4.25 here], 334 of these were from the General Membership, while 66 were from the Applied Linguistics interest Section, 62 came from Higher Education, 82 from Research, and 63 from TE. This means that the return rates for the questionnaires varied from a low of 31 percent for the Higher Education interest section to a high of 41 percent for the Research group. The last row in Table 2 indicates that 55.0 percent of the questionnaires returned to us were from the General Membership, while 10.9 percent came from the Applied Linguistics, 10.2 percent from Higher Education, 13.5 from Research, and 10.4 from TE.

Notice in Table 2 [Table 4.25 here] that the Research interest section had the highest return rate. This may be because the members of this interest section were naturally more interested in research issues, or it may be because they were somewhat more sympathetic to participating in research. Regardless of the reason they were represented slightly more than the other groups involved.

Unfortunately, in retrospect, I realize that the results presented in Table 4.25 and the prose discussion of that table provide a prime example of one of the dangers in interpreting simple descriptive statistics. Because we did not use any statistical tests to determine whether the difference between the Research interest section and the other interest sections was significant, we really had no way of knowing whether the difference in frequencies that we observed between the Research interest section and the other three was simply a chance fluctuation.

Using the chi-square statistic now, I find that the expected value for the frequencies 66, 62, 82, and 63 is 68.25 and that the chi-square observed for these four frequencies would be 3.82 and the chi-square critical for three degrees of freedom (df = 4 − 1 = 3) at $p < .05$ is 7.8147. So there are no significant differences in these frequencies from the expected frequencies. But what if I include the frequencies for the general membership? To do so, I would have to adjust the frequency (334) for the general membership to reflect the per 200 people used in the interest sections (instead

TABLE 4.26. RESEARCH BACKGROUND CHARACTERISTICS OF GROUPS SAMPLED

		Interest sections				
Characteristic	*Gen Mem*	*AL*	*HE*	*RE*	*TE*	*Total*
Taken a testing course? (%)						
Yes	56.1	57.8	50.8	66.2	63.9	57.9
No	43.9	42.2	49.2	33.7	36.1	42.1
Taken a statistics course? (%)						
Yes	60.4	77.3	58.1	95.1	71.4	67.9
No	39.6	22.7	41.9	4.9	28.6	32.1
Current with research? (%)						
Yes	70.5	70.3	64.5	89.0	77.0	73.1
Sometimes	4.6	4.7	6.5	4.9	9.8	5.4
No	24.9	25.0	29.0	6.1	13.1	21.6
Conduct research? (%)						
Yes	51.1	80.3	48.3	97.5	66.1	61.9
No	48.9	19.7	51.7	2.4	33.9	38.1

of per 1,000) by dividing 334 by 5, which equals 66.8. Then I could compare the resulting 66.8 with the other four frequencies for the interest sections by analyzing the following frequencies: 66.8, 66, 62, 82, and 63. In this case, the chi-square observed for these four frequencies would be 3.86 and the chi-square critical for 4 degrees of freedom (df = 5 − 1 = 4) at $p < .05$ is 9.4877. So there are no significant differences in these frequencies from the expected frequencies either. Thus, the observed differences in frequencies in Table 4.25 for the five groups can only be said to be random fluctuations, and much of what we said in the second paragraph of the quotation immediately above was not justified. That is why it is important to think about using such statistical tests. In this case, a statistical test could have helped to avoid overinterpreting the descriptive statistics.

Table 4.26 (Table 5 in the original report) reports the research background characteristics of the groups. Notice that the questions were posed as yes/no questions, and the results for three of the questions are couched in those terms. However, one of the questions (the third one) has a *sometimes* category that was forced on us by the respondents, 4.6 percent to 9.8 percent of whom wrote in qualifying words such as *sometimes, usually,* and *often*. This phenomenon was fairly widespread on our yes/no questions. We report this as the "sometimes" category as you see it in Table 4.26. The problem is that only those who wrote something in had this option, so it does not reflect what the percentages might have been if all of the respondents had been give three options (yes/sometimes/no)

TABLE 4.27. AVERAGE RATINGS (1–5) FOR TESOL PUBLICATIONS

| Characteristic | Gen Mem | Interest sections | | | | |
		AL	HE	RE	TE	Total
TESOL Quarterly overall	3.8	3.9	3.8	4.1	4.0	3.8
Component:						
Book reviews	3.5	3.5	3.5	3.7	3.4	3.5
Brief reports	3.6	3.6	3.5	3.6	3.4	3.6
Classroom research articles	4.0	4.0	3.9	4.2	4.3	4.0
Classroom teaching articles	4.1	3.8	3.8	3.6	4.3	4.0
Statistical research articles	2.6	3.3	2.3	4.1	2.8	2.8
TESOL Matters overall	3.6	3.4	3.7	3.1	3.6	3.5

instead of the two (yes/no) that they were given. Following is what we said about Table 4.26 in the original report.

Other interesting results of this survey (shown in Table 6 [Table 4.26 here]) are that more that 56 percent of the General Membership have taken a language testing course, over 60 percent have taken a statistics course, over 70 percent feel that they stay current with the research in the field, and more than 51 percent conduct research themselves. The other groups reported similar percentages with the exception of the Research interest section for which the percentages were at least 10 points higher than the other groups in all categories. It is not surprising that about 98 percent of the Research interest section reported doing their own research. It appears that, if any group is likely to contain a very high proportion of researchers, it is the Research interest section – followed to a lesser degree by the Applied Linguistics interest section. However, it is clear from these results that research of one sort or another is conducted by many members in various parts of the organization.

Table 4.27 (Table 7 in the original report) begins the reporting of the repondents' answers with the average ratings for two TESOL publications, *TESOL Quarterly* and *TESOL Matters* (results for the main sections of the *TESOL Quarterly* are also reported separately). Notice that the questions were Likert-scale questions, and the results are summarized as average Likert-scale ratings.

Following is what we said about Table 4.27 in the original report.

In general, Table 7 [Table 4.27 here] indicates that the ratings for the *TESOL Quarterly* components averaged 3.3 to 4.3 on a five-point scale (1–5). However, there were several exceptions. Statistical Research Articles were rated lower by the General Membership as well as by the Higher Education and Teacher Education interest sections with averages ranging from 2.3 to 2.8. In contrast, such articles were rated 4.1 on average by the Research interest section and 3.3 by Applied Linguistics. At the same time, the Research interest section rated *TESOL Matters* somewhat lower than the other groups with an average of 3.1.

Note that the other tables in the original report give statistics similar to those in the tables already shown here.

First rotating example: Analyzing survey data using means comparisons

Sasaki (1996) examined the differences between teacher preferences in student classroom behaviors and their perceptions of those behaviors. To do so, she administered a questionnaire containing 25 five-point Likert-scale questions (see the second column of Table 4.28 for abbreviated versions of these questions; they took the form *Never* = 1 to *Always* = 5). Notice that the table gives the questions, shows the number of respondents to each question (to account for missing data), shows the mean preferences, shows the mean perceptions, and their difference, along with the associated *t*-test, the statistical significance of which is indicated by the presence or absence of an asterisk, which references $*p < .0001$ just below the table and to the left. It would have been helpful if, in addition to the means, Sasaki had reported the standard deviations for each question in both the teacher preferences and teacher perceptions questionnaires.

Notice how the table is laid out so that it can be clearly understood. Also note that she was able to show that all but two of the mean differences were statistically significant. But, why did she choose to set here alpha level so low ($p < .0001$)? Doesn't that limit the possibilities of her finding a significant difference? Yes, it does, but she did so for a specific reason, which is explained in the following quotation:

A multivariate analysis of variance (MANOVA) was performed on the Tperc and Tperf data. . . . Pillais, Hotellings and Wilks (PHW) indicated a multivariate significant difference at $p < .0001$. . . . Twenty-five paired *t*-tests were used to compare means of TPerf and Tperc. A Bonferroni adjustment to the alpha level of .05 was made to avoid Type II errors [she should have said Type I errors, that is, finding a significant difference, which is, in fact, spurious]. The resulting alpha value of .002 was determined by dividing .05 by 25. TPerf and Tperc were found to be significantly different ($p < .0001$) on 23 of the 25 items (Sasaki, 1996, p. 232).

Note that the MANOVA referred to by Sasaki in the previous quotation is not covered in this book. MANOVA procedures are most effectively used along with the Bonferroni adjustment to doubly ensure that you correctly interpret the p values from multiple *t*-tests. Unfortunately, explaining MANOVA is well beyond the scope of this book. For further explanations, see Tabachnick and Fidell (1996).

TABLE 4.28. MEANS COMPARISONS

#	Student behavior	n	Teacher preferences	Teacher perceptions	Difference	t
1	Volunteer to answer teacher's questions	79	4.55	2.19	2.36	21.08*
2	Readily volunteer to share opinions	76	4.41	1.91	2.50	24.32*
3	Seek clarification from teacher	80	4.73	2.35	2.38	23.83*
4	Verbally indicate not understanding	81	4.61	2.31	2.30	21.36*
5	Wait to be called on before speaking	79	2.36	4.20	-1.84	13.39*
6	Listen quietly when teacher speaks	79	4.48	3.87	0.61	6.56*
7	Listen quietly to classmates	78	4.76	3.28	1.48	13.15*
8	Do assigned homework	78	4.83	3.54	1.29	15.09*
9	Arrive over 15 minutes tardy	73	1.48	2.41	-0.93	8.38*
10	Speak audibly in English	79	4.81	3.33	1.48	15.18*
11	Respond to teacher without consulting with others first	77	4.23	3.05	1.18	8.07*
12	Take risks, are unafraid to make mistakes	79	4.50	2.51	1.99	18.25*
13	Try to use English as much as possible	78	4.73	2.56	2.17	17.20*
14	Ask teacher for help	80	4.38	2.74	1.64	14.16*
15	Mimic what teacher says or does	71	2.83	2.36	0.47	3.10
16	Avoid sitting in front rows	68	1.80	3.49	-1.69	8.79*
17	Resist working with students other than friends	72	1.63	2.61	-0.98	7.42*
18	Respond to teacher spontaneously	75	4.38	2.53	1.85	16.61*
19	More comfortable with structured tasks than loosely structured ones	63	2.68	3.68	-1.00	6.12*
20	Relaxed when teacher monitors	74	4.33	3.41	0.92	8.47*
21	Show nonverbal signs of not understanding	79	3.62	3.15	0.47	3.43
22	Make needs in classroom clear	78	4.37	1.86	2.51	21.06*
23	Rely more on classmates for instruction than teacher	76	2.42	3.41	-0.99	7.50*
24	Initiate interaction with teacher in English	80	4.40	2.71	1.69	15.32*
25	Early finishers extend in-class practice activities	73	4.38	2.10	2.28	17.58*

* p < .0001.
Source: Adapted from Sasaki, 1996, Tables 1 and 2.

In the running example given earlier, I provided an example of how chi-square analysis can be used in analyzing survey data, and in this section I showed Sasaki's (1996) strategy for comparing means using MANOVA, multiple *t*-tests, and Bonferroni adjustments. You will see in the next example one way that correlational analysis can be used and several ways that reliability and validity can be handled.

Second rotating example: Analyzing survey data using correlation and factor analyses

The second rotating example in this chapter is a survey conducted in Brazil to investigate the relationship between various types of motivation (as measured on a version of the MSLQ that we translated into Portuguese and called the QEMA) and overall English language proficiency as measured by a cloze test. The following subscales were part of the original MSLQ and hence subscales on the QEMA as well:

Motivation section	*35 items*
Value components	
Intrinsic goal orientation	(4 items)
Extrinsic goal orientation	(4 items)
Task value	(6 items)
Expectancy components	
Control beliefs	(8 items)
Self-efficacy	(5 items)
Expectancy for success	(3 items)
Affective components	
Test anxiety	(5 items)
Learning strategies section	*50 items*
Cognitive strategies	
Rehearsal strategies	(4 items)
Elaboration strategies	(6 items)
Organization strategies	(4 items)
Critical thinking strategies	(5 items)
Metacognitive strategies	(12 items)

Table 4.29 shows the descriptive statistics from Brown et al. (in press) Notice that the first column contains labels for the various subscales and the second column gives the number of participants (*N*), which is the same (*N* = 89) on all 16 subscales and the cloze. The third column indicates the number of questions (*k*) involved in each subscale, and the successive columns give the mean (*M*), standard deviation (SD), minimum (Min) or lowest answer given, maximum (Max) answer given, median (Mdn), mode, and skew statistics. All of those statistics were explained earlier in the chapter, so I will not dwell on them here, except to say that TASK, SELF, and EXPT appear to be somewhat negatively skewed as indicated

TABLE 4.29. DESCRIPTIVE STATISTICS

	N	k	M	SD	Min	Max	Mdn	Mode	Skew
INTR	89	4	5.41	1.04	2.25	7.00	5.50	6.00	−0.78
EXTR	89	4	3.86	1.37	1.00	6.75	4.00	4.25	−0.22
TASK	89	6	6.16	0.90	2.50	7.00	6.50	7.00	−1.86
CONT	89	8	4.09	0.70	2.50	6.25	4.00	4.00	−0.06
SELF	89	5	5.57	1.05	1.40	7.00	5.80	6.20	−1.15
EXPT	89	3	5.61	0.92	3.00	7.00	5.67	6.00	−1.04
TEST	89	5	3.27	1.15	1.00	6.20	3.20	3.80	−0.03
REHR	89	4	4.99	1.34	1.75	7.00	5.25	4.25	−0.45
ELAB	89	6	5.38	1.07	2.00	6.83	5.50	6.67	−0.95
ORGS	89	4	5.49	1.24	1.50	7.00	5.75	7.00	−0.97
CRIT	89	5	5.08	1.19	1.60	7.00	5.20	5.00	−0.56
META	89	12	4.58	0.89	2.25	6.33	4.75	3.17	−0.47
TIME	89	8	4.89	0.68	2.88	6.25	5.00	5.25	−0.75
EFFT	89	4	3.51	0.88	1.50	5.50	3.75	3.75	−0.37
PEER	89	3	3.01	1.41	1.00	6.00	3.00	1.00	0.17
HELP	89	4	4.98	1.07	2.00	7.00	5.25	5.50	−0.62
CLOZE	89	50	16.31	5.80	1.00	31.00	17.00	14.00	−0.08

Source: From Brown et al., in press.

by the skew statistic (over 1.00 in a negative direction) and the relationships among their mean, mode, median, and standard deviations.

Table 4.30 gives a variety of different reliability estimates for the subscales on the QEMA and for the cloze test used in this study. Notice that the first column again contains labels for the various subscales and that the authors consistently used these labels in exactly the same order in all of their tables (Tables 4.29 to 4.33 in this chapter) to help their readers interpret the tables more easily. Notice also that the second column once again gives the number of questions (*k*) in each subscale and the cloze. This information is provided here even though it was shown in the previous table because, all other factors held constant, as the number of questions on a scale increases, so does the reliability of that scale. Thus, differences in the reliability of scales may be due to actual variations in reliability or to simple differences in the numbers of questions. Hence, interpreting the relative reliability of various subscales on a survey instrument must always be done with the relative numbers of questions in mind.

In the third column of Table 4.30, the authors also give the reliability estimates (Cronbach alpha estimates in all cases shown here) reported by original authors of the MSLQ (some of which were not provided as indicated by the NG, or not given). Then, they provide the reliability estimates for their own QEMA version of questionnaire. Notice that the reliabilities

TABLE 4.30. SUBSCALE AND CLOZE RELIABILITIES

Variable	k	MSLQ ALPHA	QEMA ALPHA	S-B (k = 12)	S-B (k = 50)	SEM
INTR	4	0.71	0.55	0.79	0.94	0.70
EXTR	4	NG	0.59	0.81	0.95	0.76
TASK	6	0.91	0.79	0.88	0.97	0.44
CONT	8	NG	0.38	0.48	0.79	0.53
SELF	5	0.89	0.82	0.92	0.98	0.45
EXPT	3	NG	0.67	0.89	0.95	0.53
TEST	5	0.82	0.45	0.67	0.89	0.86
REHR	4	0.65	0.61	0.82	0.95	0.86
ELAB	6	0.75	0.68	0.81	0.95	0.63
ORGS	4	0.73	0.66	0.85	0.96	0.74
CRIT	5	0.83	0.78	0.90	0.97	0.63
META	12	0.83	0.79	0.79	0.94	0.47
TIME	8	0.82	0.58	0.67	0.90	0.60
EFFT	4	0.70	0.43	0.70	0.91	0.93
PEER	3	NG	0.60	0.86	0.96	0.91
HELP	4	0.70	0.42	0.68	0.90	0.97
CLOZE	50	—	0.79	0.35	0.79	2.67

NG = not given in the manual for the original MSLQ.
Source: From Brown et al., in press.

for the QEMA are consistently lower than those reported for the original MSLQ, which may be due to more homogeneity in the answers of the Brazilian students (that is, more homogeneous motivations in this population) or to more errors (for instance, more students not taking the questionnaire seriously and answering more or less randomly). Knowing for sure what causes such unreliability is impossible. However, knowing the degree of reliability is possible. So, for instance, as explained earlier in the chapter, the .55 Cronbach alpha estimate given for INTR means that that scale is 55% reliable and by extension 45% unreliable (100% − 55% = 45%).

In addition, notice that, using a statistic called the Spearman-Brown Prophecy formula (for a full explanation, see Brown, 1996, pp. 195, 204–205), the authors illustrate in Table 4.30 what the reliabilities of the subscales would be if those reliability estimates were adjusted for differences in the numbers of questions. The fifth column shows what the reliabilities would be if all the subscales had 12 questions, and the sixth column shows what the reliabilities would be if all the subscales had 50 questions. Notice that, with the exceptions of CONT and TEST, all of the subscales have respectable reliability when such an adjustment is made. Thus, the authors argue, when subscale length (in terms of numbers of questions) is controlled, it appears that differences in reliability largely disappear. Conversely, differences in reliability appear to be accounted for largely by the differences in numbers of questions in the various subscales.

The last column of Table 4.30 shows the standard error of measurement (SEM) for each scale. This statistic provides a band of scores (plus and minus one SEM) within which participants' answers can be expected to vary about 68 percent of the time; their answers can also be expected to vary two SEMs plus and minus about 95 percent of the time. Thus, for the INTR, which has a SEM of 0.70, a participant answering with an average of 4.30 on that subscale could be expected to answer between 5.00 (4.30 + 0.70 = 5.00) and 3.60 (4.30 – 0.70 = 3.60) 68 percent of the time if they were hypothetically made to answer this questionnaire repeatedly. That is quite a large band of variation for such a scale and is due to its relative unreliability ($\alpha = .55$). Thus, this statistic provides some idea of what the reliability of a subscale means in terms of how many points of variation the researchers would expect due to random error if the scale were administered repeatedly.

Table 4.31 shows the correlation coefficients for each subscale and the cloze with all others. Notice that the rows are labeled in the leftmost column and that the columns are labeled at the bottom. Note also that there is a series of 1.00s running diagonally across and down the table. These numbers are cleverly referred to as **the diagonal,** and they simply show the place where the correlation of each variable with itself is 1.00. Basically, the diagonal helps the readers orient themselves in reading such a table. Consider one example: in the upper left corner, the .22 indicates that EXTR and INTR are correlated at .22. One more example: The .52 just below the previous example indicates that TASK and INTR are correlated at .52. The fact that there is an asterisk next to a particular coefficient indicates that it is significant at $p < .05$.

Table 4.32 shows the same correlation coefficients in the same way. However, this time, a **correction for attenuation** was applied, which means that the correlation coefficients were adjusted to eliminate the unreliable variance in one or the other of the scales, or both. In this particular study, the adjustment was made for both. The adjustment is relatively easy, as shown in the following three formulas.

The correction for attenuation (unreliability) in scales X and Y:

$$r_{\substack{\text{corrected} \\ \text{for } X \& Y}} = \frac{r_{xy}}{\sqrt{(r_{xx'})(r_{yy'})}}$$

where $r_{\substack{\text{corrected} \\ \text{for } X \& Y}}$ = coefficient corrected for unreliability in variables X and Y

TABLE 4.3I. INTERCORRELATIONS OF ALL SUBSCALES AND CLOZE

	INTR	EXTR	TASK	CONT	SELF	EXPT	TEST	REHR	ELAB	ORGS	CRIT	META	TIME	EFFT	PEER	HELP
INTR	1.00															
EXTR	.22*	1.00														
TASK	.52*	.40*	1.00													
CONT	.35*	.16	.01	1.00												
SELF	.25*	.19	.32*	.08	1.00											
EXPT	.39*	.32*	.45*	.23*	.65*	1.00										
TEST	-.10	.14	-.20	.08	-.23*	-.22*	1.00									
REHR	.12	.25*	.16	.14	-.02	-.07	.16	1.00								
ELAB	.34*	.14	.39*	-.02	.36*	.28	.01	.36*	1.00							
ORGS	.34*	.19	.33*	.06	.15	.10	.08	.49*	.64*	1.00						
CRIT	.48*	.07	.23*	.10	.27*	.34*	-.11	.31*	.65*	.59*	1.00					
META	.53*	.25*	.37*	.18	.22*	.19	-.06	.53*	.63*	.58*	.72*	1.00				
TIME	.37*	.14	.33*	.09	.12	.32*	-.08	.41*	.43*	.42*	.36*	.51*	1.00			
EFFT	.25*	.35*	.40*	.09	.23*	-.12	.05	.28*	.43*	.49*	.31*	.43*	.51*	1.00		
PEER	.07	.30*	-.01	.16	-.13	.12	.16	.35*	.08	.19	.14	.33*	.04	.10	1.00	
HELP	.19	.22*	.13	.12	.07	.19	.23*	.37*	.32*	.31*	.31*	.39*	.20*	.26*	.44*	1.00
CLOZ	.30*	.05	.23*	.11	.19	.22*	-.15	.07	.29*	.20	.20	.34*	.31*	.15	-.04	-.10

$p < .05$.

Source: From Brown et al., in press.

TABLE 4.32. INTERCORRELATIONS OF ALL SUBSCALES AND CLOZE (CORRECTED FOR ATTENUATION)

	INTR	EXTR	TASK	CONT	SELF	EXPT	TEST	REHR	ELAB	ORGS	CRIT	META	TIME	EFFT	PEER	HELP
INTR	1.00															
EXTR	.38	1.00														
TASK	.79	.59	1.00													
CONT	.77	.34	.01	1.00												
SELF	.37	.28	.40	.15	1.00											
EXPT	.64	.51	.62	.45	.87	1.00										
TEST	-.21	-.28	-.34	.20	-.38	-.39	1.00									
REHR	.20	.41	.23	.30	-.02	-.11	.30	1.00								
ELAB	.56	.22	.53	-.04	.48	.41	.01	.56	1.00							
ORGS	.57	.30	.45	.12	.20	.15	.14	.78	.96	1.00						
CRIT	.72	.10	.30	.18	.33	.47	-.19	.45	.89	.82	1.00					
META	.80	.36	.47	.34	.28	.27	-.10	.76	.87	.80	.91	1.00				
TIME	.65	.24	.49	.19	.17	.51	-.15	.69	.68	.67	.53	.76	1.00			
EFFT	.52	.69	.69	.23	.39	-.23	.11	.55	.79	.93	.53	.74	.99	1.00		
PEER	.12	.50	-.01	.34	-.19	.19	.31	.58	.13	.31	.21	.48	.07	.20	1.00	
HELP	.39	.43	.23	.31	.12	.35	.53	.73	.60	.59	.54	.68	.40	.62	.88	1.00
CLOZ	.46	.08	.29	.20	.23	.30	-.26	.10	.39	.28	.25	.43	.46	.25	-.06	-.17

Source: From Brown et al., in press.

r_{xy} = correlation coefficient between variables X and Y

$r_{xx'}$ = reliability of variable X

$r_{yy'}$ = reliability of variable Y

For example, the correlation between INTR and TASK is .52 as reported in Table 4.31, and as shown in Table 4.30, the Cronbach alpha reliabilities for the INTR and TASK on the QEMA were .55 and .79, respectively. In order to correct for attenuation in both measures, the attenuation equation above would be applied as follows:

$$r_{\substack{\text{corrected} \\ \text{for } X\&Y}} = \frac{r_{xy}}{\sqrt{(r_{xx'})(r_{yy'})}} = \frac{.52}{\sqrt{(.55)(.79)}} = \frac{.52}{\sqrt{.4345}} = \frac{.52}{.6591661}$$

$$= .7888755 \approx .79$$

And, you will note that .79 is the result shown in Table 4.33 for the correlation between INTR and TASK corrected for attenuation in both measures.

To correct for attenuation in only one of the measures (X or Y), but not both, only the square root of the reliability of that measure would go in the denominator. Thus correcting for attenuation only in INTR (the X variable in this case) would be as follows:

$$r_{\substack{\text{corrected} \\ \text{for } X}} = \frac{r_{xy}}{\sqrt{r_{xx'}}} = \frac{.52}{\sqrt{.55}} = \frac{.52}{.7416198} = .7011679 \approx .70$$

And, correcting for attenuation only in TASK (the Y variable in this case) would be as follows:

$$r_{\substack{\text{corrected} \\ \text{for } Y}} = \frac{r_{xy}}{\sqrt{r_{yy'}}} = \frac{.52}{\sqrt{.79}} = \frac{.52}{.8888194} = .5850457 \approx .59$$

Table 4.33 presents the results of a factor analysis (after a VARIMAX rotation). The clearest results in that analysis are for the Cognitive section of the survey, where all five of the subscales loaded above .30 (a traditional cut-point) on Factor 1, as indicated by the asterisks. One variation is found in the REHR subscale, which also loaded on Factor 3 at .52.

The results for the Management section are almost as clear because three of the four subscales loaded most highly on Factor 3. However, the TIME subscale loaded most highly on Factor 1. Hence, the TIME subscale appears to be more closely related to Factor 1 and the subscales on the Cognitive section than the other subscales of Management. Since the HELP subscale also loaded above .30 on factors 1, 2, and 3, this subscale may not be as unique and discrete as the original authors thought when

TABLE 4.33. VARIMAX ROTATION OF THE FOUR-FACTOR SOLUTION

	Factor				
Variable	*1*	*2*	*3*	*4*	*h²*
Motivation					
INTR	.47*	.39*	−.09	.51*	.64
EXTR	−.00	.64*	.57*	.01	.73
TASK	.31*	.73*	−.00	−.09	.64
CONT	.00	.06	.19	.87*	.80
SELF	.12	.69*	−.27	.05	.57
EXPT	.12	.77*	−.14	.33	.74
TEST	−.07	−.22	.59*	−.04	.40
Cognitive					
REHR	.55*	−.06	.52*	−.03	.58
ELAB	.79*	.27	.00	−.15	.72
ORGS	.78*	.11	.23	−.11	.69
CRIT	.82*	.13	−.10	.18	.73
META	.82*	.03	.22	.25	.78
Management					
TIME	.62*	.22	−.20	.12	.49
EFFT	−.10	−.14	.54*	.02	.32
PEER	.18	.00	.61*	.26	.47
HELP	.40*	.31*	.62*	.04	.64
Proportion of variance	*.24*	*.16*	*.14*	*.08*	*.62*

*Loadings above .30.
Source: From Brown et al., in press.

the instrument was designed, or alternatively, something may have been lost in the translation into Portuguese.

Five of the seven component subscales of the Motivation section loaded above .30 on Factor 2. However, one of these component subscales (TEST) loaded most heavily on Factor 3 and hence may be more highly related to the Management section than to the Motivation section. Furthermore, the INTR and CONT subscales loaded most heavily on another, entirely different, fourth factor. Finally, the INTR and TASK loaded above .30 on Factor 1, which probably indicates that these two scales were also related to the Cognitive section. In short, five of the seven subscales of the Motivation section loaded on Factor 2, but the patterns of additional loadings above .30 made the results for the Motivation section more difficult to interpret than the other two sections of the QEMA version of the MSLQ.

However, in general, the loadings for motivation are predominantly on Factor 2, the loadings for the Cognitive section are almost exclusively on Factor 1, and the loadings for Management are predominantly on Factor 3. Thus these analyses provide some evidence for the validity of these subscales. The results also indicate subscales that might profitably be modified to better fit the model implied by the subscales of the survey and their organization.

Summary

In this chapter, I showed a number of ways to analyze survey data statistically. I began by explaining the calculation and interpretation of descriptive statistics, including frequencies and percentages, graphical display of data, symmetrical and skewed distributions, as well as statistics of central tendency (the mean, mode, and median) and dispersion (range, low–high, and standard deviation). Next, I explained strategies for calculating and interpreting statistical tests for examining the correlation of two sets of numbers, comparing the means of different groups in a set of results, and comparing frequencies to expected frequencies. Then, I explored some of the available techniques for estimating the reliability of your survey instruments statistically. After reliability, I covered some of the approaches available for exploring and defending the validity of your instruments (including content, criterion-related, construct, and decision validity arguments). As usual, I ended the chapter with examples. In the running example, I described the use of descriptive statistics to analyze the TESOL research survey. I also presented two running examples: In the rotating example from Sasaki (1996), I focused on analyzing survey data by making means comparisons and, in the rotating example from Brown et al. (in press), I showed how survey data can be analyzed using correlation and factor analysis techniques.

Suggestions for further reading

Many hundreds of books have been written over the years on statistics and statistical applications in education and psychology. Some books have even focused on statistical methods for language researchers. Naturally, I recommend Brown (1988) if you are interested in developing your skills in critically reading statistical language studies. However, for conducting statistical language research and analyzing the results, I recommend Hatch and Lazaraton (1991). One text, Fink (1995b), focuses on the research designs available to survey researchers. Another, Jacoby (1997) emphasizes techniques for developing effective graphs. One other book, Fink (1995e), explains simple statistical analyses for survey data in general. Litwin (1995) and Fowler and Mangione (1993) take different approaches to the issues of survey reliability and validity. Other books focus on secondary analysis of survey data (Kieholt & Nathan, 1985), study of complex survey data (Lee, Forthofer, & Lorimor, 1989), or examination of repeated surveys (Firebaugh, 1997). For much more depth on many different types of statistical analyses suitable for survey research, see the collection of articles by Rossi, Wright, and Anderson (1983).

Important terms

agreement
agreement coefficient
alpha decision level (α)
alpha level (α)
bar graph
bimodal (distribution)
biserial coefficient
Bonferroni adjustment
central tendency
column graph
communalities (h^2)
concurrent criterion-related validity
construct validity
content validity
convergent validity
convergent/discriminant validity
  studies
correction for attenuation
correlation
correlation coefficient
criterion-related validity
critical value
Cronbach alpha (α)
curvilinear relationship
decision validity
descriptive statistics
the diagonal
differential-groups validity studies
discriminate validity
dispersion
distribution
donut graph
eigenvalues
equivalent-surveys method
error variance
experts
face validity

factor analysis
frequencies
frequency comparison statistics
independence
independent
independent *t*-test
internal-consistency method
intervention validity studies
linearity
linear relationship
loadings
low–high
marginals
mean
means comparison statistics
mean function
median
median function
mode
mode function
multitrait-multimethod (M-M)
  strategy
negatively skewed (distribution)
n-way χ^2 designs
one-tailed decision
one-way χ^2 designs
paired
paired *t*-test
Pearson product–moment correlation coefficient
percentages
percent of agreement
phi coefficient (φ)
pie chart
point-biserial correlation coefficient
positively skewed (distribution)
predictive criterion-related validity

principal components analysis	statistical tests
range	survey reliability
raw frequencies	survey validity
reliability	symmetrical (distribution)
repeated-surveys method	tetrachoric coefficient
scatterplot	3-D bar graph
skewed (distribution)	3-D pie chart
social consequences in decision validity	t-test
	two-tailed decision
Spearman rho (ρ) correlation coefficient	two-way χ^2 designs
	validity
standard deviation (SD)	value implications in decision
statistical significance	validity

Review questions

1. What are frequencies and percentages? How are they different?
2. What are at least five different ways to display numerical data graphically?
3. What are symmetrical and skewed distributions?
4. How do you calculate (by hand or in a spreadsheet) and interpret the three indicators of central tendency (the mean, mode, and median)?
5. How do you calculate (by hand or in a spreadsheet) and interpret the three indicators of dispersion (range, low–high, and standard deviation)?
6. How do you calculate (by hand or in a spreadsheet) and interpret the correlation of two sets of numbers?
7. How do you calculate (by hand or in a spreadsheet) and interpret differences between the means of different groups in a set of results?
8. How do you calculate (by hand or in a spreadsheet) and interpret differences between frequencies and expected frequencies?
9. What is survey reliability? What are repeated-surveys, equivalent-surveys, and internal consistency reliability, and how can they be estimated?
10. What is survey validity? What are face, content, construct, and criterion-related validity, and how can they be assessed? Why is decision validity important in terms of value implications and social consequences?

Application exercises

A. Read the following description of a beginning plan for a study.

The purpose of this survey study is to assess the French language learning and situation needs of American students who will arrive in August in France for a year of study at various universities throughout the country. They will all be together in Paris for one month of intensive training in language and culture. You plan to do some interviews with students who went through last year's program and then studied for one year in French universities. Then, you plan to mail a questionnaire out to all the students who participated last year and another questionnaire to those students who will participate in the coming August. You plan for the questionnaire to include at least 75 percent closed-response questions.

1. Who in addition to the students, might you want to interview?
2. How will you maximize the return rate on your mail questionnaire?
3. How will you code the quantitative data so they can most easily be analyzed?
4. What descriptive statistics will you calculate? What correlational statistics? Means comparisons statistics? Frequency comparisons statistics?
5. What graphical displays might prove useful in explaining your results to others?

B. Imagine a quantitative survey study of any kind at your institution. Sketch out the purpose, participants, and methods that you will use to conduct the study. What kinds of statistical analyses will you use in conducting this study? What steps will you take to maximize the reliability and validity of your questionnaires and the study as a whole? How will you investigate the reliability and validity of your instruments?

C. Plan a survey research study of your own for your own purposes. Be sure to include some quantitative and qualitative data. What is your purpose? Overall, what steps will you follow? How will you gather, code, and analyze the data? In particular, what strategies will you use to ensure the reliability and validity of your instruments, and how will you study their reliability and validity? Better yet, actually conduct this study, and calculate and interpret all necessary statistics.

5 Analyzing survey data qualitatively

As with the statistical analyses discussed in Chapter 4, the purpose of conducting qualitative analyses is to find interesting and useful patterns in your data. In this chapter, however, the concern is with patterns in your qualitative data. Qualitative data are not just those that cannot be quantified. Indeed, qualitative data can and should sometimes be quantified (for example, see Taylor's 1983 chapter on analyzing qualitative data). According to Lynch (1997), qualitative data can be gathered in many ways, including observations, journals, logs, retrospective narratives, document analyses, interviews, and questionnaires. For the purposes of this book, **qualitative survey data** will be the focus of this discussion, and they will be defined as all of the information that comes from the open-response questions on interviews and questionnaires (as discussed at length in Chapter 2). As Lynch (1992, p. 75) put it:

Questionnaires are not always considered sources of *qualitative* data. Especially when the questionnaires are to be answered on some sort of a rank-ordered scale, the researcher is obviously forcing the data into pre-existing categories. However, when the questions are general and open-ended enough, the resulting data begin to resemble what people actually say in response to such questions in interviews [in his view, interviews provide qualitative data, pp. 74–75].

According to Glesne and Peshkin (1992, p. 127), **qualitative data analysis** "involves organizing what you have seen, heard, and read so that you can make sense of what you have learned. Working with the data, you create explanations, pose hypotheses, develop theories, and link your story to other stories. To do so, you must categorize, synthesize, search for patterns and interpret the data you have collected." Bogdan and Biklen (1997) characterize qualitative data analysis as "the process of systematically searching and arranging the interview transcripts, field notes, and other materials that you accumulate to increase your own understanding of them and to enable you to present what you have discovered to others" (p. 145). Naturally, in this book, qualitative data analysis will refer exclusively to **qualitative survey data analysis,** which is the process of systematically searching and arranging the answers to open-ended survey questions (that is, questions in interviews or on questionnaires).

Analyzing qualitative data and doing qualitative research in general are providing increasingly important tools for researchers to use. The qualitative techniques explained in this chapter should be the tools of choice in some cases, whereas quantitative procedures may be more appropriate in other cases. Perhaps the best approach in still other cases will be to combine qualitative and quantitative methods (see, for instance, Lynch, 1992, 1997, or the three studies cited by Lazaraton, 1995, p. 464, as combining qualitative and quantitative methods: Jacob, 1982; Johnson, 1987; and Lazaraton & Saville, 1994). Generally speaking, researchers should select their approach based on the purpose of their study (Lazaraton, 1995, p. 467). Unfortunately, I suspect that many researchers select their approach based more on their training than on the purpose of their study. Indeed, much of my early work relied almost exclusively on quantitative methods, but beginning with Brown and Bailey (1984), I learned from my research partner the value of using at least some qualitative techniques. In all cases, where I have employed qualitative data along with my quantitative results, I have been better able to understand the numerical (quantitative) results based on the non-numerical (qualitative). So, similar to the advice I gave in Chapter 2 for open-response and closed-response question formats, I advise you to use both qualitative and quantitative research methods whenever possible, because both methodologies can serve useful, different, and complementary purposes in any given survey project.

Huberman and Miles (1994, pp. 428–429) divide qualitative data analysis into three subordinate processes and argue that all three of these subordinate processes should be occurring before, during, and after data collection. The three subordinate processes, which will serve as primary organizing headings of this chapter, are (1) data reduction, (2) data display, and (3) conclusion drawing and verification. Other major topics that will be covered in this chapter include methods for estimating the reliability of qualitative survey data and guidelines for qualitative studies.

Data reduction

Data reduction is the process whereby the huge universe of all possible data is reduced in advance to manageable dimensions by choices that the researcher makes in terms of "conceptual framework, research questions, cases, and instruments" (Huberman & Miles, 1994, p. 429). All researchers inevitably make choices in setting up their studies that reduce the proportions of the data. They do so to save time, energy, and resources. In quantitative analyses, one common choice, for instance, is to randomly select, say, 100 participants from a pool of 1,000 available students in the whole population, in order to save time, energy, and resources.

Similarly, in all types of survey research, choices are made, as discussed in previous chapters, that can help to reduce the dimensions of the work involved: (1) the number and types of conceptual frameworks involved, (2) the number and types of respondents sampled, (3) the number and types of instruments used, (4) the number and complexity of the research questions addressed, (5) the number and types of analyses attempted, (6) the length of the research report, and so forth. Even within a particular survey instrument, something as simple as deciding on the ratio of open-response to closed-response questions (or the number and types of open-response questions to include) may make a big difference in the amount of work involved in the project as a whole.

For example, you can choose to use a shotgun approach by asking a number of general open-response questions that will help you find your way through the data and figure out what the important questions and issues are. That is a perfectly legitimate choice, but you must recognize that making such a choice may limit the number of responses you get back and will inevitably mean a great deal of work carefully combing through the large amounts of data to find useful and informative patterns. Sometimes this approach is preferable, especially if you want to keep the possibilities wide open for what you will find. This approach will certainly be preferable if the primary purpose of your survey project is **hypothesis-forming research** – that is, you start out without research questions and you want to find out, in the process of doing your research, what the pertinent issues, research questions, and/or hypotheses are.

Alternatively, you may feel that you already know what the relevant issues are, in which case you may be able to limit the amount of data necessary by carefully choosing your research questions and/or hypotheses. You may also choose to invest more effort at the beginning of your survey project and carefully plan a small number of precisely aimed and pertinent open-response questions. In such a case, you may have saved yourself a great deal of work later in the project, when you are analyzing the data. This too is a perfectly legitimate choice, but here you must recognize that making such a choice may limit the possibilities for what you will ultimately find. Sometimes this approach is preferable, especially if you know what the issues are and do not mind narrowing the possibilities for what you will find in your data. This approach will also be preferable if the primary purpose of your survey project is **hypothesis-confirming research** – that is, you start out with research questions and/or hypotheses that you want to confirm or test.

As with so many choices that we make in our work, and indeed in our lives generally, there are clearly trade-offs involved in data reduction. Thus, before making such choices, it is important to think carefully through the purposes of your research and then why, how, and how much you want to reduce your data. Much of the information you need for making those choices appears elsewhere in this book.

Data display

Researchers inevitably need to display their data in various ways so they can analyze and synthesize the information. In previous chapters, I explained how quantitative survey data analysis involves entering the data into a spreadsheet. That is one way of displaying the data so you can begin to analyze them. Quantitative data analysis also involves using tables and graphical displays of various aspects of the data throughout the data analysis processes to help you understand the patterns.

Qualitative analyses rely on other means for displaying data. Qualitative **data display** is the systematized and summarized collection and sorting of data that makes possible "conclusion drawing and/or action taking" (Huberman & Miles, 1994, p. 429). For instance, you may need to transcribe your data in order to display your survey data in such a way that you can begin to analyze them. Another way of reducing and displaying the data is in matrices, which can also help you analyze and synthesize your data so that useful and informative patterns emerge. Transcribing data and using matrices will be primary topics of this main section. However, I will also consider some of the tools that can be applied by entering and analyzing your data on a computer.

Transcribing

Recall from Chapter 3 that the nature and purpose of open-response questions on a survey often results in transcribing the data obtained. **Transcribing** means making a copy, arrangement, or record of the data with the purpose of reducing the data to a form that can easily be stored, accessed, sorted, and analyzed. Briefly, the three steps discussed in Chapter 3 for this process were:

1. Determining the categories to be used in transcribing, which involves putting all the participants' answers for each question together and perhaps planning ahead far enough to sort and group the answers on the basis of your variables of interest before transcribing them. Note that, in qualitative analyses, it is also perfectly legitimate to start out with little idea in advance what categories might turn out to be of interest in your data.
2. Choosing a set of transcribing tools, which consists of choosing either a paper-and-pencil approach or a computer word processor approach (the latter having the distinct advantage of making lexical tallies, readability estimates, concordance analysis, and other analyses easily available).
3. Doing the actual transcribing, which involves (a) for handwritten data, deciding on whether you want to clean up the data as you enter them

or type them just as they are (the latter course of action is generally advised because an accurate record of the data can be very important and they can always be cleaned up later), and (b) for taped oral interview data, considering using a cassette player with a start/stop foot pedal so that you can control the machine while keeping your hands free to type the transcription.

Consider the possibilities if you are working with written answers to open-response questionnaire questions and you decide to transcribe your data the old-fashioned way, that is, using paper and pencil or a typewriter. It might prove useful in such a situation to write or type each person's response to each question on a separate card or sheet of paper. That way you can arrange and rearrange the cards, sort through them, consider groups of cards together, and so forth. If you know in advance the categories or groupings you want to analyze, you can sort the cards as you transcribe the data. If not, you may discover those categories or groupings while you are transcribing, or later by working with the cards. For taped oral data from open-response questions in a survey, you might decide to write or type the recorded comments on pieces of paper using the tape player's start/stop button (or foot pedal if you have such a machine) as best you can. Otherwise, the processes for entering oral data on cards or pieces of paper are exactly the same. The point is that you want to get the data together in one place, but in a flexible form that will allow you to organize and rearrange it as necessary for analysis.

Using matrices to analyze qualitative data

Once you have your qualitative data transcribed in a usable format, you may decide to use matrices to help you analyze them. **Matrices** in this sense are arrays or tables, usually in two dimensions, with one set of categories labeled across the top and another down the left-hand side and with data arranged or summarized in columns and rows that can help the researcher discern patterns in the data. You may end up trying more than one such matrix, or revising, rearranging, or changing the categories in the process of analyzing your qualitative data, before you settle on the matrix or matrices that best illustrate the patterns or conclusions that you have drawn from the data. If the data are entered using paper and pencil, you may choose to use the cards described in the previous section and sort them into columns and rows on a big table (or on the floor, as I used to do on my hands and knees). Alternatively, you might find it more useful to use the butcher-paper approach that I have seen other researchers use, whereby they sketch out categories and enter data using a pencil to write and erase as necessary for sorting, rearranging, and changing the matrix.

Lynch's (1992) study was an evaluation study:

... designed to investigate the two major approaches to program evaluation: quantitative, experimental (in the traditional sense of the term) evaluation and qualitative, naturalistic evaluation. The data came from the University of Guadalajara (UdeG)/University of California, Los Angeles (UCLA) Reading English for Science and Technology (REST) Project (p. 61).

Lynch showed matrices of two types for the qualitative analysis in his evaluation study. The first type of matrix he called an **effects matrix,** that is, a matrix used to describe various effects and processes in the data, as shown in Figure 5.1.[1] As Lynch pointed out, such a matrix does "not come with preordained means for interpretation as the quantitative analyses do" (p. 84). He chose to analyze the effects matrix in Figure 5.1 by scanning the data for three types of patterns (pp. 84–87): general patterns (for example, simply counting the plus and minus signs in the matrix indicates more negative factors in the process/methods column than in the objectives/goals column and an even higher proportion of negative factors in the relations/climate column); specific difference patterns (one of several examples cited by Lynch was the fact that the coordinator listed more positive factors than did the teachers/researchers in the process/method column, whereas the reverse was true in the objectives/goals column); and specific similarity patterns (one of several examples provided by Lynch is the use of authentic English texts in chemical engineering classes, which was listed as a positive idea by both students and teachers/researchers in the objectives/goals column).

The second type of matrix Lynch (1992, p. 87) labeled a site dynamics matrix, that is, a matrix used to try to uncover the underlying causes and dynamics of the effects and processes previously found in the effects matrix. The analysis of this dynamics matrix (shown in Figure 5.2) was at a somewhat higher level than the analysis of the effects matrix. As Lynch put it:

By the time the Site Dynamics Matrix ... has been filled in, a great deal of analysis and interpretation has already occurred. In order to determine the flow of entries across the rows of the matrix, the researcher must come to some understanding of the dynamics involved. This happens as a logical course of movement back and forth between the data and the matrix that the construction requires (p. 87).

Lynch chose to analyze the effects matrix in Figure 5.2 by scanning the data for two types of patterns (pp. 87–89): predominant outcomes (for

1 Defining some of the abbreviations in Figures 5.1 and 5.2 might help readers: UdeG Coord is the University of Guadalajara Coordinator; UdeG T/B Asst's appears to be the University of Guadalajara teaching/research assistants (where the *B* appears to be a typo; UCLA T/Rs are the University of California, Los Angeles teacher/researchers; and the four Ss Groups are different groups of students at three different levels.

As seen by	Objectives/goals	Process/methods	Relations/climate
UdeG Coord	+ A curriculum framework to improve Ss ability to read EST. - Ss did *not* 'master' anything just introduced to. - did *not* convince Ss that they don't need to read word-by-word.	+ Use grammar in context as a *strategy* for reading. + Use read. strat's, e.g., preview, prediction, skim, scan. + Teach functions of log. Connectors: rhetorical modes. + Use authentic Chem. E. texts, but *not* exclusively.	+ (Coord) overall positive to Project. + T/Ts hard workers - Cultural misunderstandings: T/Rs 'took it personally'. - Ss more demanding than most & 'a few bad apples'. - T/Rs did *not* get along well as a group.
UdeG T/B Asst's	+ Interesting curric: helpful to Ss.	+ Well supported mat'ls: prep'd well by UCLA - (REST) Too dependent on other Univ. Dept's - Problems w/ classrms and schedules - tedious classes; too much time spent on some points; excessive repetition - need to allow more talking & listening in English & expand grammar module.	+ Good attitude – all T/Rs. - lack of communication: T/R Assts - lack of understanding (UCLA T/Rs) of Mex. S behavior.
UCLA T/Rs	+ S confidence to 'attach' Engl. Texts + signif. improv't in gen. ESL prof., reading & grades in REST + Ss Chem. E. profs now expect them to read texts in Engl., w/o transla-tions, and do 'practicas' based on readings. + basic elements of a curriculum. + Lots of ideas and infor. For a thesis. - Not enough time for research. - Ss will *not* be 'prof. Readers' of EST in 2 years	+ Using texts as basis for grammar discuss. ++ Give Ss more basic linguistic skills. + Began to use more '4-skills' type activit's for reading. - Lack of mat'ls. - Lack of focus & organization. - Relied too much on theory: didn't know how to implement it. - A clum of strat's: did them w/ every text. - T/Rs hindered by need to all do same mat'ls same way, same rate.	++ UCLA support. ++ Some staff members dedicated. - Lack of UdeG admin. Support. - S resentment of Project & T/Rs. - REST staff 'not taken seriously or taken advantage of' ? Lack of cooperation between T/Rs (1 'yes', 2 'no') - Frustration

	– 'we didn't do enough for them'. – not able to give real training to Mexican T/Rs.	+ Use of the OHP. – Need a different system for understanding grammar. – At times, too much mat'l too fast: no time to take notes. + Read, strat's do help us w/reading.	– At times, we feel a little bored.
Ss Group B/Begin	+ Were able to use some Chem. E. texts (sugg'std by C.E. prof's) in their 'practicas' – helped them. + Now we can use the *strategies* taught. + Overall, course help us 'bastante'		
Ss Group B/Adv	+ Used texts (Engl.) in our 'practicas'.	+ Use of the OHP. – Read. *strat's* approach doesn't work: 'we look at articles but don't *read* them'. – Need a review of grammar. – Need more participation on part of Ss.	
Ss Group A/C Int.	+ Now we know how to form/write a sentence in Engl. – Nothing well-defined in the development of the course. – Very little covered first 1/2 year.	+ More grammar & vocab. (since Feb.) = "going in circles': same basic activities. – Reading strat's 'a waste of time': already known. – 'Timed' factor on tests unfair.	– 'boring' – Lack of attend.: because not what expected/wanted; i.e., '4-skills' & bad schedule for Engl. class.

Figure 5.1. Effects matrix: First-year outcomes of the UdeG/UCLA REST project (Lynch, 1992).

Dilemma/problem	Underlying themes	How coped with	Resolution/change
REST Curriculum not what Ss expected/wanted.	'Reading strategies approach' vs. traditional '4-skills'	Tried to 'win Ss over' to new appro; gradually moved to more grammar & vocab. While constantly recycling reading strategies; (at times a feeling of now knowing how to put theory into practice).	Curriculum change: Focus on 'grammar in context', 1st year (decision that Ss need a minimum level of English before taking advantage of reading strats).
REST Ss' EFL proficiency level: a wide range & many 'false beginners'.	Need for grammar before read strategies; relationship of linguistic knowledge to reading.	Divided classes into 2 levels of prof.; eventually levels (1st hour classes); TEAM TEACH-ING; use of Spanish in class.	Rethink curriculum in terms of 2 levels of prof.
Lack of classrooms – class sizes too large	Combined with 'prof. level' dilemma, above.	Pleaded for extra classrooms; tried to used group work and TEAM TEACHING to deal with size problems.	Given 1 extra room (Feb. '86); formed 3rd/'Int.' level (1st hr.); split one 'Team' to cover new class.
Lack of EFL prof. for most Ss makes use of Engl. for teaching reading strat's ineff; 2/3 of UCLA Ts are not capable of 'teaching in Spanish'.	Combines with innovative reading strats approach vs. grammar and relationship of ling. know. To reading; use of Engl. vs. Span. In the clssrm.	TEAM TEACHING (1 Nat. Span. Speaker in each class); Use of more Span. than Engl. to start with; move to use of more and more English.	UCLA Ts (non-nat. Span. speakers) became more confident of ability to use Span. in classrm. (by end of year); Ss became more confident about understanding Engl. in clssrm.
Lack of S attendance.	S motivation & attitude; cultural differ's btwn UCLA T/Rs and Ss.	Allow/ask Ss to change 'levels'; individual 'talks' w/Ss; formal rollcall; referral of Ss not attending to Academic Adv.; 'talks' with Ss and RESt coord's.	Creation of a grading policy that includes a 40% attend. & participation factor.

Bad relations between T/Rs and Ss; disc. problems in class	Interacts w/ attend. Prob. & S mot/att. & mismatch btwn. REST & S expectations; cultural diff's.	Seating Chart (1 class) separate 'problem Ss'; referral of Ss to Academic Ad; individual 'talks' T to S; 'talks' betwn. REST Coord's and Ss.	Grading policy (see above); some Ss petition to leave program; no real solution.
Lack of cooperation betwn T/Rs; tension; arguments	Group planning vs. indiv. plan; 'competition' brtwn. Teams & individuals.	Various group planning schemes. Individuals 'withdraw' from group; ignore/deny prob.; individual 'talks' with REST coords.	Change TEAM TEACH. by splitting one 'team' into 2 individual Ts/class (relates to 3rd classrm avail); Mexican T/R leaves Project; no real solution.
Cramped work/office space; lack of equip. & materials.	Lack of support from UdeG.	Reliance on extra help from UCLA; personal expend's; waiting for new work/office bldg.	No real solution; (new work/ office bldg. still under construction); increased depend. on UCLA and indep. from UdeG.

Figure 5.2. Site dynamics matrix: First year of curriculum development for the REST Project (Lynch, 1992).

example, in Figure 5.2, changes appear to be mostly in terms of procedures such as grading, teachers using more Spanish in class, dividing classes into levels, team teaching, and so forth); and repeating or overlapping elements (for example, the word *lack* repeats often in the data in the dilemma/problem column, including lack of classrooms, lack of EFL proficiency, lack of student attendance, lack of cooperation between teachers and students, and so forth).

To summarize a bit, the techniques Lynch used for interpreting his matrices were as follows: (1) scan for general patterns, (2) peruse the data for more specific difference patterns, (3) look for specific similarity patterns, (4) check for predominant outcomes, and (5) examine the data for repeating or overlapping elements.

Using computers to analyze qualitative data

If transcription is done using computer software, the resulting file(s) can readily be analyzed in a number of ways. The simplest of these forms of analysis, which for many people will not involve learning new computer skills, is to use your word processor for reading through the transcript and finding patterns. Once a potential pattern is noticed, the word processor search function, or search and replace function, may prove helpful in searching through the transcript. A **search function** is simply a series of keystrokes or icon/menu selections that allow you to use the computer to find a particular word or phrase. Say, for instance, that you notice the word *lack* coming up often in the transcript (as in the Lynch matrix shown in Figure 5.2). You could use the search function to help you locate each instance in which the word *lack* occurs. By reading what is said in each instance, you might begin to understand why it comes up so often, why it is important to the respondents, how different respondents feel differently about it, and so forth. Better yet, the search function is not limited to words, so you could equally well search for a recurring phrase, such as trust "in others" or "trust in me" if you find those recurring in interesting ways. Note that searches of this type can only be made for exact strings of letters. Thus, a search for "trust in others" will not reveal the phrase "trust in other people." As a consequence, you will have to think of such alternatives yourself as you go along.

You can also use a computer to do lexical counts that might prove useful. For instance, I sometimes use the RightWriter computer program (RightWriter, 1990) to calculate the readability of texts. Conveniently, RightWriter also provides a **lexical count,** which means that it can analyze a computer file and determine how many times each word occurs. The computer then generates an alphabetical list of all the words in the file along with the number of times each word appeared. Obviously, words such as *the, of, a, an,* and *on* all appear very frequently, and counts of these words are usually not very illuminating. However, it might turn out that the word *trust* came up 275 times in the responses of 400 people to a particular question. That would be useful information in its own right. After all, content words that occur often are probably salient or prominent in the data. Such a result would probably also lead you to use the search function in your word processor to see what people were saying about *trust*.

Another useful computer tool is known as a concordance. A **concordance** is a computer software tool that, in addition to listing occurrences of any words or phrases in which you may be interested in, can list them in a column straight down the middle of the computer screen while showing the context on each side of those occurrences so you can analyze what people are saying about the word or phrase. Thus, concordances have the distinct advantage of providing lists of words with immediate environment around the words displayed. One example of a concordance is MonoConc for Windows software (Barlow, 1998).

CHILDES (see, for instance, MacWhinney, 1995; Sokolov & Snow, 1994) and similar programs were specifically developed to allow you to code any feature you like within a transcript and then use those codes to analyze your data in a number of ways. For example, you could code all the instances of hesitant, impolite, and irritable responses in your transcript and code your respondents for gender and nationality. You could then use CHILDES to analyze the results. You might simply want to find the frequencies of occurrence for hesitant, impolite, and irritable responses, or you might want to break those frequencies down by gender, or by nationality, or by all combinations of gender and nationality. Programs like CHILDES involve a great deal of time coding and learning to use the program, so you should probably consider using such programs only when the transcripts are fairly large and detailed analyses with many variables and interactions of variables are of interest. CHILDES can be particularly useful if you intend to use the same data in a variety of different ways.

Conclusion drawing and verification

Conclusion drawing and verification involve interpreting and "drawing meaning from displayed data" (Huberman & Miles, 1994, p. 429). Authors writing about qualitative research often stress that a variety of tactics should be used iteratively to draw conclusions. Lynch (1992, p. 78) suggests that qualitative strategies should be iterative even as early as the coding process in a language program evaluation: "As with every stage of qualitative data collection and analysis, the coding of the data is an *iterative* process. . . . "

In addition, open and honest reporting of the procedures used for collecting data and conducting a study are important in qualitative research, just as they are in quantitative traditions. As Huberman and Miles (1994) put it:

The conventions of quantitative research require clear, explicit reporting of data and procedures. That is expected so that (a) the reader will be confident of, and can verify, reported conclusions; (b) secondary analysis of the data is possible; (c) the study could in principle be replicated; and (d) fraud or misconduct, if it exists, will be more trackable. There is an added internal need: keeping analytic strategies coherent, manageable, and repeatable as the study proceeds. That is, the reporting requirement encourages running documentation from the beginning. In our view, the same needs are present for qualitative studies, even if one takes a more interpretive stance (p. 439).

Even a cursory examination of the literature on qualitative research will indicate that issues analogous to the quantitative research concepts of reliability and validity are just as important in qualitative research as they are in quantitative research. Writers in qualitative research may use different terms, in fact, may even view the concepts of reliability and validity in a somewhat different light. Nonetheless, the general issues are very real for researchers who subscribe to and use qualitative research.

For example, Lincoln and Guba (1985, p. 145) argue that terminology borrowed from the quantitative research tradition is not appropriate for qualitative research. In their view, terminology like *internal validity, external validity, reliability,* and *objectivity* is inappropriate for qualitative research. They propose instead using four alternative terms to deal with the same, or at least analogous, research issues: *credibility, transferability, dependability,* and *confirmability.*

Within those four concepts, numerous strategies have been worked out in the qualitative research literature for drawing useful and informative conclusions from qualitative data. Credibility is loosely analogous to internal validity in quantitative studies, and you can enhance it by using various combinations of the following strategies: prolonged engagement, persistent observations, triangulation, peer debriefing, negative case analysis, referential analysis, and/or member checking. Transferability is loosely analogous to external validity in quantitative studies, and you can enhance it by using thick description (as defined in the Transferability section below). Dependability is loosely analogous to reliability in quantitative studies, and you can improve it by using overlapping methods, stepwise replications, and/or inquiry audits. Confirmability is roughly analogous to objectivity in quantitative studies, and you can improve it through use of audit trails (as described in detail by Lincoln and Guba, 1985). Thus numerous strategies can be applied iteratively to enhance the validity, or verification, of the conclusions qualitative researchers draw from their qualitative data. Since credibility, transferability, dependability, and confirmability as well as the various strategies used to enhance them are such important concepts in qualitative research, I will now explore each of the four in more depth.

Credibility

Credibility involves demonstrating that the research was carried out in a way that maximizes the accuracy of identifying and describing the object(s) of study, especially as judged by the multiple parties being studied. According to Denzin (1994, p. 513), credibility can be enhanced by prolonged engagement, persistent observation, triangulation, peer debriefing, negative case analysis, referential analysis, and member checking. Definitions for each of those terms or phrases follow.

1. & 2. **Prolonged engagement** and **persistent observation** involve the investment of sufficient time and repetitions of meetings and observations (respectively) to establish respondents' confidence and trust in the researcher, to learn adequately about the cultural context, and to check for misinformation introduced by the respondents or the researcher (Davis, 1992, p. 606; 1995, p. 445).

3. **Triangulation** is defined much more fully below, but in brief, triangulation involves studying the data in your research from different perspectives.

4. **Peer debriefing** is the critical examination and evaluation of the data collection, analysis techniques, and research methods in general by a qualified research peer.

5. **Negative case analysis** is the purposeful search for instances or participants that do not fit developing hypotheses and analysis of alternative explanations or hypotheses suggested by those negative cases.

6. **Referential analysis** uses cinematic methods to furnish a chronicle of social life in a particular context.

7. **Member checking** involves verifying the data, analyses, interpretations, and conclusions with the respondents.

Transferability

As Lazaraton (1995) notes, "Perhaps the most frequent criticism leveled against qualitative research is that the results obtained are not generalizable to other contexts (see, e.g., the arguments in Larsen-Freeman & Long, 1991; Long, 1983; Seliger & Shohamy, 1989). Davis (1992, p. 606) points out that qualitative researchers strive instead for transferability of their results. **Transferability** is the demonstration of the generalizability, or applicability of the results of a study in one setting to another context, or other contexts. Davis goes on to explain that "The degree to which working hypotheses can transfer to other times and contexts is an empirical matter, depending on the degree of similarity between the two contexts" (p. 606). She continues by explaining that the researcher is responsible for providing a "thick description" with enough detail so readers can determine for themselves if transferability is justified. "In this way, the responsibility of the original investigator ends in providing sufficient descriptive data to make such similarity judgments possible" (p. 606). **Thick description** "involves an emic perspective, which demands description that includes the actors' interpretations and other social and/or cultural information" (Davis, 1995, p. 434). Marshall and Rossman (1989, p. 145) note that the burden of demonstrating transferability rests on the person attempting to apply the results to the new context(s).

I should stress that generalizability is not just a problem in qualitative research. As Lazaraton (1995) justifiably points out, "generalizability is a serious problem in nearly all the research conducted in our field" (p. 465). Generalizability is a particular problem in quantitative studies where samples of ESL students (even large samples) are used with no attempts to control for nationality. Results based on such samples are impossible to generalize to other samples of ESL or EFL students at other institutions because they are likely to be made up of different nationalities or at least different proportions of those nationalities.

Dependability

Dependability involves accounting for the changing conditions in the objects of study as well as changes in the design of the study in order to gain more exact understanding of the context. Denzin (1994, p. 513) argues that "dependability can be enhanced through use of overlapping methods, stepwise replications, and inquiry (dependability) audits. . . . ." Definitions of each of those terms or phrases follow.

1. **Overlapping methods** involve carefully planned methodological triangulation, or the use of multiple data-gathering procedures, such that they provide overlapping, or cross-validating information.
2. **Stepwise replications** typically involve what I will later label time triangulation, or using multiple data-gathering occasions, at one site. For example, you might choose to gather data at the beginning, middle, and end of the semester, and thereby verify the consistency of your data and interpretations.
3. **Inquiry audits** are precise explanations of the consistency of agreement

among data, research methods, interpretations, and conclusions verified by an outside "auditor," who is a qualified qualitative research.

Where appropriate, dependability can also be enhanced by quantitative analyses of the consistency of coders and/or raters in the forms of intercoder/intracoder agreement or interrater/intracoder reliability (see discussion below).

Confirmability

Confirmability involves full revelation or at least the availability of the data upon which all interpretations are based. In other words, whether or not it is actually done, it must be possible for another person to confirm the results or interpretations. According to Denzin (1994, p. 513), "confirmability builds on audit trails (a 'residue of records stemming from inquiry' [Lincoln & Guba, 1985], p. 319) and involves the use of written field notes, memos, a field diary, process and personal notes, and a reflexive journal." Careful record keeping and retention of data for further scrutiny are essential to this concept.

Focus on triangulation

Because triangulation is prominent in all the discussions of rectifying the common criticisms of qualitative research (as discussed in the previous section) and putting qualitative research methods on a solid footing, I feel bound to expand on this concept. Some authorities say that the term *triangulation* was first coined by Webb, Campbell, Schwartz, and Sechrest (1965), whereas others (see Fielding & Fielding, 1986) trace it back to Campbell and Fiske (1959). Regardless of its antecedents, **triangulation** involves studying data from multiple perspectives. As Glesne and Peshkin (1992) put it, "Qualitative researchers depend on a variety of methods for gathering data. The use of multiple-data-collection methods contributes to the trustworthiness of the data. This practice is commonly called 'triangulation' (p. 24). Looking at triangulation from Rossman and Wilson's (1985) point of view: "Data from different sources can be used to corroborate, elaborate, or illuminate the research in question."

As an undergraduate studying geography field methods, I learned that triangulation is an important aspect of mapping. Triangulation in this context can help a cartographer locate a point in space. It turns out that you can get a somewhat accurate notion of the location of a point in space if you look at it from only one angle; at least you will know that it is somewhere on a particular straight line. if you plot the point from two angles, you can locate it much more accurately; at least you will know where it is on a particular flat plain. However, if you must locate the point accurately in three-dimensional space, as in the real world, you will need to triangulate, or plot it from three angles.

Similarly, if your qualitative data are examined from at least three points of view, you stand a better chance of producing credible results by limiting bias in the findings. Basically, the purpose of triangulation is to maximize the possibility of obtaining credible findings by cross-validating them. As Miles and Huberman (1984, p. 235) put it: "Stripped to its basics, triangulation is supposed to support a finding by showing that independent measures of it agree with it or, at least, don't contradict it." The discussion of issues related to triangulation will continue with explorations of the types of triangulation, problems with triangulation, and choosing what to triangulate.

TYPES OF TRIANGULATION

Denzin (1978) lists four categories of triangulation: data triangulation, investigator triangulation, theory triangulation, and methodological triangulation. Janesick (1994) suggests a fifth type: interdisciplinary triangulation. Freeman (1998) suggests yet another type of triangulation, which might actually be viewed as two types: triangulation in time and/or location.

I have summarized these seven types of triangulation by listing and briefly defining them in Table 5.1. In more detail:

1. **Data triangulation** involves using multiple sources (the sources are usually people with different roles) of data to mediate and understand biases interjected by people in different roles. For example, in a language teaching situation, you might want to consult teachers, students, and administrators.
2. **Investigator triangulation** implies using multiple researchers examining the same data; this type of triangulation helps to moderate and understand researchers' biases. For instance, two or three researchers might analyze the open-response questions on a questionnaire, write up their conclusions, and then compare what they found.
3. **Theory triangulation** entails using multiple conceptual or theoretical points of view. For example, open-ended responses from an interview could be analyzed from an error analysis viewpoint, a discourse analyses perspective, and a communicative fluency perspective.
4. **Methodological triangulation** involves using multiple data-gathering procedures (as shown in Table 5.1). For instance, you might choose to use interviews, surveys, and observations to gather data using different methods.
5. **Interdisciplinary triangulation** requires drawing on the perspectives of

TABLE 5.1. SUMMARY OF TRIANGULATION TYPES

1. Data triangulation – using multiple sources of information
2. Investigator triangulation – using multiple researchers
3. Theory triangulation – using multiple conceptual viewpoints
4. Methodological triangulation – using multiple data-gathering procedures
5. Interdisciplinary triangulation – using the perspectives of multiple disciplines
6. Time triangulation – using multiple data-gathering occasions
7. Location triangulation – using multiple data-gathering sites

multiple disciplines. For example, in studying some aspect of English for specific purposes, you might use perspectives drawn from linguistics, psychology, education, and the sciences.

6. **Time triangulation** involves using multiple data-gathering occasions. For example, you might choose to gather data at the beginning, middle, and end of the semester.
7. **Location triangulation** entails using multiple data-gathering sites. For instance, you could gather language learning data from five different high schools, or from two elementary schools, two junior high schools, and two high schools.

PROBLEMS IN TRIANGULATION

It is worth noting that the notion of triangulation has been criticized for two problems. First, criticism has been leveled at the assumption that triangulation works automatically. Fielding and Fielding (1986) point out that "using several different methods can actually increase the chance of error. We should recognize that the multi-operational approach implies a good deal more than merely piling on of instruments" (p. 31). Instead, they point out that "the important feature of triangulation is not the simple combination of different kinds of data, but the attempt to relate them so as to counteract the threats to validity identified in each" (p. 31), and therein lies its strength. Thus, triangulation, if it is to be effective, must be carefully thought through and planned.

Second, criticism has been directed at the assumption that triangulation necessarily guarantees validity of the results. Again, Fielding and Fielding (1986, p. 31) point out that:

We have argued that it is naïve to assume that the use of several different methods necessarily ensures the validity of findings. McCall and Simmons [1969] long ago pointed out the fallacy into which the characterization of qualitative data as "rich" leads the novice. The novice may neglect the fact that data are never rich in and of themselves, but are "enriched" only by their being grounded in a refined theoretical perspective.

229

Again, to make your triangulation effective, you must think it through and plan carefully, and ground your data in a clear theoretical perspective.

Third, criticism has also been leveled at the assumption that starting with a blank mind is necessarily a good thing. Fielding and Fielding (1986, p. 31) wrote: "Because of its emphasis on 'telling it like it is,' research informed by a naturalistic perspective often finds the idea of starting with a 'blank mind' rather appealing. It may be a good thing to begin with no preconceptions, if this means that we have no ax to grind, no preferred perceptual grid into which data will be forced, or for which only the conformable data will be selected. Too often, it serves as a warrant to almost blindly collect quantities of 'data,' the value of which is uncertain and trustingly thought to be discoverable after the fact." Yet again, to make your triangulation effective, you must think it through and plan carefully, and ground your data in a clear theoretical perspective.

Fourth, Fielding and Fielding (1986) point to two potential sources of bias in a qualitative researcher: a tendency to select data to fit an "idea conception (preconception)" and a tendency to select data that are salient and perhaps more exotic data, "at the expense of less dramatic (and possibly indicative) data" (p. 32). Fielding and Fielding (1986) also correctly point out that quantitative research is not free from these faults, though the nature of such research "makes the researchers' assumptions more explicit and available for inspection" (p. 32).

In their book, Fielding and Fielding, who are themselves qualitative researchers, address ways to overcome the above criticisms. In addition, the formulation and use of many of the concepts discussed earlier in this chapter were developed to overcome such criticisms. In any case, you should address all of these potential problems whenever you are dealing with qualitative data, by which I mean you should recognize that triangulation is not automatically effective, and does not necessarily guarantee the validity of your results. Moreover, you should acknowledge that your preconceptions may affect your choices of data and you may be attracted to conspicuous data, perhaps to the exclusion of less interesting but more pertinent data.

Simply being aware of the above-listed potential problems may help, but you should probably also make sure that you (1) thoughtfully plan your triangulation so as to minimize the biases of different data sources while maximizing their strengths, (2) scrupulously analyze the degree to which your preconceptions may affect your choices of data, and (3) examine the degree to which you may be attracted to salient/exotic data.

CHOOSING WHAT TO TRIANGULATE

Obviously, it will not be practical to set up a study that uses three investigators to investigate three sources of data based on three theories using three methods from three disciplines at three different times at three locations (though using all of those strategies would probably allow for a very thick description that, if handled properly, would in turn be highly credible, transferable, dependable, and confirmable).

For reasons of practicality, researchers generally have to select from among the triangulation possibilities available to them. As Huberman and Miles (1994) note: "A general prescription has been to pick triangulation sources that have different biases, different strengths, so they can complement one another" (p. 438).

In addition to paring down the number and types of triangulation in any particular study, it is important to realize that you are not limited to using three sources; you can use four, five, six, or whatever is appropriate in a particular study. It is also important to recognize that quantitative analyses can be combined with qualitative results in triangulating. Hence, combining the qualitative results of interviews and observations with the quantitative results of a questionnaire might provide a very effective form of triangulation.

Miles and Huberman (1984) summarize triangulation well when they argue the following:

> Perhaps our basic point is that triangulation is a state of mind. If you *self-consciously* set out to collect and double-check findings, using multiple sources and modes of evidence, the verification process will largely be built into the data-gathering process, and little more need be done than to report on one's procedures (p. 235).

Methods for estimating the reliability of qualitative survey data

Despite protestations to the contrary (Lincoln and Guba, 1985, p. 145), reliability can and probably should be addressed for some aspects of qualitative data collection and analysis so it will strengthen the credibility of the research. In the language fields, reliability is especially applicable for two different types of qualitative questions on surveys: (1) questions where you are investigating the language of the answers for certain characteristics and (2) questions where you are analyzing the content of the answers. An example of the former would be a question designed to elicit a correct response that would necessarily include a regular verb in the future tense. The analysis would then be a text analysis of the respondents' use of future tense with regular verbs. An example of the latter would be a question designed to elicit students' views on what they still need to learn in the language. The analysis would focus on the content of their responses and ignore any language accuracy issues such as spelling or grammar errors.

Response coding versus response rating

Regardless of which type of question is involved, analyzing qualitative responses will usually require coding or rating of the responses by some individual or individuals with expertise in the area under analysis. **Response coding** usually requires a coder or coders to examine each response and (1) decide whether it falls in one category or another (say, correct or incorrect, or grammatical or ungrammatical, or past, present, or future tense), or (2) tally the number of certain features that each answer has (for instance, the number of words, the number of sentences, the number of error-free sentences, etc.), or (3) list the key points made in each answer (for example, listing the study skills that each student wants to improve and tallying them across students). In short, response coding will generally produce nominal, or categorical, results.

Response rating, on the other hand, usually requires a rater or raters to examine each response and (1) decide on the degree to which the response matches a prototype response (for instance, the degree to which an answer is grammatical on a scale of 0 for ungrammatical to 3 for completely grammatical, or the degree to which an answer is factually correct on a scale of 1–5), or (2) the degree to which a response meets certain clearly described criteria (for instance, separate rating scales of 1–5 for pronunciation, fluency, grammaticality, vocabulary, and register with each point value for each category clearly spelled out), or (3) the degree to which a response matches certain clearly described levels (for instance, a scale ranging from 0 for no English language proficiency to 5 for native-speaker proficiency, with descriptors for each of the following six levels: 0, 1, 2, 3, 4, 5). In short, response rating will generally produce interval- or ratio-scale results.

In brief, the distinction that I am making here between coding and rating is that response coding will generally lead to results that are coded nominally, whereas response rating will generally lead to results that are interval or ratio scales (though conceivably they could also be ordinal). I discuss the difference between coding and rating because the analysis of the reliability of codings is generally handled differently from the analysis of ratings, as I will explain next.

Consistency between coders or between raters

Often, when examining qualitative responses, more consistent and believable results will follow if two or more "expert" individuals are used to do the analysis. The analysis of the consistency of such procedures is called intercoder agreement or interrater reliability.

TABLE 5.2. EXAMPLE OF CALCULATING INTERCODER AGREEMENT ON QUESTION 33

	Coder A			Coder B			Number of codings that agree	Total number of codings
Student	Past	Present	Future	Past	Present	Future		
1	1	4	2	1	3	3	12	14
2	2	2	2	2	1	3	10	12
3	3	2	1	3	2	1	12	12
4	2	2	1	2	2	1	10	10
5	3	1	1	3	1	1	10	10
6	1	2	1	1	2	1	8	8
7	2	2	2	2	1	3	10	12
8	2	2	2	2	2	2	12	12
9	3	2	1	3	2	1	12	12
10	2	2	1	2	2	1	10	10
						Sum =	106	112

INTERCODER AGREEMENT

Intercoder agreement (also known as the **intercoder agreement coefficient**) indicates the degree to which two raters agree on assigning categories. Calculating the intercoder agreement is similar to the agreement and percent of agreement discussed earlier in Chapter 4, except that intercoder agreement is based on the codes assigned by two coders rather than on the answers given on two occasions or two forms by the respondents. In the case of intercoder agreement, you need to count up the number of category assignments across all respondents that were exactly the same for both coders and divide that number by the total number of categories assigned (that is, the number of categories on which the two coders agreed plus the number on which they did not agree). Then multiply the result by 100 to get the **percent of intercoder agreement.**

For example, Table 5.2 shows the codings of two coders who, for Question 33 on a fictitious survey, were coding the number of instances of past, present, and future tense verbs in the responses of students to a particular qualitative question. For student 1, Rater A found one, four, and two instances of the three tenses, respectively, and Rater B found one, three, and three instances, respectively, for a total of 12 category assignments on which they agreed and two on which they did not agree in a total of 14 category assignments. Doing the same for all 10 students and totaling the results shows that these two raters across all students have 106 codings that agree for a total of 112 codings (see bottom right portion of Table 5.2). The intercoder agreement is the number of codings

Chapter 5

TABLE 5.3. CALCULATING INTERRATER RELIABILITY FOR QUESTION 21

Students	Rater A	Rater A
1	5	5
2	4	4
3	4	2
4	2	1
5	2	1
6	3	2
7	2	3
8	3	4
9	3	3
10	5	5
11	2	2
12	2	3
13	1	1
14	1	1
15	3	3
16	3	3
17	4	4
18	2	3
19	2	2
20	2	2
$M =$	2.75	2.70
$SD =$	1.13	1.23
$r_{xx'} =$	0.81	

that agree divided by the total number of codings, or 106/112 = .9464 ≈ .95. Multiplying that number by 100 yields the percent of intercoder agreement, or .9464 × 100 = 94.64% ≈ 95%. This means that the coders agreed on about 95 percent of their codings and disagreed on 5 percent.

INTERRATER RELIABILITY

Interrater reliability (also called the **interrater reliability coefficient**) indicates the degree to which two raters agree on assigning ratings (usually based on descriptors of what each score or rating means) to a particular survey question. Calculating the interrater reliability involves examining the correlation of the two sets of ratings. To do so, you will have to calculate a correlation coefficient for the two sets of ratings.

For example, Table 5.3 shows the ratings of two raters (cleverly labeled A and B), who were rating 20 students' answers to Question 21 on a scale of 1–5 on our fictitious survey. As you can see, their ratings averaged 2.75

234

and 2.70, respectively, and had standard deviations of 1.13 and 1.23, respectively. At the very bottom of the table, you can see that the ratings correlated at .81. In this case, the correlation of .81 means that Rater A's ratings were 81 percent reliable and 19 percent unreliable, and that Rater B's ratings were 81 percent reliable and 19 percent unreliable. In other words, the correlation coefficient represents the reliability of the ratings assigned by only one rater – either rater, but still only one.

If the ratings are being used together to form total scores (by summing or averaging) for the analyses that follow, then the reliability coefficient needs to be adjusted from one-rater reliability to two-rater reliability. The **Spearman-Brown prophecy formula** can be used to do that:

$$\text{S-B} = \frac{2 \times r_{xx'}}{1 + r_{xx'}}$$

where: S-B = Spearman-Brown prophecy formula
$r_{xx'}$ = reliability of either raters' ratings

For instance, given that the correlation of the ratings of Rater A and Rater B on Question 21 of a survey was .81, you know that Rater A's ratings were 81 percent reliable and 19 percent unreliable; you also know that Rater B's ratings were 81 percent reliable and 19 percent unreliable. If the two sets of ratings are to be averaged to form the total scores reported and analyzed in a given report, the reliability of those scores is

$$\text{S-B} = \frac{2 \times r_{xx'}}{1 + r_{xx'}}$$

$$= \frac{2 \times .81}{1 + .81}$$

$$= \frac{1.62}{1.81}$$

$$= .895 \approx .90$$

So the reliability of the scores for the two sets of ratings combined is .895, or about .90, which means that the ratings combined are about 90 percent reliable and 10 percent unreliable – a considerable increase in reliability, which, by the way, demonstrates the benefit (in terms of gained reliability) of using two or more raters.

Reliability of a single coder or rater

INTRACODER AGREEMENT

Intracoder agreement (also known as the **intracoder agreement coefficient**) indicates the degree to which one rater's ratings on two different

TABLE 5.4. EXAMPLE OF CALCULATING INTRACODER AGREEMENT FOR QUESTION 3

Student	Time 1		Time 2		Number of codings that agree	Total number of codings
	Gram.	*Ungram.*	*Gram.*	*Ungram.*		
1	x		x		2	2
2	x		x		2	2
3	x		x		2	2
4		x	x		0	2
5		x		x	2	2
6		x		x	2	2
7	x		x		2	2
8		x		x	2	2
9	x		x		2	2
10		x		x	2	2
				Sum =	18	20

occasions agree with each other in terms of assigning categories. Calculating the intracoder agreement is very similar to calculating the intercoder agreement discussed above, except that intracoder agreement is based on the codes assigned by one rater on two occasions rather than two coders on one occasion. Briefly, to calculate intracoder agreement, you need to have a single coder code whatever questions need coding on two occasions. Then, count up the number of category assignments across all respondents that were exactly the same on both occasions and divide that number by the total number of categories assigned on the two occasions (that is, the number of categories that agreed on the two occasions plus the number that did not agree). Then multiply the result by 100 to get the **percent of intracoder agreement.**

For example, Table 5.4 shows the codings of one coder on two occasions (Times 1 and 2). The coder's job was to decide if the answer produced by each student to Question 3 on our fictitious survey was grammatical or ungrammatical. The coder made these judgments on separate days, one week apart. At Time 1, the coder found that students 1, 2, 3, 7, and 9 produced grammatical answers, but the rest were ungrammatical. At Time 2, the coder decided that students 1, 2, 3, 4, 7, and 9 produced grammatical answers, while the rest did not. Totaling the results shows that the rater's judgments on two occasions across all students had 18 codings that agreed for a total of 20 codings (see bottom right portion of Table 5.5). The intracoder agreement is the number of codings that agreed divided by the total number of codings, or 18/20 = .90. Multiplying that number by 100 yields the percent of intercoder agreement, or .90 × 100 = 90 percent. This means that 90 percent of the codes agreed and 10% disagreed.

INTRARATER RELIABILITY

Intrarater reliability (also called the **intrarater reliability coefficient**) indicates the degree to which one rater assigns the same ratings on two different occasions (usually based on descriptors of what each score or rating means) to a particular survey question. Calculating the interrater reliability involves examining the correlation of the sets of ratings assigned on the two different occasions. To do so, you will have to calculate a correlation coefficient for the two sets of ratings.

For example, Table 5.5 shows the ratings assigned by one rater on two different occasions for Question 15 on our fictitious survey. The rater was rating 20 students' answers to Question 15 on a scale of 1–5. As you can see, his ratings averaged 2.85 and 2.75, respectively, and had standard deviations of 1.11 and 1.22, respectively. At the very bottom of the table, you can see that the ratings correlated at .90. In this case, the correlation of .90 means that the raters first ratings were 90 percent reliable and 10 percent unreliable and the second ratings were also reliable at 90 percent and 10 percent unreliable. In other words, the correlation coefficient represents the reliability of the ratings assigned only on one occasion – either occasion, but still only one.

If the ratings on the two occasions are being used together to form total scores (by summing or averaging) for the analyses that follow, then the reliability coefficient needs to be adjusted from one-occasion reliability to two-occasion reliability. The Spearman-Brown prophecy formula (explained above) can be used to do that as follows:

$$S\text{-}B = \frac{2 \times r_{xx'}}{1 + r_{xx'}}$$

$$= \frac{2 \times .90}{1 + .90}$$

$$= \frac{1.80}{1.90}$$

$$= .947 \approx .95$$

TABLE 5.5. CALCULATING INTRARATER
RELIABILITY FOR QUESTION 15

Students	Time 1	Time 2
1	5	5
2	4	4
3	4	3
4	2	1
5	2	1
6	3	2
7	2	3
8	3	4
9	3	3
10	5	5
11	2	2
12	3	3
13	1	1
14	1	1
15	3	3
16	3	3
17	4	4
18	3	3
19	2	2
20	2	2
$M =$	2.85	2.75
$SD =$	1.11	1.22
$r_{xx'} =$	0.90	

So the reliability of the scores for the two sets of ratings combined is
.9474, or about .95, which means that the ratings combined are about
95 percent reliable and 5 percent unreliable – a considerable increase in
reliability, which, by the way, demonstrates the benefit (in terms of gained
reliability) of doing ratings on two occasions.

Coder agreement or rater reliability and sampling

In the best of all possible worlds, coding or rating will be done by two or
more experts or on two or more occasions. However, when doing actual
research or curriculum development projects, you may find that it is in-
convenient or unreasonable to ask for coding or rating by two or more
experts or on two or more occasions. Under these circumstances, you
may want to get two people to code or rate perhaps 10 percent of the

data you have sampled so that you can get an idea of how much agreement in codings you are getting or how reliable the ratings are. Then you can have one person continue in the same way, with at least a rough idea of how much agreement the codings have or how reliable the ratings are. Alternatively, you could have one coder or rater work on 10 percent of the data you have sampled on two occasions so that you get an idea of how much agreement in codings you are getting or how reliable the ratings are. Then you can have that person continue to do all the codings/ratings in the same way, with at least a rough idea of how much agreement the codings have or how reliable the ratings are.

Some version of the consistency estimates described in the previous four sections can be done for virtually any kind of qualitative results, unless, of course, the survey researcher does not care whether the results are consistent, which would be very irresponsible indeed. Note that the big difference between quantitative and qualitative approaches to consistency is that, for quantitative answers, you will simply be comparing the numerical results of the two administrations, whereas for qualitative answers, you will need first to code the elements of each answer that you are looking for, then check for agreement or reliability of two or more coders or raters on one occasion, or one coder or rater on two occasions.

A caution about survey agreement and reliability

As with quantitative survey reliability estimates, one aspect of survey agreement and reliability is particularly important to think about: Agreement or reliability coefficients simply indicate that the respondents were answering consistently, or that the coders or raters were responding consistently. Hence, if a survey is designed with subsections that measure distinctly different things, the fact that high agreement or reliability is found for the whole survey may be bad news. Such a result would mean that the respondents were answering the same way across all the subsections. If indeed those subsections were designed to measure distinctly different things, respondents should not be answering the same way across all the subsections. Thus, high agreement or reliability for the whole survey could indicate that the subsections might not be as different as the survey designer initially thought, or alternatively, might indicate that the respondents (or a substantial number of them) were being lazy or not paying attention to the actual questions, and were consistently answering one way or another.

When coders or raters are involved, the picture can become even more complicated. In such a case, high agreement or reliability for the whole survey could also indicate that the coders or raters were not responding to the subsections as differently as the survey designer initially wanted, or alternatively, might indicate that the coders or raters were being lazy or not paying any attention to the actual responses, and were consistently coding or rating one way or another.

In general, for survey instruments that were designed to have separate subsections, calculating the agreement or reliability of each of the subsections separately will make much more sense than calculating the agreement or reliability for the whole survey instrument.

Existing guidelines for qualitative studies

Two sets of guidelines are provided here to help you collect, plan, conduct, analyze, and report any qualitative aspects of your survey project: One set of guidelines is taken from the general literature on qualitative research (Marshall, 1985), and another from the second language qualitative research literature (TESOL, 2000b).

General guidelines for assessing the trustworthiness and goodness of qualitative research

Marshall (1985) suggests guidelines for assessing the trustworthiness and goodness of qualitative research reports from the reader's perspective. Nonetheless, these guidelines can be applied by researchers to their own research.

1. Data-collection methods are explicit.
2. Data are used to document analytic constructs.
3. Negative instances of the findings are displayed and accounted for.
4. Biases are discussed, including biases of interest (personal, professional, policy-related), and theoretical biases and assumptions.
5. Strategies for data collection and analyses are made public.
6. Field decisions altering strategies or substantive focus are documented.
7. Competing hypotheses are presented and discussed.
8. Data are preserved.
9. Participants' truthfulness is assessed.
10. Theoretical significance and generalizability are made explicit.

Keeping all 10 of these guidelines in mind during the qualitative research design, data collection, data analysis, and reporting stages cannot help but improve the entire process.

*TESOL Quarterly qualitative research guidelines**

The *TESOL Quarterly* Qualitative Guidelines (TESOL, 2000b) are organized into three categories: conducting the study, analyzing the data, and reporting the data. The Qualitative Research Guidelines are as follows.

*© TESOL. Reprinted with permission.

To ensure that *Quarterly* articles model rigorous qualitative research, the following guidelines are provided.

CONDUCTING THE STUDY

Studies submitted to the *Quarterly* should exhibit an in-depth understanding of the philosophical perspectives and research methodologies inherent in conducting qualitative research. Utilizing these perspectives and methods in the course of conducting research helps to ensure that studies are credible, valid, and dependable rather than impressionistic and superficial. Reports of qualitative research should meet the following criteria:

1. Data collection (as well as analyses and reporting) is aimed at uncovering an emic perspective. In other words, the study focuses on research participants' perspectives and interpretations of behavior, events, and situations rather than etic (outsider-imposed) categories, models, and viewpoints.
2. Data-collection strategies include prolonged engagement, persistent observations, and triangulation. Researchers should conduct ongoing observations over a sufficient period of time so as to build trust with respondents, learn the culture (e.g., classroom, school, or community), and check for misinformation introduced by both the researcher and the researched. Triangulation involves the use of multiple methods and sources such as participant-observation and formal interviewing, and collection of relevant or available documents.

ANALYZING THE DATA

Data analysis is also guided by the philosophy and methods underlying qualitative research studies. The researcher should engage in comprehensive data treatment in which data from all relevant sources are analyzed. In addition, many qualitative studies demand an analytic inductive approach involving a cyclical process of data collection, analysis (taking an emic perspective and utilizing the descriptive language the respondents themselves use), creation of hypotheses, and testing of hypotheses in further data collection.

REPORTING THE DATA

The researcher should generally provide "thick description" with sufficient detail to allow the reader to determine whether transfer to other situations can be considered. Reports also should include the following:

1. A description of the theoretical or conceptual framework that guides research questions and interpretations.
2. A clear statement of the research questions.
3. A description of the research site, participants, procedures for ensuring participant anonymity, and data collection strategies. A description of the roles of the researcher(s).
4. A description of a clear and salient organization of patterns found through data analysis. Reports of patterns should include representative examples not anecdotal information.

5. Interpretations that exhibit a holistic perspective in which the author traces the meaning of patterns across all the theoretically salient or descriptively relevant micro- and macro-contexts in which they are embedded.
6. Interpretations and conclusions provide evidence of grounded theory and discussion of how this theory relates to current research/theory in the field, including relevant citations. In other words, the article should focus on the issues or behaviors that are salient to participants and that not only reveal an in-depth understanding of the situations studied, but also suggest how it connects to current related theories.

Examples of analyzing survey data qualitatively

The examples in this chapter include (1) the TESOL survey running example with a focus on the issues involved in analyzing the qualitative survey data and (2) the rotating example, which is an account of a project that compared the first and second language writing programs at a large U.S. university (Atkinson & Ramanathan, 1995).

Running example: Analyzing survey data qualitatively

In this section, I will focus on the qualitative analysis of the TESOL Research Task Force questionnaire. Earlier in this chapter, I discussed four central issues in qualitative research: credibility, transferability, dependability, and confirmability. I will organize the discussion of the TESOL questionnaire around those four topics. Then, I will explain the steps that were involved in the data transcription and analysis stages of the TESOL study.

CREDIBILITY

Recall that *credibility* means showing that a qualitative study was conducted in a way that maximizes the accuracy of identifying and describing the object(s) of study, especially as judged by the multiple parties being studied. The credibility of the TESOL Research Task Force study was enhanced by using triangulation and member checks. We used at least three sources of information in this project: meetings, closed-response questions, and open-response questions. Thus, our research included methodological triangulation (using multiple data-gathering procedures). The closed-response questions and open-response questions were addressed to members of the general membership, and each of four special interest groups. Thus, our research also included data triangulation (using multiple sources of information). Member checks occurred at various stages in this study in the form of feedback from members of each of the groups under investigation and the board of directors.

TRANSFERABILITY

Earlier in this chapter, *transferability* was defined as showing the generalizability, or applicability of the results of a study in a single setting to other contexts, "depending on the degree of similarity between the two contexts" (Davis, 1992, p. 606). Transferability was an issue in this study in two senses. The first issue was the degree to which the results could be generalized to the entire membership of the TESOL International organization. This question applied to the open-response questions as well as the closed-response questions. In part, the results of this particular study were based on random samples of 1,000 from the general membership. In addition, because we believed that researchers represented a relatively small proportion of the general membership, we took four other random subsamples (of 200 each) from the interest sections believed to have relatively larger proportions of researchers: the Applied Linguistics, Higher Education, Research, and Teacher Education interest sections. As explained in Chapter 3, random sampling is a commonly used technique for creating smaller groups from an entire population that should be representative of the total population. Thus, random samples should produce results that are transferable to the entire population from which they were sampled.

Unfortunately, because the TESOL survey was a mail survey with no follow-up mailing, we got only about a 34 percent return rate overall. The problem is that those 34 percent were not randomly selected and they may have had characteristics that biased the results. In this case, the questionnaire was fairly long and involved, so the people who responded may have tended to be those who were most interested in research issues to start with.

Second, the transferability of the results to other organizations or to teachers outside the organization might be questioned. Although this issue was not addressed directly in our report, it is interesting to speculate on the transferability of the results of our study to ESL/EFL teachers outside of TESOL International or to other organizations. The former would depend on the degree to which the members of the TESOL International organization are representative of the field as a whole and the latter would depend on the degree to which TESOL International is like other organizations. It seems much more likely that TESOL International is representative of the field as a whole, than that it is like other organizations (for instance, the Modern Language Association or the American Educational Research Association).

In our defense, we openly addressed the issue of the applicability of our results to the entire total membership of TESOL International in our report (included in Chapter 6) and left it up to the readers to judge the transferability of our results to the total membership of the TESOL

International organization. Davis (1992) advocated providing a *thick description* with enough detail so readers can determine for themselves if transferability is justified. Hence, the degree to which we openly and honestly revealed all of the steps and procedures that we followed in conducting our study can be said to contribute to the information available for readers to judge the transferability of our results to their lives, to other teachers, to other organizations, and so on.

DEPENDABILITY

Recall that *dependability* entails accounting for any changing conditions in the objects of study and any changes in the design of the study in order to gain more exact understanding of the context. In this study, we used *overlapping methods,* that is, the use of multiple data-gathering procedures, to provide overlapping, or cross-validating information. As explained in the report (see Chapter 6), we used three data-gathering procedures (meetings, closed-response questions, and open-response questions) and multiple sources of information (the closed-response questions and open-response questions were addressed to members of the general membership, and each of four special interest groups). The readers of our report must ultimately determine the degree to which these triangulation techniques were carefully planned and indeed provide overlapping and cross-validating information.

CONFIRMABILITY

As described earlier in this chapter, *confirmability* involves the complete disclosure or at least availability of the data upon which all interpretations are based so it would be possible for another researcher to confirm the results and interpretations. The questionnaires themselves were kept for a period of five years before they were destroyed. The transcripts and quantitative data files are stored permanently. Thus, it would be possible for other researchers to confirm our results and interpretations. Since careful record keeping and retention of data for further scrutiny are essential to this concept, we can be said to have addressed it.

DATA TRANSCRIPTION AND ANALYSIS

A number of steps were taken in analyzing the open-response questions in this survey instrument.

First, I transcribed the data into separate computer files for each of the open-response questions so that all the answers for all the respondents to a given question were together in one file. This was a time-consuming process, but I felt it was worthwhile, because I wanted to use the computer to help me do the analyses and because I wanted to be able to quote easily and accurately from the respondents' comments. Note also that I made a decision early on to type the transcripts just as they appeared on the questionnaires, including typographical errors, misspellings, British spellings, and incorrect punctuation.

Second, I read through the answers for each question. I did this to proof-read what I had typed, in order to ensure the accuracy of the resulting transcripts. Reading through the answers also helped me to get a general feeling for the responses.

Third, I used the RightWriter (1990) software to generate lexical counts for each file. The result of each of these computer analyses was a print-out for the file being analyzed. The printout contained a list of all the words that appeared in the file and their frequencies. Some of this information was useless. For instance, it is not very interesting to discover that *the* appeared 1,245 times or that *a* appeared 956 times. However, some of the high frequencies (especially for content words [nouns, verbs, adjectives, and adverbs]) were very revealing. For instance, interesting patterns emerged in the responses to the following question: "What do you consider to be the single biggest problem facing ESL/EFL teachers today?" In reading through this file, I realized that the individual answers ranged widely, from "burn-out" to "poorly designed curricula" to the "budget crisis." However, I noticed in the computer analysis that, in the answers of the 334 people in the general membership who responded, *recognition* appeared 44 times, *respect* was mentioned 15 times, *acceptance* had 10 instances, and *credibility* also appeared 10 times. Further examination of the frequencies found nine instances of *marginalization* or lack of *legitimacy.*

Fourth, I investigated the results of my lexical frequency analysis by using the search function of my word processor to search instances of *recognition, respect, acceptance,* and so forth, and read precisely what the respondents had said in each instance.

Fifth, I interpreted what I found in the fourth step above as follows (Brown, 1992a, p. 1):

Many ESL professionals appeared to be unhappy about the way that they are treated in their professional lives. For instance, one respondent felt that the key problems in ESL/EFL are "certification, professionalization, and recognition," while another cited "others' perception of ESL professionals" and "lack of respect" as problems. Still another person complained about lack of "legitimacy within the university structure for ESL/EFL teachers." This problem was forcefully described by one person as "R-E-S-P-E-C-T."

For many teachers, the issue of respect appears to be linked to the erroneous notion that anybody who happens to be an English native speaker can teach ESL. One respondent put it this way: "Just because you speak English, doesn't mean you can teach ESL." Another commented that the biggest problem is a "lack of professional respect within institutions – 'anyone who speaks English can teach English.'" One other person suggested that the single biggest problem was "credibility – i.e., other professionals realizing that speaking English does not equal teaching English."

In interpreting my data, I also chose to draw on some larger quotes from the data in explaining the relationship of respect to larger political issues as follows (Brown, 1992a, p. 1):

The respect issue also seems to be linked to larger political concerns, as well. As one ESL professional put it, the biggest problem is:

> Lack of prestige within one's institution – positions are non-tenured at the college level – teachers are not certified and sometimes untrained, especially in the adult ed. ESL field; public school ESL teachers often have no training or experience and have been riffed or grand-fathered into ESL positions.

Or, as stated by another person, the biggest problem is:

> The nation's current low regard (one reflection: low pay) for education/ educators compounded by the fact that few (even in education) know what we do. We're not remedial English teachers or tutors. . . . We're *foreign language* teachers (the language foreign to our students being English).

In addition to the issue of respect, qualitative analyses of the open-ended questions on our survey uncovered further information in the following areas: the biggest problems TESOL members see facing ESL/EFL teachers today, the various definitions that members have for the term *research,* the research questions that most interest TESOL members, and the roles that members see for the TESOL International organization in their professional lives. These results were published in the organization's newsletter, *TESOL Matters,* in a series of short articles (Brown, 1992a, 1992b, 1992c, 1992d, respectively) and were discussed to a lesser degree in the report discussed in Chapter 6.

Rotating example: Analyzing survey data qualitatively

The rotating example in this chapter is an account of a cooperative project that compared the first and second language writing programs at a large U.S. university (Atkinson & Ramanathan, 1995). This project grew out of a perceived problem: Serious differences existed between the University Composition Program (UCP) and the English Language Program (ELP) in how they viewed and taught writing (for more on the disjunction between ESL and English department instructors, see Brown, 1991b). Two researchers, one from each program, worked together for 10 months on this project. Each had three years of experience teaching in his or her respective program, some of which was supervisory in nature.

PROLONGED ENGAGEMENT, PERSISTENT OBESERVATIONS, AND ITERATION

A series of observations and interviews were conducted in each program by the researcher from that program. During the data-gathering process, the two researchers worked together in interpreting the results, each relying on the other as a "guide and native consultant/informant" (p. 541). That work led to further collection of data and then to further interpretation. Thus, two notions suggested by Davis (1992, p. 606; 1995, p. 445) were used in this study: *prolonged engagement* (that is, the study was 10 months in duration) and *persistent observations* (that is, there were observations and data collection were repeated). The latter characteristic would also fit with Lynch's (1992, p. 78) notion of the *iterative* nature of such research. In a sense, *peer debriefing* was also used in that a trained peer from the other department was involved in checking and cross-checking the data-collection and interpretation processes, and probably the write-up of the project as well. Prolonged engagement, persistent (iterative) observations, and peer debriefing all enhance the credibility of this study.

TRIANGULATION

Six data sets were collected and analyzed in this rotating example study:

1. Two orientation sessions were observed in each program, for a total of four.
2. Interviews ranging in length from one to two and a half hours were conducted with program administrators – four in the UCP and three in the ELP.
3. Interviews (of about the same length as for data set 2 above) were conducted with three teachers in each program, for a total of six.
4. Two writing classes for international students were observed, one for each program (for a total of 27 hours in the UCP and 20 hours in the ELP).
5. Written documents were collected, including orientation documents, students' writing assignments, drafts of essays with teacher comments on them, program memos, and course descriptions.
6. The researchers also took and compiled miscellaneous notes as they made observations in their own programs.

Thus, triangulation is quite evident in this study. *Data triangulation* can be seen in the use of multiple sources of information; *investigator triangulation* is evident in the use of multiple researchers; *methodological triangulation* is found in the use of multiple data-gathering procedures; and *time triangulation* is clear from the use of multiple data-gathering occasions. These researchers might also claim some degree of *interdisciplinary triangulation* in that the English and ESL program views were arguably so different for these two different disciplines. The use of *triangulation* and *overlapping methods* clearly enhances both the credibility and dependability of this study.

In addition, the authors provide a *thick description* from an emic perspective (Davis, 1995, p. 434), with plenty of comparative information about both programs in terms of their structure, instructional objectives, writing assignments, assessment standards, teaching practices, and so forth. Thus, the reader is provided with ample information about the two instructional cultures to determine the degree of transferability of the results to other settings.

All in all, this study must have taken some very careful planning (as advocated by Fielding and Fielding, 1986, p. 31), because prolonged engagement, persistent (iterative) observations, peer debriefing, overlapping methods, five types of triangulation, and thick description do not occur simultaneously in one study by chance alone. Given that all of the above was so carefully planned and carried out, I would be very surprised if the researchers did not also carefully document and preserve an audit trail as well, so as to enhance the confirmability of their study. Thus, there is considerable evidence for the credibility, dependability, and transferability of the results of this study, and every reason to believe in the confirmability of the study. I suppose it would have been helpful if the authors had used those terms (or some other standard set of criteria) in explaining their study, so that readers could judge the *trustworthiness* and *goodness* of the study for themselves.

Incidentally, the authors conclude from their study that (1) the UCP presupposes cultural knowledge that non-native speakers of English may not have, (2) non-natives will experience considerable differences in the conceptualization of what writing is when they cross over from ELP to UCP instruction, and (3) the substantial differences between the two programs can be mediated if appropriate instructors are used, policies are adjusted so that non-native speakers' needs and abilities are addressed, and program members work together.

Their final ringing conclusion is as follows:

In conclusion, we call for purposeful articulation among any and all intrauniversity writing programs that NNS writers must transit for academic success. We also call on such programs to examine their theoretical assumptions and curricular practices vis-à-vis NNS students. To navigate the diverse cultural territories of university writing – and to come out safely on the other side as writers – our students can do with no less.

Summary

In this chapter, I discussed a number of issues involved in the qualitative analysis of survey data. I organized the discussion around three notions: data reduction, data display, and conclusion drawing and verification. Data reduction involved making a number of choices such as whether the study is hypothesis forming or hypothesis confirming. To make such choices well, you will want first to think through the purpose of your study as well as why, how, and how much you want to reduce your data. Data display included all types of graphs and charts used to help analyze and synthesize the data. I next turned to discussion of (1) transcribing, (2) using matrices to analyze qualitative data, and (3) using computers to analyze qualitative data. Conclusion drawing and verification involved examining and interpreting the displayed data. Next, four research issues were explored because they can enhance the caliber of qualitative research: credibility (including prolonged engagement, persistent observation, triangulation, peer debriefing, negative case analysis, referential analysis, and member checks), transferability (including thick description and reader responsibility), dependability (including overlapping methods, stepwise replications, and inquiry audits), and confirmability (especially keeping careful records and retaining data for further scrutiny). I then focused on the useful notion of triangulation (including data, investigator, theory, methodological, interdisciplinary, time, and location triangulation), as well as on problems associated with triangulation and ways to select triangulation strategies. I continued by presenting some general guidelines for assessing qualitative research, and by exploring methods for estimating coder and rater reliability. The running and rotating examples focused on ways to analyze survey data qualitatively.

Suggestions for further reading

The literature on qualitative research methods is small but growing. An even smaller number of references deal with qualitative research in language studies. From among the books I read on general qualitative research, I recommend Fetterman (1989), Fielding and Fielding (1986), Glesne and Peshkin (1992), Marshall and Rossman (1989), as well as Weller and Romney (1988). For books focused on reliability and validity issues in qualitative research and survey research, respectively, see Kirk and Miller (1986) and Litwin (1995). If you are interested in much more depth on the topic of qualitative research methods, I recommend the book by Miles and Huberman (1984) and the collection of articles edited by Denzin and Lincoln (1994). Three books provide at least a

chapter-length treatment of qualitative *language* research methods: Freeman (1998), Johnson (1992), and Nunan (1992). A few articles have recently appeared in the *TESOL Quarterly* on qualitative language research
methods: Davis (1992, 1995), Johnson and Saville-Troike (1992), and
Lazaraton (1995). Finally, Lynch (1992, 1997) has clearly demonstrated
how quantitative and qualitative research methods can be combined effectively in performing language program evaluation.

Important terms

conclusion drawing and verification
concordance
confirmability
credibility
data display
data reduction
data triangulation
dependability
effects matrix
hypothesis-confirming research
hypothesis-forming research
inquiry audits
intercoder agreement
intercoder agreement coefficient
interdisciplinary triangulation
interrater reliability
interrater reliability coefficient
intracoder agreement
intracoder agreement coefficient
intrarater reliability
intrarater reliability coefficient
investigator triangulation
lexical count
location triangulation
matrices

member checking
methodological triangulation
negative case analysis
overlapping methods
percent of intercoder agreement
percent of intracoder agreement
peer debriefing
persistent observation
prolonged engagement
qualitative data analysis
qualitative survey data
qualitative survey data analysis
referential analysis
response coding
response rating
search function
Spearman-Brown prophecy formula (S-B)
stepwise replications
theory triangulation
thick description
time triangulation
transcribing
transferability
triangulation

Review questions

1. What is data reduction? What is the primary choice that you must
   make in data reduction? What must you think about before making
   that choice?
2. What is the purpose of data display? What does it mean to transcribe
   data? And, what are the three steps involved in transcribing?

3. What are matrices? How are they useful for analyzing qualitative data? And, what are the techniques Lynch used for interpreting his matrixes?

4. In doing computer analysis of qualitative data, how can you use the search function in your word processing software? How can computerized lexical count or concordance programs be used to analyze qualitative data? How might a computer program such as CHILDES (MacWhinney, 1995) be useful for analyzing qualitative data?

5. What are conclusion drawing and verification? What four strategies can be applied iteratively to enhance the validity, or verification, of the conclusions you draw from your qualitative data?

6. Why is credibility important to qualitative data analysis? What are the seven strategies discussed in this chapter for enhancing credibility?

7. Why is transferability important to qualitative data analysis? How do thick description and reader responsibility relate to the notion of transferability?

8. Why is dependability important to qualitative data analysis? What are three strategies discussed in this chapter for enhancing dependability?

9. Why is confirmability important to qualitative data analysis? How are careful record keeping and retaining data for further scrutiny related to confirmability?

10. What are the seven types of triangulation? What are the four potential problems associated with triangulation, according to Fielding and Fielding (1986)? And, how can those problems be overcome?

11. What is the difference between intercoder agreement, interrater reliability, intracoder agreement, and intracoder reliability? How are they calculated?

Application exercises

A. Read the following description of a beginning plan for a study:

The purpose of this survey is to assess the English language learning and situation needs of students in the People's Republic of China who will be 22- to 25-year-old graduate students from all the sciences and engineering fields, who need training before they leave to continue graduate training in Australia. You plan to do some interviews and then some questionnaires (with 50 percent closed-response and 50 percent open-response questions) as necessary to determine at least an initial set of language and situation needs for these students.

1. Who do you plan to interview, and to whom do you plan to administer questionnaires?
2. How will you set about reducing the scope of the data?
3. How will you display the data so you can analyze them?

4. How will you set up this study in order to maximize its credibility, dependability, confirmability, and transferability?
B. Imagine a qualitative study of any kind at your institution. Sketch out the purpose, participants, and methods that you will use to conduct the study. What kinds and how many kinds of triangulation will you use in conducting this study? How will these forms of triangulation cross-validate each other? How will these forms of triangulation contribute to the dependability and credibility of the study? What forms of problems should you anticipate having with triangulation? How will you address these potential problems?
C. Plan a survey research study of your own for your own purposes. Be sure to include some quantitative and qualitative data. What is your purpose? Overall, what steps will you follow? How will you gather quantitative and qualitative data, code the data, and analyze the data? In particular, what strategies will you use to reduce the scope of your data, or at least keep them within manageable bounds? How will you display your data for analysis?

6 Reporting on a survey project

The survey report excerpts provided later in this chapter (on the place of research in the TESOL International organization) are based on the study discussed in the running examples that appeared in all the other chapters of the book. This study, as presented here, was submitted to the board of directors of TESOL International, and a number of actions were taken. The report was also submitted as a paper to *TESOL Quarterly*, because we felt the information might be of interest to the general membership. However, the two anonymous readers did not feel the report was appropriate for the *TESOL Quarterly* (one of them was adamant about not publishing it), so it was turned down for publication. In the belief that this report is indeed interesting and that it will serve as a sound real-life model of a survey research report, I include parts of it here with the permission of the TESOL International organization. I also hope that reading through this example report will help you review many of the concepts covered in this book. Most of all, I hope that you will find this report so clear that you will realize how much you have learned in reading this book. On the other hand, if the report is not clear, you may want to review the topics for those parts you do not understand.

Before presenting the report itself, I will briefly discuss how survey reports can be organized, including the relatively strict organization of statistical survey research reports and the relatively flexible organization of qualitative research reports. I will include several examples of each to show some of the possibilities, and then discuss one way the strict statistical and relatively flexible qualitative ways of organizing a report can be combined.

How should a survey report be organized?

Different survey research reports serve different purposes and have different analytical bases. At least four analytical bases spring to mind immediately: purely statistical, statistical with some qualitative, qualitative with some statistics, and purely qualitative. Each of these analytical bases might call for a different way of organizing the report, and indeed, each study may call for further modifications. However, I think it is safe to say that the different ways of organizing such reports will fall on a continuum with the strict and fairly rigid American Psychological Association (APA) format used on the statistical end of the continuum and the relatively flexible organizational format used on the other, qualitative end of the continuum.

Strict APA format for statistical studies

On the statistical end of the continuum, reporting on a survey project should probably be just like reporting on any other statistical research project. In other words, when doing survey research, I follow the guidelines in the latest edition of the *Publication Manual of the American Psychological Association,* which as of this writing is the fourth edition (APA, 1994). Those guidelines suggest the following four main sections: Introduction, Method, Results, and Discussion (or Conclusions). Detailed descriptions of what should be included in each of the five sections are provided in Chapter 5 of Brown (1988) and in the APA manual itself (1994, pp. 7–22).

Overall, the organization of the headings and subheadings for a statistical study will typically be more or less as shown in the following outline:

I. Introduction (all headings optional in this section)
   A. Literature review
   B. Statement of Purpose
   C. Research Questions (and/or Hypotheses)
II. Methods
   A. Participants
   B. Materials
   C. Procedures
III. Results
IV. Discussion (and/or Conclusions)
   A. Direct answers to research questions
   B. Interpretation
   C. Suggestions for Future Research

In somewhat more detail, the **Introduction section** (which often has no heading) provides a framework within which to view the study, usually in the form of a literature review, but sometimes in the form of an explanation of the background of the study (that is, an explanation of where the idea for the study came from). Within the Introduction, a **statement of purpose** (which also often lacks a heading) will explain the overall goals of the research, and will usually contain the **research questions** (which are the questions that the research will answer) or **research hypotheses** (which are expected outcomes of the research).

The **Methods section** normally includes at least three subsections: (1) the **Participants subsection** provides at least a description of the participants in the survey project and how they were sampled; (2) the **Materials sub-**

section gives at least a description of the survey instrument(s) used in the study as well as any other materials used in the project (for example, tapes, transcripts, and so forth); and (3) the **Procedures subsection** explains step by step how you administered the instruments.

The **Results section** should provide a clear technical discussion of all statistical analyses and results in the project. Such results should include at least descriptive statistics, as well as reliability and validity statistics as appropriate. Then and only then, you can report any other relevant statistics. You should summarize this technical information insofar as possible in graphs and tables in a way that will help readers understand your results. In addition, where it is helpful, you should provide brief prose explanations of the graphs and tables.

The **Discussion** (or **Conclusions**) **section** should include at least direct answers in lay terms to the original research questions posed at the beginning of the study and explain those answers as necessary. This section should also bring the narration full circle. Such closure can be accomplished through discussion of the author's interpretation of the results in terms of the literature review and/or the background of the study (as was the case in the Conclusions section of the running example report below). This final section sometimes also contains a subsection headed **Suggestions for Further Research,** which provides a list of research questions that would be appropriate for any follow-up studies (note that this optional subsection was not used in the running example report).

An example of the relatively strict organization of statistical studies can be found in the TESOL report used as the running example in this book, which can be outlined as follows:

I. Introduction
   A. Background
   B. Research Questions
II. Methods
   A. Participants
   B. Materials
   C. Procedures
III. Results
IV. Discussion
V. Conclusions

In general terms, this outline is remarkably similar to the one suggested in the APA publication manual. The structure of the Introduction section is somewhat unusual in that there was no literature to draw on for this study. An acceptable substitute was the Background section, which helped frame this project much as the Literature Review provides context for other statistical research projects. In addition, unlike the APA publication manual outline, the TESOL report presents separate Discussion and

Conclusions sections for reasons that I will explain later. Incidentally, such separation into two sections, a Discussion section and a Conclusions section, is not unusual in language research.

   Another example of the relatively strict organization of statistical studies can be found in Sasaki (1996), which has the following sections:

I. Introduction (no heading)
    A. Literature review
    B. Statement of Purpose
    C. Research Questions
II. The Study
    A. Method
       1. Subjects
       2. Materials
III. Results
IV. Discussion and Conclusions

Sasaki's sections follow the APA conventions fairly closely except for a few minor details: (1) The *The Study* heading, which appears to be idiosyncratic to the *JALT Journal* (other studies published in that Japan Association for Language Teaching journal around the same time also have this heading), the *Subjects* heading used instead of *Participants,* and (3) the lack of a *Procedures* section.

Relatively flexible organization for qualitative studies

On the qualitative end of the continuum, reporting on a qualitative survey project should probably be just like reporting on any other qualitative research project. For example, Atkinson and Ramanathan (1995), the rotating example in the previous chapter, had the following sections:

I.   Introduction (no heading)
II. Motivation and Methods
III. The Culture of the UCP
IV. The Culture of the ELP
V.   Comparison and Discussion
VI. Conclusion and Applications

Note that the authors devoted a paragraph each in the second section (II. Motivation and Methods) to explaining (1) the origins of the study, (2) their reasons for selecting the research methodology they did, (3) their research questions, (4) the procedures they followed in gathering data, and (5) the six types of data they collected. Hence, their organization is not altogether different from that shown above for statistical studies. Indeed, there are many ways in which the two outlines overlap.

A quick glance at the sections of two other qualitative research studies will reveal that the organization can vary considerably more than it typically does among statistical studies. As a second example, consider the sections used by Duff (1995):

   I. Introduction (no heading)
   II. Qualitative Approaches to Research on FL Education
   III. The Present Study: Context, Purpose, and Methods
   IV. Research Methods
   V. Analysis
   VI. The Baseline Speech Event: The Hungarian Recitation
   VII. Classroom Practices in Transition
   VIII. Student Lectures: Assignment, Organization, and Interventions
   IX. Summary and Implications

As a third example, consider the sections used by Willet (1995):

   I. Introduction (no heading)
   II. Theoretical Orientation
   III. Communicative Events, Routines, and Strategies
   IV. Methodology
   V. The Context
   VI. Entering the Social and Academic World of Room 17
      A. The ESL Children in Room 17
      B. Morning in Room 17
   VII. Learning the Languaculture of Room 17
      A. Learning from Adults
      B. Learning from Friends
   VIII. Constructing Social Relations, Identities, and Ideology
   IX. Conclusion

Notice that the headings for these qualitative studies tend to be at one level, though a second level is used in two sections of the Willet (1995) study. Note also that the headings differ considerably from report to report. Thus, relative to the typical organization of statistical research reports, the section headings and organization of qualitative research reports appear to be relatively flexible. The three examples given above for qualitative research do all have Introduction, Methods, and Conclusion sections of some sort. However, the material in between these three sections (and even the material within them) varies considerably according to the type of qualitative research being done as well as the individual research project being reported. In other words, qualitative research reports will often set out to tell the story of the research, and that story may differ in structure from project to project and report to report.

Mixing the organization for quantitative and qualitative studies

Along the continuum between the strict organization of statistical studies and the relatively flexible organization of qualitative studies, numerous combinations may occur. For instance, the TESOL report running example in this book (the same one presented later in this chapter) used both statistical and qualitative types of data. In reporting the results of those two types of analyses, the overall outline shown above in two levels was very similar to that suggested by the APA. However, if I expand the outline to include all the sections of the report, it will have three levels and a mixture of the relatively strict outline of statistical studies and the relatively flexible story-telling outline (especially in the Discussion and Conclusions sections) of qualitative research:

I.   Introduction
    A. Background
    B. Research Questions
II. Methods
    A. Participants
        1. Sampling
        2. Characteristics of the Participants
    B. Materials
    C. Procedures
        1. The Mailing
        2. Return Rate
        3. Possible Reasons for the Return Rate
III. Results
    A. Educational Characteristics
    B. Occupational Characteristics
    C. Research Background
    D. Views on TESOL
    E. Views on TESOL Conventions
    F. Views on Research
IV. Discussion
    A. Which TESOL members do research?
    B. What are members' views on the state of the profession?
    C. What are members' views on TESOL publications?
    D. What are members' views on the TESOL convention?
    E. What are members' views on the place of research in TESOL?
V.   Conclusions
    A. Initiatives Already Taken
    B. Planned Initiatives
    C. Coda

All in all, the best policy with regard to organizing a survey research report is probably to decide if it is a statistical study or a qualitative study and then organize and report the study accordingly. If, on the other hand, your survey project turns out to be a mixture of the two types of studies, you may have to come up with a hybrid form of organization that can account for all the things you need to report. Perhaps, even with such a hybrid report, you may need to decide whether it is primarily a statistical study or mainly qualitative in nature. Then, you can decide on the predominant organizational structure and modify it somewhat to accommodate the mixture of both quantitative and qualitative methods.

Whether you use quantitative or qualitative methods, or a mixture of methods, you will definitely want to use headings of some sort to guide your readers through the report and help them understand the report's organization. In the next section, I present excerpts from the TESOL report of the research described in the running examples throughout this book. While you are reading about it, think about whether the organization is clear to you and observe how the headings help to make the report and its organization clearer.

Examples of reporting on a survey project

The examples in this chapter include (1) the TESOL survey running example with a focus on the issues involved in reporting on a survey project and (2) the rotating example, which is a satire of what a good survey research project report should be.

Running example: Reporting on a survey project*

The running example is once again the TESOL report referenced as Brown, Knowles, Murray, Neu, and Violand-Hainer (1992b) in this book. For the sake of space, some parts of that report will be briefly summarized. However, to illustrate how the heart of a survey study can be reported, the Methods section will be reproduced here in its entirety.

INTRODUCTION

The TESOL report begins with a chronological recounting of the formation of the TESOL Research Task Force and the general purpose of the project, which was to survey and compare the attitudes of researchers and the general membership of TESOL toward research. To those ends, five research questions were posed:

1. Which TESOL members do research?
2. What are members' views on the state of the profession?

*© TESOL. Reprinted with permission. *Note:* This material has been superseded by current TESOL efforts.

3. What are members' views on TESOL publications?
4. What are members' views on the TESOL convention?
5. What are members' views on the place of research in TESOL?

Thus, the stage was set for the Methods section that follows.

Methods

Participants

SAMPLING

A total of 1800 questionnaires were mailed out from the TESOL Central Office. In order to answer the questions listed above, it was important to first sample the views of the General Membership of TESOL. To that end, 1000 people were randomly selected from the general membership list, and questionnaires were mailed to them. Because it was believed that researchers were relatively few in number within the organization, other subsamples were taken from those interest sections which were believed to contain relatively larger numbers of researchers: Applied Linguistics, Higher Education, Research, and Teacher Education. Random samples of 200 each were selected for mailings to represent each of those interest sections, as well.

CHARACTERISTICS OF THE RESPONDENTS

Table 1 shows the gender, nationality, and first language of the respondents. These characteristics are reported in percentages for the General Membership (GEN MEM), and separately for the Applied Linguistics (AL), Higher Education (HE), Research (RE), and Teacher Education (TE) interest sections. In the column at the far right, the percentages are given for all of the respondents taken together. Note that the average ages are also presented in the last row at the bottom of the table.

In general, the groups appear to be fairly similar, with several notable exceptions: (a) Higher Education appears to have a larger proportion of females, while Research and Teacher Education have generally lower proportions, (b) Higher Education has a considerably larger proportion of people with US nationality than the other groups with a correspondingly higher percentage of first language speakers of English, (c) the Applied Linguistics and Research groups are several years younger on average than the other groups. Additional information is provided on the educational and professional characteristics of these groups in the results section of this report.

Materials

The survey instrument used in this study was developed in the following four stages:

1. In January 1991, there was a meeting of the TESOL Research Task Force in San Jose, California. At that meeting, members of the Task Force decided

TABLE I. PERSONAL CHARACTERISTICS OF GROUPS SAMPLED
INTEREST SECTIONS

| Characteristic | Gen Mem | Interest sections | | | | Total |
		AL	HE	RE	TE	
Gender (%)						
Female	72.1	72.7	82.3	62.5	62.9	71.0
Male	27.9	27.3	17.7	37.5	37.1	29.0
Nationality (%)						
US	89.6	72.7	98.4	79.0	84.1	86.7
Other	10.4	27.3	1.6	21.0	15.9	13.3
First Language (%)						
English	89.7	83.3	96.8	90.1	88.9	89.7
Latin Language	5.8	4.5	1.6	3.7	6.3	5.0
Germanic	0.9	4.5	1.6	2.5	0.0	1.5
Sino-Tibet	2.7	6.1	0.0	2.5	3.2	2.8
Semitic	0.3	0.0	0.0	1.2	0.0	0.3
Other	0.6	1.5	0.0	0.0	1.6	0.7
Average Age	44.7	41.9	45.0	42.6	45.3	44.2

on the numbers and types of questions to be used, and many suggestions were made for specific questions.

2. A preliminary draft questionnaire was developed by the chair of the Task Force.
3. Feedback on the draft questionnaire was obtained from many TESOL colleagues in the US including the members of the TESOL Research Task Force, Executive Board, and Central Office, as well as the current and future chairs of the Applied Linguistics and Research interest sections, and many others.
4. The comments and suggestions received in the feedback were incorporated into a final version of the questionnaire.

The resulting questionnaire (see Appendix B) contained 31 questions of various types, some of which had additional sub-parts. The questions required a variety of open-response, selected-response, and Likert scale answers. Some of the questions centered on the personal, educational, and occupational characteristics of the respondents, while others focused on their background in research, and still others sought their opinions on the *TESOL Quarterly,* the TESOL Convention, and research issues in general.

It should be pointed out that some of the respondents were not 100 percent happy with the format, wording of questions, etc. involved in the instrument that they were returning. It is safe to report that no single question (closed-response or open-response) went without criticism by at least one respondent.

Even the relatively innocuous YES-NO response questions were implicitly criticized by those respondents who felt that they needed to write in words like "sometimes." The Likert scale responses also drew comments that indicated that some respondents felt that there were not enough categories supplied to fit the opinions that they wished to express. In the case of the open-response questions, the criticisms tended to be about the wording of the question. Either the question was considered too broad to answer, or the wording was not clear to the particular respondent. Such criticisms were very few when viewed as a percentage, but they must nevertheless be taken into account in interpreting the results of this study as well as in developing any future questionnaires for TESOL.

Several respondents made comments that indicated that they were unhappy with the questionnaire as a whole. One respondent asked, "Will this questionnaire provide relevant data?" Another criticized the length and complexity, when stating the following: "*Very few* teachers will respond to this questionnaire. You should however, receive a response from every researcher. Congratulations." While the response patterns indicate that hundreds of teachers did indeed respond to this questionnaire, the criticism must be taken to heart in that it may be true that researchers were more likely than teachers to return it.

Another respondent pointed out that "This questionnaire has polarised, non-polar issues, so typical of the binary thinking of some political ideologies." We agree. Particularly the closed-response question formats tended to polarize the issues involved. However, there are two ways in which we would answer the above comment. First, the open-response questions were provided to allow for expression of any and all other points of view, and they seem to have done just that, as indicated by the fact that the above comment could be made. Second, the purpose of the questionnaire was to discover whether such a polar view of research versus teaching was justified within the organization. Interestingly, the conclusions drawn from the questionnaire are generally that, while such polarization is a problem within the field, most respondents think that it is not justified or that it should be remedied.

It is heartening to realize that the questionnaire also received praise. Comments like the following were not uncommon:

1. Good questionnaire. I will be looking forward to reading the report of your findings in *TESOL Matters*.
2. I like your questionnaire – I'll be interested in reading the results. . . . Your try to tap ground feeling in TESOL is a good one.
3. Congratulations on asking these questions! Keep up the good work, TESOL; I boost you wherever I go.

Perhaps, the single most important lesson to be learned from these criticisms is that opinions on the quality of a questionnaire will vary as much as opinions on any other aspect of our professional lives. In short, no questionnaire, indeed no single question on a questionnaire, will please all of the people all of the time.

TABLE 2. QUESTIONNAIRES RETURNED

Characteristic	Gen Mem	Interest sections				Total
		AL	HE	RE	TE	
Number sent out	1,000	200	200	200	200	1,800
Number returned	334	66	62	82	63	607
Return rate percent	33.4	33.0	31.0	41.0	31.5	33.7
Percent of all qestionnaires	55.0	10.9	10.2	13.5	10.4	100.0

Procedures

THE MAILING

The photocopying, collating, random sampling, and mailing of the questionnaires were efficiently handled by the TESOL Central Office. As mentioned in the *Participants* section, questionnaires were mailed to 1000 people randomly selected from the general membership database of TESOL and 200 each were targeted at random samples from the Applied Linguistics, Higher Education, Research, and Teacher Education interest sections. These questionnaires were mailed out in April 1991 with a deadline of July 31 for returning them. It was suggested by some of the respondents that we would have gotten a better return rate if we had made a shorter deadline. However, we were concerned that such a short deadline would work against the international members. In fact, any questionnaires that arrived before the TESOL Executive Board October 1991 midyear meeting were included in the study.

RETURN RATE

A total of 607 questionnaires were returned. According to Table 2, 334 of these were from the General Membership, while 66 were from the Applied Linguistics interest section, 62 came from Higher Education, 82 from Research, and 63 from TE. This means that the return rates for the questionnaires varied from a low of 31 percent for the Higher Education interest section to a high of 41 percent for the Research group. The last row in Table 2 indicates that 55.0 percent of the questionnaires returned to us were from the General Membership, while 10.9 percent came from Applied Linguistics, 10.2 percent from Higher Education, 13.5 from Research, and 10.4 from Teacher Education.

Notice in Table 2 that the Research interest section had the highest return rate. This may be because the members of this interest section were naturally more interested in research issues, or it may be because they were somewhat more sympathetic to participating in research. Regardless of the reason they were represented slightly more than the other groups involved.

POSSIBLE REASONS FOR THE RETURN RATE

The moderate overall return rate of 33.7 percent may be explained by some of the logistical issues involved in distributing and returning the questionnaires. For instance, though return envelopes were provided, postage was not. This was necessary because US and international mailings were mixed. Hence, it was decided by the Executive Board that supplying postage was not feasible. In addition, because of the extra time and cost involved, it was decided that there would be no follow-up mailing. Furthermore, the three page questionnaire was fairly long and difficult to fill out with a number of open-ended questions. In piloting, it had taken respondents between 15 and 30 minutes to fill out the questionnaire. However, in the actual survey, it was clear that some of the respondents took far more time, providing careful answers that often spilled over onto the backs of the questionnaire sheets. It was also inevitable that a number of people were accidentally sampled as General Members as well as members of one or more of the interest sections. Presumably such people sent back only one questionnaire even though they had received more than one.

All of the above factors may have contributed to the fact that only about a third of the questionnaires found their way back to us. However, such a return rate is not unusual in the social sciences, and is in fact rather high in comparison to other surveys run by TESOL. For example, the final results of the TESOL 1991 Membership Survey indicate an 11 percent response rate (12.16 percent for U.S. members, and 6.75 percent for international members). Nevertheless, the fact that only 33.7 percent of the questionnaires were returned must be considered in thinking about the results, and those results must be interpreted cautiously. [For more discussion of the sampling procedures and return rate, see Brown, Knowles, Murray, Neu, and Violand-Hainer, 1992a.]

SOME COMMENTS ON THE METHODS SECTION

First, notice in the Methods section that the Participants subsection provides information about how the respondents were selected, how they were grouped, and what their characteristics were. Second, notice that the Materials subsection describes the stages followed in developing the materials, the types of questions included, and the reactions of various respondents to the questions. Indeed, a fairly large section is devoted to criticisms leveled at the questionnaire. This sort of open and honest discussion of the problems that occurred in a project can help readers understand the project and judge its credibility. No language survey research project is ever perfect, so why not be open and honest about the problems that arise during the research process?

Third, notice that the Procedures subsection describes the mailing of the questionnaires in considerable detail, as well as the return rate and reasons why that return rate might have been relatively low. Again, the researchers were open and honest, this time about a problem with their return rate.

RESULTS

The Results section, which followed directly after the Methods section, provided a technical report of the statistical results of the study. For the sake of clarity and brevity, much of the information was summarized in eight tables (some of which appear in Chapter 4 of this book as Tables 4.26 and 4.27). The Results were subdivided into six sections with the following headings:

1. Educational Characteristics
2. Occupational Characteristics
3. Research Background
4. Views on TESOL Publications
5. Views on TESOL Conventions
6. Views on Research

In each of those sections, the relevant tables were discussed in detail in terms of the salient characteristics of particular groups and comparisons between the groups. Recall that the groups involved were the General Membership and the four special-interest groups thought to have high proportions of researchers: Applied Linguistics, Higher Education, Research, and Teacher Education.

DISCUSSION

The Discussion section provided direct answers to the five research questions posed at the beginning of the study, so naturally those five questions were used as subheadings to help organize the discussion. The direct answer given for each question was written entirely in prose and was based on a combination of summary statistical information (from the Results section prose and tables) and quotes from the answers given to the more qualitative open-response questions on the survey.

CONCLUSIONS

Because of the political nature of this survey project, the Conclusions section focused on what the organization could do with the results of the survey. Thus this section covered *Initiatives Already Taken and Planned Initiatives,* which included the formation of a new TESOL Research Advisory Committee to continue the work of the Task Force and a structure for the new committee to use in doing its work. The Conclusions section also contained a subsection on the last page entitled *Coda,* which began with the words "All in all, it was a difficult and emotionally draining task to create this questionnaire, analyze the results, and report the findings." Then the authors went on to explain some of the ways the project had been both draining and rewarding for them, which added a human touch to the otherwise academic-technical account. The report was brought to a close with the following sentence: "It is hoped that this paper will serve as a solid basis for the on-going work of a newly constituted Research Advisory Committee, which can consider the information presented here and solve some of the research-related problems that we have identified."

Naturally, the report also contained References and included the questionnaire itself in an appendix (you can find the questionnaire in Appendix B of this book).

265

Rotating example: A satire

I wrote the following satirical survey research report in response to the experience of doing the above TESOL survey research project. I find that it sometimes helps to laugh a bit about the ever-so-serious earnestness with which we sometimes take our professional selves. The degree to which you see humor in the satire that follows may be an indication of how successful I have been at explaining survey research in this book. After all, satire is funny because it violates whatever norms are involved, and the degree to which you understand such violations is probably directly proportional to the number of times you laugh.

THE TESOL QUIRKS PROJECT
JAMES DEAN BROWN
UNIVERSITY OF HAWAI'I AT MANOA

The results of the end-all TESOL QUestionnaire for Investigating Really Kaleidoscopic Samples (a.k.a. QUIRKS [pronounced quirks]) are in. This paper is designed to provide readers for the results of this project. The purpose of the study was to explore survey research investigation evaluation analysis assessment appraisal estimation techniques (i.e., to study whether there should be questions on questionnaires). To that end, the following research questions were posed:

1. Does TESOL have members?
2. If so, do those members respond to stimuli (e.g., questionnaires)?
3. If they respond to questionnaires, should they (the questionnaires) be mailed in plain brown wrappers for a better response rate?

The alpha level for all statistical tests was set at $\alpha > 1.05$ to ensure significance.

Method

Participants

An astounding total of 23,743 questionnaires were returned by the 21,152 members of the TESOL organization, which represents an unheard of return rate of 112 percent.[1] Such a return rate is clearly a record for language sciences survey research (LSSR), if not for social sciences research (SSR) as a hole.

Of the respondents, 62 percent were female and 50 percent were male. The

---

1 The astoundingly high return rate has led to accusations that some of the "university research types" surreptitiously photocopied and filled out hundreds, if not thousands, of extra questionnaires to make sure that the "researchers' point of view" (as if you could actually get any two researchers to agree on any "point of view") would continue to dominate the TESOL organization for the rest of the millennium. However, one bleary-eyed researcher (with copy machine toner on her hands) suggested that the dastardly deed may have been done by "public school teacher types" for equally nefarious reasons. This important, but mysterious, debate may never be resolved.

ages ranged from 12.5 to 107 with a median mental age of 11. However, it should be noted that 62 percent of the respondents left the age question blank, or filled in an obscenity. A number of ESL/EFL teachers turned out to have had experience in teaching ESL/EFL, though the results were similar to those found in Vitro (Unpublishable ms., cited in Brown, 1982), who found that "many teachers have only had one year of experience over, and over, and over again."

Materials

Naturally, the questionnaire used in this study was carefully designed to reflect the biases of the questionnaire designer. And, of course, it is readily available for further public inspection (see Brown, 1989, cited in Naire, 1990zzzz [which, incidentally, had a print run of five copies, all of which went to the author's mother]). The QUIRKS questionnaire had a question–requestion reliability coefficient of .01, which is clearly significant at the .01 level ($r_{xx'} = p = .01$).

The questionnaire included 30 closed-response Lick-it scale (a.k.a. Liquored scale) questions, which turned out to be fairly messy to analyze. There were also three open-ended questions which received not only drier responses, but longer ones, as well. Naturally, the open-ended questions were analyzed using the latest qualitative research methods (even though some "quantitative" researchers believe "qualitative research" is an oxymoron [not to be confused with a Cambridge moron]).

The length of time that it took respondents to answer the questionnaire was operationalized by measuring the surface area of the coffee stains and other food markings that showed up on the questionnaires. The longest time that it took any single respondent to fill out the questionnaire was 3.73 square inches.

Procedures

The questionnaires were sent out by third-class mail in plain brown envelopes in order to keep the sample size small; it was hoped that a small sample size would, in turn, help to keep the analyses simple and straightforward. [nb. While the plain brown wrappings were brown, they were not completely plain; they were accidentally marked with the word PRURIENT.] However, rather than dampening the response rate, the brown-wrapper strategy (BS) appears to have had the opposite effect on the TESOL membership. In short, there has never been such a high level of interest in any survey conducted in our field. The respondents literally ripped the brown wrappers open in their eagerness to get at the contents. Some disappointment was reported because of what they found inside (or, more accurately, what they did not find inside).

Results

The results of the Lick-it type scale were so smeared and sticky that the quantitative analyses were abandoned. In effect, this meant that it was neither possible nor necessary to use any descriptive or inferential sadistics in this study. Nonetheless, a contingency table was drawn up – just in case a table was needed.

The open-ended questions were considerably more productive, drawing a wide variety of interesting answers. The first open-ended question was WHAT DO YOU PERCEIVE AS THE GREATEST SINGLE PROBLEM IN THE FIELD OF ESL/EFL? Three example responses will illustrate the range of responses:

1. "Phooey!"
2. "Too damned many foolish questionnaires to answer."
3. "What does ESL/EFL mean, anyway?"

Other respondents, responded with different responses, but most of those had to do with the ways that administrators and educators in other fields think of us, i.e., as derelict, irresponsible professionals (or DIPs, for short). As one (1) respondent put it, "Hour salarys are two low, and hour ours are to long, and we don't get enuf respekt for peple with hour traneing and degreez."

The second question was DO YOU FIND THE RESEARCH IN THE *TESOL QUARTERLY* USEFUL? The responses were mostly positive to this question, but several questionnees said that they had not noticed that there was any research reported in the *TESOL Quarterly* (TQ), and another answeree said that it would be fine for TQ to begin printing research articles at any time. Of those who had noticed the research articles in TQ, an underwhelming minority (less than .0000421 percent, i.e., one person) felt that the research was of such bad quality that the results should be ignored, while a larger number ($N = 2$) felt that at least some of the research studies were probably actually carried out as described in the journal.

Many *teachers* indicated that they wanted more practical implications to come out of the research. *Researchers* seemed to want more serious and purely theoretical efforts not bound to producing immediate practical applications. Perhaps the best compromise solution would be for the TQ to publish more articles that are impartially practical and partially impractical.

The final question was WHAT DO YOU THINK OF THE ANNUAL TESOL CONVENTION? Those answerees who had attended 0 or less times had the strongest negative opinions, while those who had attended 1 or more times seemed to feel, on the whole, that the annual TESOL Convention happens every year. Twelve of the respondees (out of 23,743) felt that the "breakfast with the stars" events were a great idea. [These 12 were later found to be the "stars" themselves.]

Discussion/conclusions

Once the results were in, the alpha level was raised to the 5.55 level, and the research questions were changed. Direct answers to these new research questions, were as follows: yes, yes, and maybe.

Clearly, the most remarkable result to come out of this research was that the use of a plain brown envelope and/or the stamping of the word *PRURIENT* on the envelope resulted in an extraordinarily high return rate. It is important to note that the word *PRURIENT* may only work with English teachers, because they are more likely than other educators to have that word in their vocabularies (though it is currently not listed in the Claire [1990] dictionary of indispensable ESL vocabulary). It is also important to note that this research did not disambiguate whether it was the plain brown wrapper or the word *PRURIENT* that caused the high level of interest.

Suggestions for future research

Future researchers might consider sending out their questionnaires half in truly plain brown envelopes, half in white envelopes marked *PRURIENT,* and half in envelopes that are both brown and marked *PRURIENT.* All of these machinations would help to determine which condition results in the most remarkable return rates. Perhaps, an interaction of Prurience and Brownness is necessary, and I was just lucky enough to hit on this combination in my study. Only carefully designed empirical survey investigation evaluation analysis assessment appraisal estimation research can answer this vital question – a question clearly important to the future of the entire language teaching profession.

Final conclusion

Without a doubt, the most important result of this study is the finding, which coincidentally agrees with the conclusions of Brown (1982, p. 12), who put it this way: "ESL/EFL teachers are significantly better people . . . because they have learned through absolute necessity to laugh at themselves and poke fun at their own seriousness."

References

Real citations

Brown, J. D. (1982). An empirical analysis of psychological constructs underlying the desire to teach ESL/EFL: A satire. *TESOL Newsletter (16),* 3, 9, 12.
Claire, E. (1990). *An indispensable guide to dangerous English for language learners and others* (2nd ed.). Dundee, IL: Delta Systems.

Surreal citations

Naire, Q. (1990zzzz). *Questionnaire design: A study in deception and demagoguery.* Rarely, Miss: Nonesuch Press.
Vitro, N. (Unpublishable ms.) Poverty: The baseline in ESL/EFL teaching. *Language Leering (4571),* 657. Previously cited in Brown, J. D. (1982). An empirical analysis of psychological constructs underlying the desire to teach ESL/EFL: A satire. *TESOL Newsletter (16),* 3, 9, 12.

Summary

In this chapter, I discussed ways to organize survey research reports, among them the relatively strict organization of statistical survey research reports (after the APA guidelines), which include an Introduction section (with optional headings for three sections: Literature Review, statement of purpose, and research questions and/or hypotheses), Methods section (including Participants, Materials, and Procedures), Results section, and Discussion (or Conclusions) section. I also examined the relatively flexible organization of qualitative research reports, which typically include an Introduction, (Research) Methods, and Conclusion sections, but are otherwise organized (between the Methods and Conclusions sections) to tell the story of the research. I included several examples of both the strict statistical organization and the more flexible qualitative organization to show how even the predominant patterns can vary in each case. Then, I discussed one way in which the strict statistical organization and its relatively flexible qualitative organization can be combined in one report. The remainder of the chapter provided two examples: the TESOL report running example, and a lighter, perhaps frivolous, satirical rotating example.

Suggestions for further reading

The general books listed in this section in Chapter 1 all cover the topic of reporting survey results. Only one book that I have found, Fink (1995f), focuses solely on the issues involved in reporting survey results.

Important terms

Introduction section
statement of purpose
research questions
research hypotheses
Methods section
Participants subsection

Materials subsection
Procedures subsection
Results section
Discussion (or Conclusions)
   section
Suggestions for Further Research

Review questions

1. For which type of research, qualitative or quantitative, is the organizational framework generally more flexible?
2. What is the purpose of the Introduction section of a statistical survey research report? What should the Introduction section contain?

3. How do the statement of purpose and research questions (or research hypotheses) fit into the Introduction section?
4. What three subsections should be included in the Methods section of a statistical survey research report?
5. What types of information should be included in the Participants subsection of a statistical survey research report?
6. What should the Materials subsection of a statistical survey research report contain?
7. What types of information should the Procedures subsection of a statistical survey research report provide?
8. What is the purpose of the Results section of a statistical survey research report?
9. At minimum, what should be accomplished in the Discussion (or Conclusions) section of a statistical survey research report?
10. What three sections did the three example outlines from qualitative research have in common?

Application exercises

A. Look again at the rotating example in this chapter (the satire), and outline its organization. Does it follow the strict statistical organization, or the more flexible qualitative type? How does this example handle the qualitative information?
B. Find one of the survey research reports mentioned in this book (e.g., Bailey & Brown, 1995; Bernbrock, 1979; Jacob, 1982; Lynch, 1992) and outline its organization. Is it a qualitative or a statistical study? How does it deviate from the guidelines provided in this chapter? Does that deviation enhance or detract from its clarity?
C. Outline a report, either for a study that you have already done or for a study that you would like to propose. Will your outline follow the strict statistical organization, or the more flexible qualitative type? How does your outline deviate from the examples shown in this chapter?

Appendix A Language testing course description questionnaire

Name _____ Sex _____ Age _____
Nationality_____ Office Phone: (___) _____
Institution _____
Address _____
_____

Have you ever taught an INTRODUCTORY level language testing course
of any kind? (circle one)   YES   NO

If your answer is NO, please stop and mail the questionnaire in the self-
addressed envelope provided. Remember, it is important that we hear from
those of you who are not language teaching testing courses, too. If your
answer was YES, please continue!

About the instructor

What degrees do you hold (include the field of study for each)?
_____
_____
_____
_____

How many testing/statistics courses have you taken? And, what were they?
_____
_____
_____
_____

What other types of noncourse testing experiences or preparation have
you had? _____
_____
_____
_____
_____

Source: Bailey & Brown, 1995.

About the course

How much time do the students spend actually getting hands-on experience with the following in your course? (circle number)

	Amount of time					
	None	Some	Moderate		Extensive	
Type of experience						
item writing	0	1	2	3	4	5
test administration	0	1	2	3	4	5
test scoring	0	1	2	3	4	5
test score interpretation	0	1	2	3	4	5
test revision	0	1	2	3	4	5
test critiquing	0	1	2	3	4	5
test taking	0	1	2	3	4	5

How much time do you spend on the following topics? (circle number)

	Amount of time					
	None	Some	Moderate		Extensive	
General						
norm-referenced testing	0	1	2	3	4	5
criterion-referenced testing	0	1	2	3	4	5
achievement testing	0	1	2	3	4	5
aptitude testing	0	1	2	3	4	5
diagnostic testing	0	1	2	3	4	5
placement testing	0	1	2	3	4	5
proficiency testing	0	1	2	3	4	5
measuring attitudes	0	1	2	3	4	5
measuring the different skills	0	1	2	3	4	5
assessment at different levels	0	1	2	3	4	5
critiquing published tests	0	1	2	3	4	5
others? _____	0	1	2	3	4	5
_____	0	1	2	3	4	5
_____	0	1	2	3	4	5
Item analysis						
item writing	0	1	2	3	4	5
item writing for different skills	0	1	2	3	4	5
item content analysis	0	1	2	3	4	5
item quality analysis	0	1	2	3	4	5
item facility (a.k.a. item difficulty or easiness)	0	1	2	3	4	5

	Amount of time					
	None	Some	Moderate	Extensive		
item discrimination (traditional)	0	1	2	3	4	5
biserial correlation	0	1	2	3	4	5
item agreement	0	1	2	3	4	5
item beta	0	1	2	3	4	5
distractor efficiency analysis	0	1	2	3	4	5
one-parameter IRT	0	1	2	3	4	5
two-parameter IRT	0	1	2	3	4	5
three-parameter IRT	0	1	2	3	4	5
others? _____	0	1	2	3	4	5
_____	0	1	2	3	4	5
_____	0	1	2	3	4	5
Descriptive statistics						
mean	0	1	2	3	4	5
mode	0	1	2	3	4	5
median	0	1	2	3	4	5
midpoint	0	1	2	3	4	5
range	0	1	2	3	4	5
standard deviation	0	1	2	3	4	5
variance	0	1	2	3	4	5
stanines	0	1	2	3	4	5
z scores	0	1	2	3	4	5
T scores	0	1	2	3	4	5
CEEB scores	0	1	2	3	4	5
others? _____	0	1	2	3	4	5
_____	0	1	2	3	4	5
_____	0	1	2	3	4	5

	Coverage					
	None	Some	Moderate	Extensive		
Test consistency						
sources of testing error	0	1	2	3	4	5
reliability and test length	0	1	2	3	4	5
reliability and ranges of talent	0	1	2	3	4	5
test–retest reliability	0	1	2	3	4	5
parallel forms reliability	0	1	2	3	4	5
internal consistency reliability	0	1	2	3	4	5
standard error of measurement	0	1	2	3	4	5
Split-half adjusted method	0	1	2	3	4	5

Appendix A

	Coverage			
	None	Some	Moderate	Extensive

	None	Some	Moderate	Extensive	
Spearman-Brown Prophecy formula	0	1	2	3	4	5
K-R 20	0	1	2	3	4	5
K-R 21	0	1	2	3	4	5
Cronbach alpha	0	1	2	3	4	5
Rulon	0	1	2	3	4	5
Flanagan	0	1	2	3	4	5
Guttman	0	1	2	3	4	5
interrater	0	1	2	3	4	5
intrarater	0	1	2	3	4	5
phi coefficient	0	1	2	3	4	5
phi (lambda)	0	1	2	3	4	5
agreement coefficient	0	1	2	3	4	5
kappa	0	1	2	3	4	5
generalizability coefficient	0	1	2	3	4	5
others? _____	0	1	2	3	4	5
_____	0	1	2	3	4	5
_____	0	1	2	3	4	5

Validity

content validity	0	1	2	3	4	5
item-objective congruence	0	1	2	3	4	5
item-specification congruence	0	1	2	3	4	5
construct validity	0	1	2	3	4	5
criterion-related validity	0	1	2	3	4	5
correlational analysis	0	1	2	3	4	5
simple regression analysis	0	1	2	3	4	5
standard error of estimate	0	1	2	3	4	5
principle components analysis	0	1	2	3	4	5
rotated factor analysis	0	1	2	3	4	5
confirmatory factor analysis	0	1	2	3	4	5
multi-trait/multi-measure	0	1	2	3	4	5
others? _____	0	1	2	3	4	5
_____	0	1	2	3	4	5
_____	0	1	2	3	4	5

What percentage of the course do you devote to these general areas:
Criterion-referenced testing issues? _____
Norm-referenced testing issues? _____

The students

What type(s) of students take your course? (graduate/undergraduate, majors, etc.)

_____

_____

Does the course count toward a degree or other certification?

_____

_____

Is the course required or optional? (circle one)   required   optional

How do your students feel about language testing before taking the course?

_____

_____

How do your students feel about language testing after having taken the course?

_____

_____

In general, do you think that your students find your course (check all of the ones you think apply):

_____ interesting

_____ too theoretical

_____ easy

_____ useful

_____ too practical

_____ difficult

_____ a nice balance between theory and practice

_____ challenging

_____ others?

Do you teach any other more advanced courses in language testing at your institution (briefly describe course and level)?

_____

_____

What other questions do you think should have been on this questionnaire, and how would you answer them?

_____

_____

OTHER COMMENTS OF ANY KIND (use back of sheet if you need more space):

_____

_____

Please remember to attach a copy of a recent course syllabus or other material describing your course? And check the box if you would like a copy of our final report on this project. ☐

**THANK YOU IN ADVANCE FOR
YOUR HELP WITH THIS PROJECT!**

Appendix B TESOL Research Task Force questionnaire

You have been selected as part of a random sample of the entire membership of TESOL. The questionnaire below is part of the work of the TESOL Research Task Force, which was set up by the Executive Board of TESOL. The purpose of the questionnaire is to investigate the membership's views on the place of research in the TESOL organization and TESOL convention. Your cooperation is essential because we need a high return rate on this questionnaire so that the views of all TESOL members will be represented. Please take a few minutes to fill out the attached questionnaire and mail it (no later than July 31st) in the enclosed envelope. Remember your views are important, and the only way that they will be known to the TESOL organization is if you send this questionnaire back. Rest assured that your responses are anonymous and will be kept entirely confidential. A summary report of the results of this survey will appear in *TESOL Matters* in the coming year. Thank you in advance for returning this questionnaire promptly.

   —J. D. Brown, Emma Hainer, Marjorie Knowles, Denise Murray, Joyce Neu (TESOL Research Task Force)

Gender _____ Age _____ Nationality _____
                                   First language _____

1. In the space provided, please list all college/university degrees or teaching credentials that you hold.

   Degree/credential   *Field*   *Granting institution*   *Year*

2. Do you currently work in a TESOL-related field? (circle one)
   YES   NO
3. Which of the following is your primary field of interest? (circle one)
   TESOL   BILINGUAL ED.   OTHER FOREIGN LANGUAGES
   OTHER _____

Source: Brown et al., 1992b. ©TESOL. Reprinted with permission. *Note:* This material has been superseded by current TESOL efforts.

4. Please indicate approximately the percentage of your work time that you spend doing the following:
   ADMINISTRATION _____
   CLASSROOM TEACHING _____
   COMMUNITY SERVICE _____
   COUNSELING STUDENTS _____
   MATERIALS WRITING _____
   MEETINGS _____
   RESEARCH _____
   SERVICE (INSTITUTIONAL) _____
   TEACHER TRAINING _____
   OTHER _____ _____
   TOTAL _____ [Please check that your TOTAL is 100%, even if you put in 200% days.]

5. On what basis are you employed? (circle one)
   FULL-TIME   PART-TIME

6. How many years of ESL teaching have you done (in predominantly English speaking countries)? _____

7. How many years of EFL teaching have you done (outside of the English speaking countries)? _____

8. Type(s) of Institution(s) where you do most of your TESOL-related work (circle as many as applicable):
   ADULT ED.   ELEMENTARY   HIGH SCHOOL
   INTERMEDIATE   REFUGEE
   UNIVERSITY (UNDERGRAD)
   UNIVERSITY (GRADUATE)
   OTHER _____

9. Have you ever taken an introductory level language testing course of any kind? (circle one)   YES   NO

10. Have you taken any statistics or research design courses? (circle one)
    YES   NO
    What were the course titles (roughly)?

11. Do you feel that you stay current with the research in EFL/ESL?
    YES   NO

12. Do you regularly read the *TESOL Quarterly*?   YES   NO

13. Do you feel that the research reported in *TESOL Quarterly* is of high quality?   YES   NO

14. Do you believe that *TESOL Quarterly* provides you with usable research information?   YES   NO

15. Do you conduct research of any kind?   YES   NO
    If so, what kind:

16. Would you support the creation of a Research Advisory Committee within the TESOL organization designed to increase communication between researchers and teachers, encourage sound research on theory and practice, involve TESOL in seeking research grants, increase cooperation with other organizations, etc.?   YES   NO

17. Do you think you would be better/worse off if research were not a part of TESOL?   WORSE   BETTER

18. In general, do you find research in the language teaching field to be (check all which apply):

_____ boring   _____ pointless
_____ challenging   _____ too theoretical
_____ difficult to understand   _____ too practical
_____ easy to understand   _____ about the right mix
_____ interesting   of theory and
_____ useful   practice
_____ others

19. Professionally, how much importance do you attach to each of the following items? (Circle the number that best describes the degree of importance that you attach to the item on the left.)

	None	Little	Mod.		Very
TESOL Quarterly	0	1	2	3	4	5
book reviews	0	1	2	3	4	5
brief reports	0	1	2	3	4	5
classroom research articles	0	1	2	3	4	5
classroom teaching articles	0	1	2	3	4	5
statistical research articles	0	1	2	3	4	5
TESOL Matters	0	1	2	3	4	5
TESOL Convention	0	1	2	3	4	5
breakfasts with the "stars"	0	1	2	3	4	5
colloquia on various topics	0	1	2	3	4	5
field trips to local institutions	0	1	2	3	4	5
job placement	0	1	2	3	4	5
concurrent sessions	0	1	2	3	4	5
personal networking	0	1	2	3	4	5
plenary speeches	0	1	2	3	4	5
publishers' displays (booths)	0	1	2	3	4	5

	Importance						
	None	Little		Mod.		Very	
publishers' presentations	0	1	2	3	4	5	
research presentations	0	1	2	3	4	5	
workshops (pre-convention)	0	1	2	3	4	5	
workshops (during convention)	0	1	2	3	4	5	

20. What do you consider to be the single biggest problem facing ESL/
    EFL teachers today?

21. What do you think the principal purpose(s) of the TESOL organiza-
    tion should be?

22. How would you define the word *research?*

23. If you had a magic wand, what single research question would you
    like answered?

24. How can the TESOL organization best foster communication of the
    researchers' perspectives to teachers?

25. How can the TESOL organization best increase communication of
    the teachers' views to researchers?

26. How many TESOL conventions have you attended? _____
27. If you have attended a TESOL Convention, what types of sessions
    do you best like to attend?

    And, are there enough sessions of the types you most like to attend?
    YES   NO

28. Regarding future TESOL Conventions, would you be interested in attending any of the following? (check as many as applicable)

_____ research fair (a setting where anyone can consult about his or her research ideas/projects with experienced researchers)

_____ research roundtables (group discussions with researchers about current research concerns)

_____ research workshops (workshops on how to conduct simple research projects)

_____ other _____

29. Why do you think that some research articles are inaccessible to some of the readers in our field?

30. What article (research or non-research) have you read recently that you found stimulating or interesting, and where was it published?

31. Which journals do you read regularly?

OTHER COMMENTS (use back of sheet if you need more space):

PLEASE MAIL (POSTMARKED NO LATER THAN JULY 31ST) TO:
J. D. BROWN
TESOL RESEARCH SURVEY
1600 CAMERON STREET, SUITE 300
ALEXANDRIA, VIRGINIA 22314-2751
—OR FAX TO: 703-836-7864

Appendix C   Reading course evaluation questionnaire for students

ELI 72 student questionnaire

Please take some time to answer the following questions. We need your opinions so that we can improve the ELI Reading Class. Many thanks for your help.

Background information

Status: Graduate student _____ Undergraduate _____
Major _____
Native language _____
Other languages _____
Time in the U.S.A. (in years) _____
Time at University of Hawaii _____
(in semesters)

Time at other U.S. colleges or universities_____
(in semesters)

Other English Language Programs_____
(specify)

Indicate the ELI classes taken (check one)
   ELI 70 (listening comprehension I)   _____
   ELI 80 (listening comprehension II)   _____
   ELI 73 (writing for foreign students)   _____
   ELI 83 (writing for foreign graduate students) _____
   ELI 100 (expository writing: A Guided Approach)   _____
What kind of recreational reading do you enjoy? (please specify)
_____
_____

1. Please check the kind of reading you do most in your non-ELI classes.
   textbooks   _____
   articles from academic journals _____
   others (please describe) _____

Source: Loschky et al., 1989.

284

2. On an average day, approximately how many pages of reading material do you read in your classes other than in the ELI classes?

   _____

3. Do you think that being able to read English better is important to you in your major? Why or why not?

   _____

   _____

4. What is your biggest problem with reading? (please check the appropriate blanks)

	very serious	moderate	slight
a. understanding main idea	_____	_____	_____
b. understanding details	_____	_____	_____
c. making inferences	_____	_____	_____
d. interpreting figures of speech and idioms	_____	_____	_____
e. summarizing or synthesizing materials	_____	_____	_____
f. recognizing the author's point of view	_____	_____	_____
g. recognizing the author's purpose	_____	_____	_____
h. understanding sentence structure	_____	_____	_____
i. understanding paragraph structure	_____	_____	_____
j. vocabulary			
i. general	_____	_____	_____
ii. academic	_____	_____	_____
iii. technical	_____	_____	_____
k. reading speed	_____	_____	_____
l. other problems	_____	_____	_____

5. Do you think this class will help you solve your reading problems? Why or why not?

   _____

   _____

6. Do you think the textbook, *Advanced Reading and Writing* (Baumwoll & Saitz), is good for this class? Why or why not?

   _____

   _____

7. Approximately how many of the vocabulary words in *Meaning by All Means* (Mason) did you already know before you enrolled in this class?

   most _____   some _____   not many _____

8. Do you think the extra reading materials your teacher brings to class (such as, newspapers, magazines, or articles) are useful? Please explain your opinion.

   _____

   _____

9. Of these extra reading materials which do you enjoy most?

   _____

   _____

10. Are there additional reading materials you would like to use in this class? If so, please specify.

   _____

   _____

11. Do you think the speed-reading cards are helping you increase your reading speed? _____

12. How important are the following for your ELI or other course work?

	very important	moderately important	not important
skimming and scanning	_____	_____	_____
reading charts, graphs, pictures, etc.	_____	_____	_____
library skills	_____	_____	_____
class discussions	_____	_____	_____

13. What are the most effective classroom activities your teacher uses? Please describe.

   _____

   _____

14. If you could add or change anything about this reading class, what would your changes be? Please explain your ideas.

   _____

   _____

15. If you would like to make any additional comments regarding the reading class, please use the space below.

Appendix D Reading course evaluation interview questions for ESL teachers

1. What are your personal goals for the students in your class?
2. What would you say their needs are?
3. What are your biggest problems in teaching reading?
4. How do you feel about the objectives?
5. Has having the objectives altered your teaching approach?
6. How would you describe your teaching approach?
7. What kind of learner does best in this class?
8. What do you think is the key to successful teaching in this class?
9. Do you use either of the textbooks extensively? What is your opinion of the texts?
10. What kind of text(s) would you like to see the reading program use? (Do you have any specific recommendations?)
11. Do you prepare a lot of supplemental materials? (If yes, is that because of the limitations of the text or because of your ideas about teaching reading?)
12. What kinds of supplemental materials do you bring to class?
13. What other kinds would you make if you had the time?
14. Do you favor closer coordination of materials preparation among teachers? (If yes, do you have any ideas as to how this coordination might be accomplished?)
15. How do you evaluate students' progress?
16. Do you perceive a need for two levels of reading classes?
17. If you could restructure the reading program, how would you do it?

Source: Loschky et al., 1987.

Appendix E Reading course evaluation: Non-ESL faculty questionnaire

1. Field of study: _____
2. Please indicate course level: Undergraduate _____
   Graduate _____
3. Do many non-native speakers of English take this course?
   Y   N
4. Please indicate the type of reading you primarily assign (use percentages if applicable).
   a. textbook _____
   b. articles from academic journals _____
   c. other (please specify) _____

5. *Approximately* how many pages of required reading material do you assign each week? _____
6. How important is the reading skill to a student's success in your department?

   _____

7. How important is the reading skill to success in your field after graduation?

   _____

   _____

8. What types of tests do you give?
   a. multiple-choice _____
   b. fill-in-the-blank _____
   c. short-answer _____
   d. essay _____
   e. other _____
9. What types of reading materials are your tests based on? (use percentages if applicable)
   a. textbooks _____
   b. articles _____
   c. lecture notes _____

Source: Loschky et al., 1987.

10. Please indicate by rank order the amount of time your students must spend for each of the following areas (1= most time; 4= least time).
listening to lectures _____
speaking in class _____
reading for class _____
writing for class _____
11. Do your non-native students have more severe reading problems than your native English speaking students? Y   N
12. If yes, how would you characterize these problems?

_____
_____

13. Would you be willing to share any of your colleagues' comments regarding non-native students' reading-related studying problems? If yes, please indicate below.

_____
_____

14. Can you offer any advice for the English Language Institute (ELI) regarding these issues? If yes, please indicate below.

_____
_____

Appendix F Foreign TA training project needs analysis: Interview questionnaire sheet

Brief description of project

This project is an analysis of the English language needs of foreign Teaching Assistants (henceforth FTAs) at the University of Hawaii at Manoa. The primary goal of the project was to rationally formulate tentative objectives to be used in the design and implementation of an orientation program for FTAs. The overall purpose of the orientation program will be to ease the transition of FTAs into the unique demands of instruction in a U.S. university classroom.

The analysis was formulated using data gathered from a variety of different sources: (1) from personal interviews with those current FTAs; (2) from questionnaires distributed to present students of FTAs; (3) from in-class observations of present FTAs; and (4) from the specific interests and expectations of professors, advisors, administrators and University policy makers. Furthermore, correspondence was carried out with other institutions with existing programs of this kind to ascertain what has and has not worked in other locations. Finally, an extensive literature search was done to find out what had been written on this subject in the past. The encouragement and helpful insights received from these various sectors in the initial stages and throughout our project have greatly facilitated our goal of ameliorating the difficulties of FTAs here at the University of Hawaii.

Intro

Interviewer introduces herself, explains what the purpose of the interview is (the formulation of guidelines for a training course for FTA's, thus 30 FTAs are being interviewed to give an accurate assessment of needs).

Biographic info

1. Name:
2. Major: Degree objective:

Source: Weaver et al., 1987.

3. Native language(s):
4. Length of residence in Hawaii:
5. Length of time here at UH:
6. Is the United States as a whole what you thought it would be, or different? In what ways?
7. How is the classroom environment here in the U.S. different from what it is in your home country? What are the similarities?

Teaching info

1. For what courses are you a TA here at UH?
2. What are your responsibilities as a TA? (e.g., running a lab, grading exams, helping students with experiments, lecturing, leading discussions)
3. Is the position you hold as a TA directly related to your field of interest?
4. Do you have previous teaching experience in the United States or elsewhere?
5. Did you run into any unexpected problems when you began as a TA here at UH? What were they?
6. What is the most difficult aspect of your position as a TA:
   –cultural differences?
   –different classroom expectations/behavior?
   –language difficulties – understanding and being understood?
7. If there had been some sort of training/orientation course before you began as a TA, what kind of information would have been helpful to you? Do you have any suggestions for things to include in a possible course in the future?
8. In your opinion, what problems do FTAs encounter with their students that native-speaking TAs do not?
9. What particular strengths do you think that FTAs can bring to the classroom in an American university?
10. In order to complete this survey of the needs of foreign TAs, we would like to have your students fill out a brief (10-minute) questionnaire. This would not affect you in any way, but would be another means for us to plan to better the educational experience for all concerned. Would it be better for you to have us come at the beginning or at the end of your class to give this questionnaire?

Thanks very much for your help!

Appendix G   Example cover letter

UNIVERSITY OF HAWAII AT MANOA
College of Languages, Linguistics and Literature
Second Language Teaching and Curriculum Center
Webster 203, 2528 The Mall
Honolulu, Hawaii 96822

May 15, 1990

Dear Language Course Coordinator,

The Second Language Teaching and Curriculum Center was formed to provide coordination and support for language teaching within the College of Languages, Linguistics and Literature (LLL). One project that the committee has decided to tackle is the coordination of activities to support the graduate teaching assistants and lecturers, who teach many of the first and second year language courses.

As a first step in that process, we are sending you information about the orientation services available to your new TAs and graduate student lecturers each summer at UHM. You will find a packet of materials enclosed on that yearly project. While this orientation is designed for incoming graduate students who will be teaching in their respective departments, I am told that students continuing in those positions can participate on a space available basis. We hope that you will take advantage of this unique orientation program to help some of your new staff get their feet on the ground.

You will also find enclosed a copy of the *ELI Teachers Manual*. This document was developed by the Director, Assistant Director and Lead Teachers in the ELI (Department of ESL) to serve as a handy reference for all ELI teachers. It is normally distributed as part of the orientation for incoming ELI instructors, most of whom are GAs or lecturers. We are sending it to you only as a source of ideas. Perhaps there is similar information that could be put together to help in orienting your teaching assistants and lecturers.

We are also working on a report about the present state of support for teaching assistants and lecturers in language departments. This report will be sent out to you this summer. It will serve as a summary of the current practices in orienting,

Source: SLTCC, 1990.

292

training, and supporting the TAs and lecturers in LLL language courses. As part of that project, we have enclosed a questionnaire. Please take a few moments to fill it out as completely as possible and return it within one week in the enclosed envelope. The sooner we have complete information from each of you, the sooner we can prepare the report and disseminate it to all of you.

Thank you in advance for your cooperation.

Sincerely,

J. D. Brown, Ph.D.
SLTCC

Appendix H Second language teaching and curriculum survey: Teaching assistant and lecturer support services in Manoa language courses

1. COORDINATOR'S NAME _____
2. ACADEMIC RANK _____ 3. WORK PHONE _____
4. DEPARTMENT _____ 5. LANGUAGE _____
6. DO YOU GET RELEASE TIME FOR COORDINATING GAs AND LECTURERS? _____
7. NUMBER OF GAs COORDINATED EACH YEAR? _____ LECTURERS? _____
8. NUMBER OF SECTIONS EACH GA COVERS? _____ LECTURERS? _____
9. TYPICAL NUMBER OF CLASSROOM CONTACT HOURS PER WEEK _____
10. TYPICAL NUMBER OF OFFICE HOURS EXPECTED TO MAINTAIN _____
11. NUMBER OF DUTY HOURS PER WEEK (INCLUDING PREP TIME, MATERIALS DEVELOPMENT, ETC.) GAs? _____ LECTURERS? _____
12. ARE OFFICES PROVIDED? GAs? _____ LECTURERS? _____
13. WHAT LEVELS OF TEACHING DO GAs DO IN YOUR DEPARTMENT (FIRST YEAR, SECOND YEAR, OTHER)?
    _____
    LECTURERS? _____
14. TOTAL NUMBER OF FIRST AND SECOND YEAR SECTIONS IN YOUR DEPARTMENT PER YEAR _____
15. NUMBER OF SECTIONS TAUGHT PER YEAR BY GAs? _____ LECTURERS? _____
16. ORIENTATION SERVICES PROVIDED:
    A. ORIENTATION SESSIONS: LENGTH _____
       CONDUCTED HOW OFTEN PER YEAR? _____
       TYPES OF INFORMATION PROVIDED (USE BACK OF SHEET IF NEEDED):
       _____
       _____
       _____
       _____

Source: SLTCC, 1990.

294

B. ORIENTATION MATERIALS: LENGTH _____
TITLE OF MATERIALS _____
TYPES OF INFORMATION PROVIDED (USE BACK OF
SHEET IF NEEDED):

_____
_____
_____
_____

C. COURSES ON LANGUAGE TEACHING METHODOLOGY,
PEDAGOGY, OR PRACTICE TAKEN BY THESE GAs AND
LECTURERS:
CATALOG NUMBER _____ REQUIRED? _____
DESCRIPTION: _____
D. DESCRIBE ONE-ON-ONE HELP AVAILABLE TO GAs AND
LECTURERS:

_____
_____

JOB AND RANK OF PERSON PROVIDING SUCH HELP:

_____

17. WHAT ARE GAs AND LECTURERS GIVEN AT THE BEGIN-
NING OF THE SEMESTER TO HELP THEM GET GOING?
(CHECK AS MANY AS IS APPLICABLE)
ORIENTATION MATERIALS _____
COURSE OBJECTIVES _____ TEXTBOOK(S) _____
ACCESS TO SUPPLEMENTARY MATERIALS FILES _____
EXAMPLE SYLLABUSES _____
SUPPLEMENTARY MATERIALS _____
SUPPLEMENTARY READINGS ON LANGUAGE TEACHING
METHODOLOGY _____
OTHER _____

18. ARE UNIT TESTS OR FINAL EXAMS PROVIDED,
COORDINATED, OR OTHERWISE DEVELOPED
COLLECTIVELY? _____ PLEASE DESCRIBE:

_____
_____

19. DESCRIBE CLASSROOM OBSERVATIONS CONDUCTED BY
COORDINATORS:

_____
_____

JOB AND RANK OF PERSON DOING OBSERVATION:

_____

20. WHAT OTHER EVALUATION PROCEDURES ARE USED
TO GIVE GAs AND LECTURERS FEEDBACK ON THEIR

TEACHING? (E.G., END-OF-TERM STUDENT EVALUATION QUESTIONNAIRES)

---

21. ARE THERE ANY OTHER GA COORDINATORS IN YOUR DEPARTMENT WHOM WE SHOULD CONTACT? (PLEASE GIVE NAME AND OFFICE NUMBER IF AVAILABLE):

---

22. WHAT, IF ANY, FINANCIAL LIMITATIONS ON HIRING DO YOU HAVE THAT HAMPER YOUR EFFORTS?

---

23. WHAT CHANGES HAVE YOU OBSERVED SINCE THE NEW LANGUAGE REQUIREMENT WAS IMPLEMENTED AT UHM?

Appendix I Language teaching activity preference survey

1. In the language class I teach, I like to have students learn by reading.   no   a little   good   best
2. In class, I like to use cassettes for listening practice.   no   a little   good   best
3. In class, I like to use games.   no   a little   good   best
4. In class, I like to have students practice conversation.   no   a little   good   best
5. In class, I like to use pictures, films, video.   no   a little   good   best
6. I think students should write everything in their notebook.   no   a little   good   best
7. All students should each have their own textbook.   no   a little   good   best
8. As a teacher, I like to explain *everything* to the students.   no   a little   good   best
9. I like to give the students problems to work on.   no   a little   good   best
10. I like to help students talk about their interests.   no   a little   good   best
11. I like to correct all the students' errors.   no   a little   good   best
12. I like to let the students find their own mistakes.   no   a little   good   best
13. I like students to study English by themselves (alone).   no   a little   good   best
14. I like students to learn by talking in pairs.   no   a little   good   best
15. I like students to learn in small groups.   no   a little   good   best
16. I like students to learn with the whole class.   no   a little   good   best
17. I like to take the students out as a class to practice English.   no   a little   good   best
18. I like to teach grammar.   no   a little   good   best

Source: Based on Willing, 1988, pp. 106–107.

19. I like to teach many new words.	no	a little	good	best
20. I like to teach the sounds and pronunciation of English.	no	a little	good	best
21. I like to teach English words through students *seeing* them.	no	a little	good	best
22. I like to teach English words through students *hearing* them.	no	a little	good	best
23. I like to teach English words through students *doing* something.	no	a little	good	best
24. At home, students should learn by reading newspapers, etc.	no	a little	good	best
25. At home, students should learn by watching TV in English.	no	a little	good	best
26. At home, students should learn by using cassettes.	no	a little	good	best
27. At home, students should learn by studying English books.	no	a little	good	best
28. I like students to learn by talking to friends in English.	no	a little	good	best
29. I like students to learn by watching and listening to native speakers.	no	a little	good	best
30. I like students to learn by using English in shops and daily life.	no	a little	good	best

References

Access. (2000). Access for Windows. Redmond, WA: Microsoft.

Anderson-Bell. (1989). ABSTAT. Parker, CO: Anderson-Bell Corp.

Angleitner, A. (1991). Personality psychology: Trends and developments. *European Journal of Personality, 5*, 185–197.

APA. (1994). *Publication manual of the American Psychological Association* (4th ed.). Washington, DC: American Psychological Association.

Atkinson, D., & Ramanathan, V. (1995). Cultures of writing: An ethnographic comparison of L1 and L2 university writing/language programs. *TESOL Quarterly, 29*(3), 539–568.

Babbie, E. R. (1973). *Survey research methods*. Belmont, CA: Wadsworth.

Babbie, E. R. (1975). *The practice of social research*. Belmont, CA: Wadsworth.

Babbie, E. R. (1990). *Survey research methods* (2nd ed.). Belmont, CA: Wadsworth.

Bachman, L. F., & Palmer, A. S. (1983). The construct validity of the FSI oral interview. In J. W. Oller, Jr., *Issues in language testing*. Rowley, MA: Newbury House.

Bailey, K. (1982). *Methods of social research* (2nd ed.). New York: Free Press.

Bailey, K., & Brown, J. D. (1995). Language testing courses: What are they? In A. Cumming & R. Berwick (Eds.), *Validation in language testing*. Clevedon, England: Multilingual Matters.

Barlow, M. (1998). MonoConc for Windows. Houston, TX: Athelstan (http://www.nol.net/~athel/mono.html).

Berdie, D. R., Anderson, J. F., & Niebuhr, M. A. (1986). *Questionnaires: Design and use*. Metuchen, NJ: Scarecrow.

Bernbrock, C. W. (1979). Determining the English language needs for curriculum planning in a Thai business college. Unpublished master's thesis, University of California, Los Angeles, CA.

Bogdan, R. C., & Biklen, S. K. (1997). *Qualitative research for education: An introduction to theory and methods* (3rd ed.). Boston: Allyn & Bacon.

Bohrnstedt, G. W. (1983). Measurement. In P. H. Rossi, J. D.Wright, & A. B. Anderson (Eds.), *Handbook of survey research* (pp. 69–121). San Diego, CA: Academic Press.

Bourque, L. B., & Clark, V. A. (1992). *Processing data: The survey example*. Newbury Park, CA: Sage.

Bourque, L. B., & Fielder, E. P. (1995). *How to conduct self-administered and mail surveys*. Thousand Oaks, CA: Sage.

Brown, J. D. (1988). *Understanding research in second language learning: A teacher's guide to statistics and research design*. Cambridge, England: Cambridge University Press.

Brown, J. D. (1989). Language program evaluation: A synthesis of existing possibilities. In K. Johnson (Ed.), *The second language curriculum* (pp. 222–241). London: Cambridge, University Press.

Brown, J. D. (1990). The use of multiple *t*-tests in language research. *TESOL Quarterly, 24*(4), 770–773.

Brown, J. D. (1991a). Statistics as a foreign language: What to look for in reading statistical language studies – Part 1. *TESOL Quarterly, 25,* 569–586.

Brown, J. D. (1991b). Do English and ESL instructors rate writing samples differently? *TESOL Quarterly, 25,* 587–603.

Brown, J. D. (1992a). The biggest problems TESOL members see facing ESL/EFL teachers today. *TESOL Matters, 2*(2), 1, 5.

Brown, J. D. (1992b). Using computers in language testing. *Cross Currents, 19,* 92–99.

Brown, J. D. (1992c). What is research? *TESOL Matters, 2*(5), 10.

Brown, J. D. (1992d). What roles do members want TESOL to play? *TESOL Matters, 2*(5), 16.

Brown, J. D. (1992e). What research questions interest TESOL members? *TESOL Matters, 2*(6), 20.

Brown, J. D. (1992f). Statistics as a foreign language – Part 2: More things to look for in reading statistical language studies. *TESOL Quarterly, 26,* 629–664.

Brown, J. D. (1995). *The elements of language curriculum: A systematic approach to program development.* Boston: Heinle & Heinle.

Brown, J. D. (1996). *Testing in language programs.* Upper Saddle River, NJ: Prentice-Hall.

Brown, J. D., & Bailey, K. M. (1984). A categorical instrument for scoring second language writing skills. *Language Learning, 34,* 21–42.

Brown, J. D., Cunha, M. I. A., & Frota, S. de F. N. (in press). The development and validation of a Portuguese version of the Motivated Strategies for Learning Questionnaire. In Z. Dönnyei & R. Schmidt (Eds.), *Motivation and second language acquisition.* Honolulu, HI: University of Hawaii.

Brown, J. D., Knowles, M., Murray, D., Neu, J., and Violand-Hainer, E. (1992a). TESOL research questionnaire sent to 1,800 members. *TESOL Matters, 2*(1), 1, 5.

Brown, J. D., Knowles, M., Murray, D., Neu, J., & Violand-Hainer, E. (1992b). *The place of research within the TESOL organization.* Unpublished ms. Alexandria, VA: TESOL.

Brown, J. D., Robson, G., & Rosenkjar, P. (1996). Personality, motivation, anxiety, strategies, and language proficiency of Japanese students. *University of Hawai'i Working Papers in ESL, 15*(1), 33–72.

Campbell, D. T., & Fiske, D. W. (1959). Convergent and discriminant validation by the multitrait-multimethod matrix. *Psychological Bulletin, 56,* 81–105.

Carroll, J. B., & Sapon, S. M. (1958). *Modern Language Aptitude Test.* New York: Psychological Corporation.

Converse, J. M., & Presser, S. (1986). *Survey questions: Handcrafting the standardized questionnaire.* Beverly Hills, CA: Sage.

dBaseIII Plus. (1986). Torrance, CA: Ashton-Tate.

Davis, K. A. (1992). Validity and reliability in qualitative research on second language acquisition and teaching: Another research comments. . . . *TESOL Quarterly, 26,* 605–608.

Davis, K. A. (1995). Qualitative theory and methods in applied linguistics research. *TESOL Quarterly, 29,* 427–453.

Denzin, N. K. (1978). *The research act: A theoretical introduction to sociological methods* (2nd ed.). New York: McGraw-Hill.

Denzin, N. K. (1994). The art and politics of interpretation. In N. K. Denzin & Y. S. Lincoln (Eds.), *Handbook of qualitative research* (pp. 500–515). Thousand Oaks, CA: Sage.

Denzin, N. K., & Lincoln, Y. S. (Eds.). (1994). *Handbook of qualitative research.* Thousand Oaks, CA: Sage.

Dick, W., & Carey, L. (1985). *The systematic design of instruction* (2nd ed.). Glenview, IL: Scott, Foresman.

Duff, P. A. (1995). An ethnography of communication in immersion classrooms in Hungary. *TESOL Quarterly, 29,* 505–537.

Excel. (2000). Excel for Windows. Redmond, WA: Microsoft.

Eysenck, H. J. (1959). *Maudsley personality inventory.* London: University of London.

Eysenck, H. J. (1990). *Maudsley personality inventory* (6th ed.). Tokyo: MPI Kenkyû-kai.

Fetterman, D. M. (1989). *Ethnography: Step by step.* Newbury Park, CA: Sage.

Fielding, N. G., & Fielding, J. L. (1986). *Linking data.* Beverly Hills, CA: Sage.

Fink, A. (1995a). *The survey handbook.* Thousand Oaks, CA: Sage.

Fink, A. (1995b). *How to design surveys.* Thousand Oaks, CA: Sage.

Fink, A. (1995c). *How to ask survey questions.* Thousand Oaks, CA: Sage.

Fink, A. (1995d). *How to sample in surveys.* Thousand Oaks, CA: Sage.

Fink, A. (1995e). *How to analyze survey data.* Thousand Oaks, CA: Sage.

Fink, A. (1995f). *How to report on surveys.* Thousand Oaks, CA: Sage.

Firebaugh, G. (1997). *Analyzing repeated surveys.* Thousand Oaks, CA: Sage.

Fisher, R. A., & Yates, F. (1963). *Statistical tables for biological, agricultural and medical research.* London: Longman.

Fowler, F. J., Jr. (1993). *Survey research methods* (2nd ed.). Newbury Park, CA: Sage.

Fowler, F. J., Jr., & Mangione, T. W. (1993). *Standardized survey interviewing: Minimizing interviewer-related error.* Newbury Park, CA: Sage.

Fox, J. A., & Tracy, P. E. (1986). *Randomized response: A method for sensitive surveys.* Beverly Hills, CA: Sage.

Freeman, D. (1998). *Doing teacher research: From inquiry to understanding.* Boston, MA: Heinle & Heinle.

Frey, J. H., & Oishi, S. M. (1995). *How to conduct interviews by telephone and in person.* Thousand Oaks, CA: Sage.

Gallup, G. (1947). *Qualitative measurement of public opinion: The quintamensional plan of question design.* Princeton, NJ: American Institute of Public Opinion.

Gardner, R. C., & Smythe, P. C. (1981). On the development of the attitude/motivation test battery. *The Canadian Modern Language Review, 37,* 510–525.

Glesne, C., & Peshkin, A. (1992). *Becoming qualitative researchers: An introduction.* London: Longman.

Gorsuch, R. L. (1983). *Factor analysis* (2nd ed.). Hillsdale, NJ: Lawrence Erlbaum.

Hatch, E., & Lazaraton, A. (1991). *The research manual: Design and statistics for applied linguistics.* Rowley, MA: Newbury House.

Huberman, A. M., & Miles, M. B. (1994). Data management and analysis methods. In N. K. Denzin & Y. S. Lincoln (Eds.), *Handbook of qualitative research* (pp. 428–444). Thousand Oaks, CA: Sage.

Iwai, T., Kondo, K., Lim, D. S. J., Ray, G., Shimizu, H., & Brown, J. D. (1999). *Japanese language needs assessment 1998–1999* (NFLRC NetWork #13) [HTML document]. Honolulu: University of Hawai'i, Second Language Teaching & Curriculum Center. Retrieved March 3, 2000 from the World Wide Web: http://www.lll.hawaii.edu/nflrc/NetWorks/NW13/

Jacob, E. (1982). Combining ethnographic and quantitative approaches: Suggestions and examples from a study in Puerto Rico. In P. Gilmore & A. A. Glatthorn (Eds.), *Children in and out of school: Ethnography and education* (pp. 124–147). Washington, DC: Center for Applied Linguistics.

Jacoby, W. G. (1997). *Statistical graphics for univariate and bivariate data.* Thousand Oaks, CA: Sage.

Janesick, V. J. (1994). The dance of qualitative research design: Metaphor, methodology, and meaning. In N. K. Denzin & Y. S. Lincoln (Eds.), *Handbook of qualitative research* (pp. 209–219). Thousand Oaks, CA: Sage.

Johns, A. M. (1981). Necessary English: A faculty survey. *TESOL Quarterly, 15,* 51–57.

Johnson, D. M. (1987). The organization of instruction in migrant education: Assistance for children and youth at risk. *TESOL Quarterly, 21,* 437–459.

Johnson, D. M. (1992). *Approaches to research in second language learning.* New York: Longman.

Johnson, D. M., & Saville-Troike, M. (1992). Validity and reliability in qualitative research on second language acquisition and teaching: Two researchers comment. . . . *TESOL Quarterly, 26,* 602–605.

Kalton, G. (1983). *Introduction to survey sampling.* Newbury Park, CA: Sage.

Kieholt, K. J., & Nathan, L. E. (1985). *Secondary analysis of survey data.* Newbury Park, CA: Sage.

Kimzin, G., & Proctor, S. (1986). An ELI academic listening comprehension needs assessment: Establishing goals, objectives, and microskills. Honolulu, HI: Unpublished scholarly paper, Department of ESL, University of Hawaii at Manoa.

Kirk, J., & Miller, M. L. (1986). *Reliability and validity in qualitative research.* Beverly Hills, CA: Sage.

Knowles, M., & Brown, J. D. (1991). Abstracts for TESOL '92 convention at Vancouver to be processed in seven steps. *TESOL Matters, 1*(2), 1.

Larsen-Freeman, D., & Long, M. H. (1991). *An introduction to second language acquisition research.* London: Longman.

Lavrakas, P. J. (1993). *Telephone survey methods: Sampling, selection, and supervision.* Newbury Park, CA: Sage.

Lazaraton, A. (1995). Qualitative research in applied linguistics: A progress report. *TESOL Quarterly, 29,* 455–472.

Lazaraton, A., & Saville, N. (1994, March). Process and outcome in oral assessment. Paper presented at the 14th Language Testing Research Colloquium, Washington, DC.

Lee, E. S., Forthofer, R. N., & Lorimor, R. J. (1989). *Analyzing complex survey data.* Newbury Park, CA: Sage.

Lincoln, Y. & Guba, E. (1985). *Naturalistic inquiry.* Beverly Hills, CA: Sage.

Litwin, M. S. (1995). *How to measure survey reliability and validity.* Thousand Oaks, CA: Sage.

Long, M. H. (1983). Inside the "black box": Methodological issues in classroom research on language learning. In H. W. Seliger & M. H. Long (Eds.), *Classroom oriented research in second language acquisition* (pp. 3–36). Rowley, MA: Newbury House.

Loschky, L., Stanley, J., Cunha, C., & Singh, S. (1987). Evaluation of the University of Hawaii English Language Institute Reading Program. Honolulu, HI: Unpublished ESL 630 project, Department of ESL, University of Hawaii at Manoa.

Lotus 1-2-3, Release 2.01. (1985). Cambridge, MA: Lotus Development Company.

Lynch, B. (1992). Evaluating a program inside and out. In J. C. Alderson & A. Beretta (Eds.), *Evaluating second language education.* Cambridge, England: Cambridge University Press.

Lynch, B. K. (1997). *Language program evaluation: Theory and practice.* Cambridge, England: Cambridge University Press.

MacWhinney, B. (1995). *The CHILDES project: Tool for analyzing talk* (2nd ed.). Hillsdale, NJ: Lawrence Erlbaum.

Mager, R. F. (1975). *Preparing instructional objectives.* Belmont, CA: Fearon-Pitman.

Marshall, C. (1985). Appropriate criteria of trustworthiness and goodness for qualitative research on education organizations. *Quality and Quantity, 19,* 353–373.

Marshall, C., & Rossman, G. B. (1989). *Designing qualitative research.* Newbury Park, CA: Sage.

McCall, G., & Simmons, J. (1969). *Issues in participant observation.* Reading, MA: Addison-Wesley.

McDonald, R. P. (1985). *Factor analysis and related methods.* Hillsdale, NJ: Lawrence Erlbaum.

McKeown, B., & Thomas, D. (1988). *Q methodology.* Newbury Park, CA: Sage.

Messick, S. (1988). The once and future issues of validity: Assessing the meaning and consequences of measurement. In H. Wainer & H. I. Braun (Eds.), *Test validity* (pp. 33–48). Hillsdale, NJ: Lawrence Erlbaum.

Miles, M. B., & Huberman, A. M. (1984). *Qualitative data analysis: A sourcebook of new methods.* Beverly Hills, CA: Sage.

Nunan, D. (1986). Communicative language teaching: The learner's view. Paper presented at the RELC Regional Seminar, Singapore, April 1986.

Nunan, D. (1991). *The learner-centred curriculum.* Cambridge, England: Cambridge University Press.

Nunan, D. (1992). *Research methods in language learning.* Cambridge, England: Cambridge University Press.

Ochsner, R. (1980). Job-related aspects of the M.A. in TESOL degree. *TESOL Quarterly, 14,* 199–207.

Oppenheim, A. N. (1966). *Questionnaire design and attitude measurement.* New York: Basic Books.

Paradox. (1991). Scotts Valley, CA: Borland.

Patton, M. Q. (1987). *How to use qualitative methods in evaluation.* Newbury Park, CA: Sage.

303

Parry, T. S., & Stansfield, C. W. (Eds.). (1990). *Language aptitude reconsidered*. Englewood Cliffs, NJ: Prentice Hall Regents.

Pearson, E. S., & Hartley, H. O. (1963). *Biometrika tables for statisticians* (2nd ed.). Cambridge, England: Cambridge University Press.

Politzer. R. L., & McGroarty, M. (1985). An exploratory study of learning behaviors and their relationship to gains in linguistic and communicative competence. *TESOL Quarterly, 19*(1), 103–123.

Quattro Pro. (1991). Scotts Valley, CA: Borland.

Richterich, R., & Chancerel, J.-L. (1980). *Identifying the needs of adults learning a foreign language*. Oxford: Pergamon Press.

RightWriter. (1990). Carmel, IN: Que Software.

Robson, G. (1992). Individual learner differences. Tokyo: Temple University Japan, Unpublished ms.

Rossett, A. (1982). A typology for generating needs assessments. *Journal of Instructional Development, 6*(1), 28–33.

Rossi, P. H., Wright, J. D., & Anderson, A. B. (1983). *Handbook of survey research*. San Diego, CA: Academic.

Rossman, G. B., & Wilson, B. L. (1985). Numbers and words: Combining quantitative and qualitative methods in a single large-scale evaluation study. *Evaluation Review, 9*, 627–643.

Rubin, H. J., & Rubin, I. S. (1995). *Qualitative interviewing: The art of hearing data*. Thousand Oaks, CA: Sage.

Saris, W. E. (1991). *Computer-assisted interviewing*. Newbury Park, CA: Sage.

Sasaki, C. L. (1996). Teacher preferences of student behavior in Japan. *JALT Journal, 18*, 229–239.

Seidman, I. (1998). *Interviewing as qualitative research: A guide for researchers in education and the social sciences* (2nd ed.). New York: Teachers College, Columbia University.

Seliger, H. W., & Shohamy, E. (1989). *Second language research methods*. Oxford: Oxford University Press.

Skehan, P. (1989). *Individual differences in second-language learning*. London: Edward Arnold.

SLTCC. (1990). Second language teaching and curriculum survey: Teaching assistant and lecturer support services in Manoa language courses. Unpublished ms., Second Language Teaching and Curriculum Center, University of Hawai'i at Manoa, Honolulu, HI.

Sokolov, J., & Snow, C. (Eds.). (1994). *Handbook of research in language development using CHILDES*. Hillsdale, NJ: Lawrence Erlbaum.

SPSS. (1999). SPSS for Windows (Release 9.0). Chicago: SPSS.

Stacey, S. E., & Moyer, K. L. (1982). *A guide to survey development: Manual on writing a survey*. Harrisburg, PA: Pennsylvania State Department of Education. [Also ERIC Document ED 222 538].

SYSTAT. (1996). SYSTAT 6.0 for Windows: Statistics. Chicago: SPSS.

SYSTAT. (1999). SYSTAT 7.0 for Windows. Chicago: SPSS.

Tabachnick, B. G., & Fidell, L. S. (1996). *Using multivariate statistics* (3rd ed.). New York: Harper Collins College Publishers.

Taylor, D. G. (1983). Analyzing qualitative data. In P. H. Rossi, J. D. Wright, & A. B. Anderson (Eds.), *Handbook of survey research*. San Diego, CA: Academic Press.

TESOL. (2000a). *TESOL Quarterly* statistical guidelines. *TESOL Quarterly, 31*(2), 386–387.

TESOL. (2000b). *TESOL Quarterly* qualitative guidelines. *TESOL Quarterly, 31*(2), 387–388.

Uhl, N. P. (1990). Delphi technique. In H. J. Walberg & G. D. Haertel (Eds.), *The international encyclopedia of educational evaluation* (pp. 81–82). Oxford: Pergamon Press.

Weaver, J., Pickett, A., Kiu, L., & Cook, J. (1987). Foreign TA training project needs analysis. Honolulu, HI: Unpublished ESL 630 project, Department of ESL, University of Hawaii at Manoa.

Webb, E. J., Campbell, D. T., Schwartz, R. D., & Sechrest, L. (1965). *Unobtrusive measures.* Chicago: Rand McNally.

Weiss, R. S. (1994). *Learning from strangers: The art and method of qualitative interview studies.* New York: Free Press.

Weller, S. C., & Romney, A. K. (1988). *Systematic data collection.* Newbury Park, CA: Sage.

Willing, K. (1988). *Learning styles in adult migrant education.* Sydney, Australia: NSW Adult Migrant Education Service.

Willet, J. (1995). Becoming first graders in an L2: An ethnographic study of L2 socialization. *TESOL Quarterly, 29*(3), 473–503.

Word. (2000). Word for Windows. Redmond, WA: Microsoft.

WordPerfect (1991). WordPerfect (version 5.1). Orem, UT: WordPerfect.

Name index

Subject index

abilities questions, 33
ABSTAT, 93–94, 98
Access (2000), 97
achievement tests, 4
address, on mail survey questionnaire,
    88
administrators, as source of data,
    21–22
advisory meetings, 5
agreement, 172
    caution about, 239–40
    intercoder, 233–34
    intracoder, 235–38
agreement coefficient, 172
alpha decision level, 137
alpha level, 137
alternative-answer questions, 39–40
American Psychological Association
    (APA), 12, 254–56
analysis of data
    qualitative, 11–12, 212–52
    statistical, 10–11, 114–211
analysis of variance (ANOVA), 157
appearance, of interviewers, 81
aptitude tests, 4
Attitude/Motivation Test Battery
    (A/MTB), 177–78, 185–88
attitudes questions, 33

bar graphs, 116, 117
behavior/experience questions, 30
behavior observations, 4
biased questions, 52
bimodal distributions, 118
biodata surveys, 34
biserial coefficient, 143
Bonferroni adjustment, 170, 182

case studies, 4
categorical scales, 17

central tendency, 118–22
    defined, 118
    mean, 119–20, 121
    median, 120–21, 122
    mode, 120, 121–22
    selecting indicators of, 121–22
checklist questions, 42–43
CHILDES, 223
chi-square (χ^2) statistic, 158–69
    assumptions of, 168–69
    calculating, 159–64
    combining two-way and one-way
        analyses, 165–67
    multiple comparisons, 169–71
    n-way, 159
    one-way, 158–61, 165–67
    statistical significance of, 165
    two-way, 159, 161–64, 165–67
clarity
    of questionnaire directions, 59–60
    of questionnaire format, 57–59
    of questions, 46–47
closed responses
    coding, 93–98
    compiling, 104–7
    forms of questions, 39–43
    nature of, 35–36
    pros and cons of, 36–38
cloze procedure, 185–88
coding, 93–98
    assigning codes to data, 94–95
    categories for, 93–94
    choosing tools for, 97–98
    deciding on approach, 95–97
    defined, 93
    recording data, 98
    response, 232
collapsing of data, 94–95
column graphs, 116, 117, 118
columns, defined, 95